Going Places
With Children
In Washington, DC

Fiftieth Anniversary Edition

EDITORS
Kathie Meizner · Lisa Nevans Locke · Meg Thale

BOOK DESIGN AND LAYOUT
Peter Braverman

COVER ART
Jennifer O'Connell

PUBLISHED BY GREEN ACRES SCHOOL
ROCKVILLE, MARYLAND
PRINTED ON FSC-CERTIFIED PAPER

SEVENTEENTH EDITION

Mixed Sources
Product group from well-managed
forests and other controlled sources
www.fsc.org Cert no. SW-COC-1530
© Forest Stewardship Council

Going Places with Children in Washington, DC

Green Acres School
11701 Danville Drive
Rockville, Maryland 20852
301 881-4100
www.greenacres.org

Cover art by Jennifer O'Connell

Photography by Peter Braverman and Cynthia Seymour

Illustrations by Green Acres School students

Metrorail map (inside back cover) courtesy of
Washington Metropolitan Area Transit Authority

ISBN 978-0-9608998-7-6

First edition, 1958; Second edition, 1961; Third edition, 1963;
Fourth edition, 1965; Fifth edition, 1968; Sixth edition, 1971;
Seventh edition, 1974; Eighth edition, 1976; Ninth edition, 1979;
Tenth edition, 1982; Eleventh edition, 1984; Twelfth edition, 1988;
Thirteenth edition, 1992; Fourteenth edition, 1995;
Fifteenth edition, 1998; Sixteenth edition, 2003.

Seventeenth edition, 2008.

Printed in the United States by Automated Graphic Systems.

We have made every reasonable effort to ensure the accuracy of this
book. However, information of this type changes frequently, and even
the most careful people sometimes make mistakes. We are sure readers understand that we regret any errors.

Going Places is dedicated, as always, to the children of Green Acres School.

GUIDE TO SYMBOLS

The following symbols are used throughout this book as a way for readers to narrow their choices. In each case, we have tried to provide the most accurate information available. As always, we encourage visitors to confirm policies and expectations for each site before visiting.

 Editors' Choice
Sites we recommend most enthusiastically

 New listings
Sites not included in the previous edition of Going Places

 Free

 Gift shop or other store

 Group rates or tours available

 Handicapped-accessible
Includes sites with broad accessibility

 Metrorail-accessible

 Musical performance or program

 Picnic facilities

 Recommended for certain age ranges
Please note that specific ages may vary by site

 Restaurant, café or snack bar

 Theater or dance performance

Grateful acknowledgment is made to many people whose contributions to this book have been invaluable:

Assistant Editors Julie Clevenger, Marjorie Haas, Christine Koubek and Claudia Nagan

Contributing Editors Karyn Blad, Kara Combs, Christine Greenlees, Nancy Kim, Ted Mackay, Bob Margolis, Nancy Morgan, Grace Park, Leon Rodriguez and Lois Sacks

Contributors Hope Adler, Margaret Beckwith, Betsy Brach, Cindy Brach, Karen Buglass, Sue Eckhart, Alexander Fraser, Anne Fretz, Brianne Friel, Gwen Garfinkle, Gynny Katon, Francesca Kim, Marcelle James, Adriana Murphy, Amanda Monsour, Parker Orr, Laura Richardson , Jessica Rogers, Darin Schonzeit, Cynthia Seymour, Clarence Smith, Robin Smith, Terry Strand, Rebecca Tobin, Bega Toolanen, Leslie Traub, Laura Trivers and Steve Waldhorn

Thanks are due as well for photographs by Peter Braverman and Cynthia Seymour, for illustrations by Green Acres School students, for capable assistance lent by Green Acres staff and parents and for encouragement by Green Acres Head of School Louis Silvano.

Finally, the editors are indebted to Green Acres School's Director of Development, Joan Adler, for her ongoing support of this project over the many editions and countless hours she has spent encouraging, coordinating, accommodating—and especially feeding—all of us.

CONTENTS

EDITORS' NOTE

When the first edition of *Going Places with Children in Washington, DC* was published in 1958, Green Acres School was already well established as a progressive school, committed to hands-on, experiential learning. From the School's founding in 1934, Green Acres welcomed children from many backgrounds into the community of learning. In fact, Green Acres was the first integrated school in Montgomery County, Maryland.

Green Acres teachers and families have always recognized that visiting places outside the classroom is an important way children and adults alike learn about the world. For half a century, our community has upheld a tradition of sharing our splendid adventures in and around Washington. In that time, *Going Places* has grown from a mimeographed pamphlet to a guidebook of more than 400 places to visit. It is the longest-running and most comprehensive guide to family outings and explorations in and around Washington.

The book is the work of a collaborative community, and we are grateful to the parents, grandparents, teachers, staff and friends who contributed to this book, naming their favorite places and sharing insiders' knowledge of the best the region has to offer.

Above all, Green Acres students have been our partners and our inspiration. They joined us in visiting the sites in this book, telling us what works and what doesn't, urging us to recommend visiting these places and giving us many of the words we have used to describe them. Our children gave us the motivation and the ideas for this book, drew the pictures, tried new experiences and revisited favorite places with us. We couldn't have done it without their enthusiasm and curiosity!

Kathie Meizner
Lisa Nevans Locke
Meg Thale

November 2007

STARTING OUT

Three important keys to successful family trips—whether for the afternoon, the weekend or longer—are planning ahead, stopping for rest and food, and finding the balance among traveling, seeing, learning and entertainment.

Take care of the environment and of yourself wherever you go—the places you visit today with your children will be part of their legacy to their children.

Locations, hours, fees and security procedures are all subject to change. We encourage you to check critical information before you go.

MAPS, VIRTUAL TOURS, EVENTS

One good place to begin an adventure away from home is to check out current information about services, hours, and special events online, either from home or at your local public library.

www.nps.gov The National Park Service online guides to the National Monuments as well as to the national parks are easy to use and provide helpful tips for visitors. Visit www.nps.gov/nr for an online tour of National Historic Places in Washington.

www.washington.org The Washington DC Convention and Visitors Association website provides a comprehensive introduction for visitors, including information about transportation, events and places to eat and stay.

www.dcpages.com/Tourism Visit for a 360-degree look at 10 buildings and monuments on the National Mall.

www.ahp.gatech.edu/dc_map.html "America's Homepage" is a quick way to find online information about and tours of the landmarks on the Mall along with resources for students and teachers, including a collection of historic documents.

www.mdisfun.org The Maryland Office of Tourism offers a free travel kit with state map, calendar of events, and a Destination Maryland Travel Guide. Other maps and guides to scenic routes, bicycling, golf and camping are available.

www.virginia.org The Virginia Tourism Corporation offers a transportation map and "Virginia is for Lovers" guide with recommendations for traveling and visiting throughout the Commonwealth.

www.cvbmontco.com The Conference and Visitors Bureau of Montgomery County, MD website is an excellent guide to events, history, and sights in the county.

www.mc-mncppc.org and **www.pgparks.com** The Maryland National Capital Park and Planning Commission websites provide guides to the parks and park facilities in Montgomery and Prince Georges counties in Maryland.

www.dnr.state.md.us and **www.dcr.virginia.gov** Maryland Department of Natural Resources and Virginia Department of Conservation and Recreation: State parks, including information about reserving campsites and cabins

www.waba.org and **www.bikewashington.org** Washington Area Bicyclist Association and Bike Washington: Online maps to bike trails and routes throughout the metropolitan area along with suggestions for recreational rides.

INFORMATION AND VISITORS CENTERS

Two visitors centers in particular are especially good sources of information and ideas about places to visit, activities for families and entertaining facts to add to the enjoyment of sightseeing.

Alexandria Convention and Visitors Bureau
Ramsay House Visitors Center

The restored home of William Ramsay, Scottish merchant and city founder, offers information on historic Old Town Alexandria, annotated maps, lists of galleries and shops, and tour information.

www.funside.com

703-838-5005

221 King Street, Alexandria, VA

Daily, 9–5.

Annapolis Conference Center and Visitors Bureau

Information about the U.S. Naval Academy, museums, boating, arts festivals, field trips, historic homes, and workshops for kids, picnic areas, kid-friendly local restaurants, athletic fields, parking, and playgrounds.

www.visitannapolis.org

410-280-0445

26 West Street, Annapolis, MD

Daily, 9–5.

SIGHTSEEING/TOURS

Real-life tour guides can greatly enhance your experience of a visit to Washington and neighboring historic places. The stories and facts shared by well-informed tour guides can provide a memorable introduction to the sites, and a multi-stop tour can help you squeeze in a few more sites during a day's visit.

Ⓜ DC Duck Tours

Take a land and water tour on an amphibious vehicle. The "Ducks" carried troops and supplies in World War II and are fully restored and Coast Guard–approved. The fully narrated tour spends one hour on land and 30 minutes on the water covering the White House and the Capitol before the Potomac River portion of the tour.

www.trolleytours.com

202-966-3825

Union Station, Washington, DC

Take Note

Children like the yellow quacker whistles given to each passenger. Bring hats, and be aware that it can be very hot on the water.

9:30 a.m.–5 p.m. Tours are offered April–October and depart hourly from Union Station.

Adults, $29; children 4–12, $14; children under 4, free.

Metrorail Red line (Union Station).

Neighborhood Heritage Trails

Do-it-yourself themed walking tours—just follow the signs. A list of these, along with downloadable trail maps and descriptions, is available at **www.culturaltourismdc.org**.

Old Town Trolley Tours of Washington, DC

Old Town Trolley Tours offers a wide-ranging tour of 100 points of interest in Washington, including Georgetown, Embassy Row, the Washington National Cathedral, Capitol Hill, Dupont Circle and the Mall. Passengers can get off and re-board at their leisure at 16 stops all day long, or use the same ticket to take separate trolleys to and from National Cathedral and Arlington National Cemetery.

www.trolleytours.com

202-832-9800

Tours depart from Union Station, Washington, DC

Trips daily every 30 minutes, 9 a.m.–5:30 p.m. The complete route takes 2:15. Evening tours are available by reservation.

Adult, $32; children 4–12, $16. Children under 4, free. Tickets are good for one day only.

Metrorail Red line (Union Station).

Wheelchair-accessible trolleys: call 24 hours in advance.

Tourmobile Sightseeing Incorporated

Tourmobile is a concessionaire of the National Park Service, offering a convenient way to get from one main attraction to another. The 85-passenger open-air vehicles, accompanied by guides, stop at 22 major sights along the Mall, Union Station, MCI Center, Ford's Theatre, FBI Building, Lincoln Memorial, John F. Kennedy Center and Arlington National Cemetery. The Arlington National Cemetery tour includes the Kennedy Family Grave Sites, the Tomb of the Unknowns, the Arlington House, and the Robert E. Lee Memorial. For an additional fee, you may add Mount Vernon and the Frederick Douglass Historic Site to your tour. You are allowed unlimited stops along the route and re-boarding is free throughout the day. This is an efficient and energy-saving way to see numerous attractions. Several Tourmobile stops are located near Metro stations.

www.tourmobile.com

202-554-5100

Daily, 9:30–4:30, except December 25 and January 1

Board every 15 to 30 minutes, depending on the season, at any stop. The complete tour, without the swing to Arlington, takes about 90 minutes.

Adults, $25; children 3–11, $12. Tickets can be purchased from the driver at any stop.

Priority seating and wheelchair storage (2–3 steps required) on all buses.

Lift-equipped buses: call 703-979-0690.

Ⓜ Washington Walks

Washington Walks offers one-hour family tours on Fridays, Saturdays and Sundays, with stories and scavenger hunts to add to children's understanding of sites like the Lincoln Memorial and the White House. For older children and teens try the two-hour easy walking tours like "Before Harlem there was U Street" (a look at Duke Ellington's home neighborhood and Washington's African-American heritage) and "Capital Hauntings" (a tour of ghostly hauntings in and around Lafayette Square).

www.washingtonwalks.com

202-484-1565

Most tours embark near a Metro station; see the website for details.

$10; children under 3, free.

TRANSPORTATION

Public transportation

Taking city buses and Metrorail trains, like traveling by other means, can be an adventure in itself, and it has its own fascination and pleasures for children. There is the fun of getting a ticket or a transfer, learning to use a route map and read a schedule, planning travel time in a different way, the adventure of leaving the car behind, and the enjoyment of the journey itself.

Many of the sites listed in Going Places are easily accessible by public transportation, and many others are accessible with a bit of planning. Whether you have a single destination—or are planning a day in

Washington, Alexandria, Baltimore, or Harper's Ferry—you may want to leave the car and parking hassles at home, and try the region's extensive public transportation system.

 ## Bethesda Circulator

Visitors to Bethesda's many shops and restaurants can park the car and ride the free, brightly colored trolleys instead. The route takes about eight minutes to travel through Woodmont Triangle and Bethesda Row, the two sections known collectively as "Downtown Bethesda."

www.bethesda.org

301-215-6661

Monday–Thursday, 7 a.m.–midnight; Friday, 7 a.m.–2 a.m.; Saturday, 6 p.m.–2 a.m.

DASH

DASH operates buses along several routes within the City of Alexandria, Virginia, connecting Metro stations with locations throughout the city, including the Old Town shopping and restaurant area.

www.dashbus.com

703-370-DASH

Base fare, $1; up to two children under 4 free with a full fare.

The DASH About free weekend shuttle runs between the King Street Metro station and Market Square in Alexandria, Friday, 7 p.m.–midnight; Saturday, 11 a.m.–midnight; Sunday, 11 a.m.–10 p.m.

DC Circulator Bus

The big windows on the Circulator Buses let travelers see the city as you travel the loops around the major monuments and destinations in town.

www.dccirculator.com

202-962-1423

$1; $0.50 senior and disabled; $3.00 one-day pass available from ticket machines

Daily, 7–9 p.m. between the DC Convention Center and the Waterfront and between Georgetown and Union Station. Daily, 10–4 between the Smithsonian and National Gallery of Art.

MARC Trains

The three lines of this commuter rail service link Washington DC's Union Station with Baltimore and points in Maryland and West Virginia on weekdays only with inbound service in the morning and outbound service in the afternoon and evening.

The Camden Line from Baltimore includes stops at College Park and Riverdale.

The Penn Line from Penn Station in Baltimore includes stops at BWI Airport and New Carrollton.

Returning along the West Virginia Line, MARC terminates in Duffields, West Virigina, with stops in Silver Spring, Kensington, Gaithersburg, Germantown, Boyds and Harpers Ferry.

MARC trains also run between Union Station and the stadium area in Baltimore for sporting events with the Orioles and Ravens.

www.mtamaryland.com

800-325-RAIL

 ## Metrorail

Parking in many downtown areas is expensive and difficult to find. Metro can be an excellent alternative for getting to and around downtown Washington. Children will enjoy the Metrorail train rides and the spacious vaulted underground stations. Metro parking lots, adjacent to many suburban stations, are convenient places to leave a car while riding Metro on weekends. For a discounted parking fee at some lots, you must obtain a bus transfer at the beginning of your return rail trip when you enter the station. Many Metro parking lots fill early on weekday mornings, but space is available on weekends at no cost. Metro offers interactive trip planning on its website.

Entrance to Metrorail is by farecard, which can be purchased at any Metro station or online. The amount charged as you exit at your destination depends on the distance traveled and the time of day. Be sure to keep your farecard until you exit the Metrorail system. Each passenger (including children five and over) must have a farecard; two children age four and under ride free with a paying passenger. The farecard vending machines will take bills in denominations of $1, $5 and $10 as well as credit cards. The highest fares are charged during weekday rush hours with fare savings during non-rush hours.

Take Note

If you can get a seat in the first car of the train, children can peer through the front window to see the tunnels ahead illuminated by the train's headlights.

Metro has elevators and train space for wheelchairs, features to assist the blind, and devices to assist the deaf, as well as reduced fares for senior/disabled Metro ID holders.

Metrorail opens at 5 a.m. Monday–Friday, and at 7 a.m. Saturday and Sunday. Metrorail closes at midnight Sunday–Thursday, and at 3 a.m. Friday and Saturday nights.

The five Metrorail lines are designated by color: Red, Blue, Yellow, Green and Orange. Transferring between lines is possible at several points.

Metrorail pocket guides are available from the Washington Metropolitan Area Transit Authority or at any Metro station.

Metrobus routes dovetail with Metrorail and together they provide a comprehensive transportation system for both city and suburbs. Exact fare ($1.25 in DC) is encouraged on Metrobus; operators do not make change. There are no transfers from bus to rail.

The website includes videos of attractions near each Metro station.

www.wmata.com

202-637-7000; 202-638-3780 (TTY)**; 301-562-5360** (MetroAccess Para-transit)

$6.50 Metrorail one-day passes are good after 9:30 a.m. weekdays and all day weekends and federal holidays.

Ride-On Buses, Montgomery County, MD

Montgomery County's Ride-On bus system connects with 12 Metro stations throughout the county and operates 80 bus routes.

Children under 5 ride free. Students (through high school) ride free from 2 p.m. to 7 p.m. weekdays with I.D.

www.montgomerycountymd.gov/dpwt

240-777-7433

Virginia Railway Express

The two VRE lines run from Fredericksburg and Manassas to Union Station in Washington DC on weekday mornings and out of Washington on weekday afternoons. Trains do not run on federal holidays.

www.vre.org

703-684-0400; 800-684-0400

PUBLICATIONS

The Washington Post (**www.washingtonpost.com**): The Friday Weekend Section column, "With the Kids," highlights children's programs and family activities, and the rest of the Weekend section is a great source of information about current exhibits, festivals and music events.

Washington Parent (**www.washingtonparent.com**) and *Washington Family* (**www.washingtonfamily.com**) are free monthly magazines about raising children in the area; those publications can be found at area grocery stores and many libraries. Each includes a calendar of events, along with special features on activities with children.

A Literary Map of Washington DC

Published by The Women's National Book Association Washington Chapter in partnership with the Library of Congress Center for the Book, this poster-sized map brochure features authors who lived, worked or are buried in the Washington area along with literary establishments and landmarks. The map is $7.95 and sold in local bookstores and tourism centers. Information about individual purchases is online.

www.wnba-books.org/wash/map.html

2

MAIN SIGHTS IN WASHINGTON

Washington, DC is home not only to the three branches of the United States government and to the monuments and museums surrounding the National Mall, but to a wonderful collection of historical and cultural resources of its own. As our country's capital city, Washington is host to embassies and organizations from around the world—and it is a city rich in the fine and performing arts, in natural resources, and in recreational opportunities. The sights and museums in this section express the enormous diversity of the city, from the National Mall to Capitol Hill and to the city beyond.

On the Mall

The National Mall is the heart of Washington, home to many of the monuments, museums and main attractions that draw visitors to the nation's capital. The Mall is almost two miles of open space and there is no such thing as a quick walk from one end to the other, especially in the heat of the summer. A good stroller is a must for young children, as are comfortable shoes for everyone else.

On a fine day, pick two or three museums to visit for an hour or two. Take a break or picnic at the carousel near the Air and Space Museum, in the two marvelous sculpture gardens near the Hirschhorn and at the National Gallery of Art, and at the outdoor fountain at the East Wing.

If time is short, a good way to squeeze in all the main attractions is to save the Washington Monument, and Lincoln, Jefferson and FDR Memorials for the cool of the evening, when they are dramatically lit. They are impressive, historical and together give a powerful sense of the wisdom and courage of four U.S. Presidents. Take a minute at the Lincoln Memorial to contemplate, and to stand in the place where Marian Andersen sang and where Martin Luther King, Jr. delivered the words, "I have a dream." Then choose from among the Smithsonian's treasures: the Spirit of St. Louis and the Lunar Lander at the Air and Space Museum; the impressive Alexander Calder mobile at the East Wing of the National Gallery; and the dinosaurs at the Natural History Museum. If you are visiting with older children, be sure to take time for a memorable tour of the U.S. Holocaust Memorial Museum (see p. 67).

A visit to the Smithsonian Information Center, in the Castle, will provide you with an orientation to all 15 Smithsonian locations in Washington, including the zoo (see p. 58).

Admission to all museums and monuments on the Mall is free. Parking on Mall streets is very limited, so use Metrorail if possible. Otherwise, try your luck or find a nearby parking garage.

Arthur M. Sackler Gallery and Freer Gallery of Art

Chinese jades, bronzes, and paintings; Buddhist sculpture; Japanese screens; early Biblical manuscripts; and miniatures from India and Persia are exhibited at the distinguished Asian collections at the Sackler and Freer. Exhibits are continuously rotated since only a fraction of the catalogued artwork can be displayed at one time. The Freer also is noted for its collection of important work by American artists, especially James Whistler. Whistler's "Peacock Room," with its lavish golds and blues, will particularly fascinate children. The Sackler is in an underground quadrangle formed by the Arts and Industries Building and the Freer Gallery.

www.asia.si.edu

202-633-4880

1050 Independence Avenue, SW, Washington, DC

Recommended for children ages 6–14 is ImaginAsia, a hands-on art project for adults and children, which takes place on selected Saturdays and Sundays. Check website for details.

Daily, 10–5:30. Closed December 25.

Metrorail Blue or Orange line (Smithsonian, Mall exit).

Security: All bags will be searched.

Highlight tours are given every day (except Wednesday and federal holidays) at 12:15 p.m.

Constitution Gardens

A large mall area, on which temporary government buildings once stood, has been transformed into a memorial to the Founders of the United States. The informal design includes a six-acre lake with a landscaped island (the site of the 56 Signers of the Declaration of Independence Memorial). The unusual design was intended to create the effect of a park within a park. This is a pleasant place to stop and take a break from sightseeing. Take a stroll, play some outdoor games, and give the children a chance to stretch their legs, but please do not feed the ducks and seagulls.

www.nps.gov/coga

202-426-6841

Between the Washington Monument and the Lincoln Memorial on Constitution Avenue, NW, Washington, DC
Park on Ohio Drive along the river. On evenings, weekends, and holidays, parking is available on Constitution Avenue.

Daily, 24 hours.

Rangers can be found at the nearby Vietnam Veterans Memorial every day from 9:30 a.m.–11:30 p.m.

Franklin Delano Roosevelt Memorial

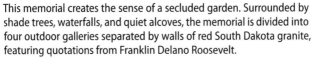

This memorial creates the sense of a secluded garden. Surrounded by shade trees, waterfalls, and quiet alcoves, the memorial is divided into four outdoor galleries separated by walls of red South Dakota granite, featuring quotations from Franklin Delano Roosevelt.

www.nps.gov/fdre

202-426-6841

Ohio Drive, West Potomac Park, NW, Washington, DC
Follow Independence Avenue (heading west) past the Washington
Monument and the Tidal Basin. Just past 17th Street, turn left on West
Basin Drive. The FDR Memorial is on the left.

Daily, 24 hours.

*Metrorail Blue or Orange line (Smithsonian, Mall exit). It is a 15–20 min-
ute walk from the Metro.*

Tourmobile stop.

Ranger Talks and Tours available on request.

Rangers on duty from 9:30 a.m.–11:30 p.m.

*Wheelchairs available upon request (first come, first served). Handi-
capped parking at front entrance of the memorial (West Basin Drive, off
Ohio Drive).*

★ Hirshhorn Museum and Sculpture Garden

This monumental collection of 19th- and 20th-century paintings and
sculpture, displayed in an unusual circular building, offers children an
exciting introduction to art. Many of the paintings are massive, vivid,
and often very colorful—making a direct impact on viewers young
and old. Exhibits from the comprehensive permanent collection (nearly 14,500 paintings, sculptures, and works on paper) and changing loan
shows provide opportunities to study major modern artists such as
Rodin, Calder, Eakins, and Matisse. Diverse art movements including
realism, pop and abstract expressionism can be studied in depth.

The building's architectural design immediately fascinates visitors.
Special exhibitions and early 20th-century paintings are displayed in
windowless outer galleries on the second and third floors. Sculptures
fill inner ambulatories, which offer comfortable chairs in which to
relax and view the central courtyard and fountain through window-
walls. Or you can relax on benches in the outdoor sculpture garden
and plaza. Contemporary paintings and sculptures are displayed in the
lower-level galleries.

Be sure to obtain a free family guide to the museum at the Information
Desk. This series of sturdy, colorful cards includes facts and activities

related to an artwork shown in a color photograph. The format encourages children to tell stories about what they see and offers information of interest to adults.

Young at Art Family Workshops are geared to ages 6–12, but programs for children as young as 3 are also offered. Check website for current offerings and information.

www.hirshhorn.si.edu

202-633-4674 (museum office), **202-633-1000** (information)

Independence Avenue at 7th Street, SW, Washington, DC
Located on the National Mall between Jefferson Drive and Independence Avenue at the corner of 7th Street.

Daily 10–5:30. Plaza hours 7:30–5:30. Sculpture garden hours 7:30–dusk. Closed December 25.

Metrorail Blue, Orange, Green or Yellow line (L'Enfant Plaza, Smithsonian Museums exit to Maryland Avenue and 7th Street SW).

Exhibition tours are offered every day at 1 and 3. Collections tour is offered every day at 2.

Wheelchair access through swinging doors on plaza. Sculpture garden accessible from the Mall. Sculpture tours for the blind and visually impaired, and sign-language tours are available by appointment, 202-357-3235.

Security: All bags will be searched.

Jefferson Memorial

The pillared rotunda is a tribute to our third President, Thomas Jefferson, who was also the author of the Declaration of Independence. Like the Lincoln Memorial, it is impressively lit at night. Park Service rangers are available to provide visitor services and present interpretive programs every hour.

www.nps.gov/thje

202-426-6841

Southern edge of the Tidal Basin, Washington, DC
Parking on Ohio Drive and limited parking at memorial.

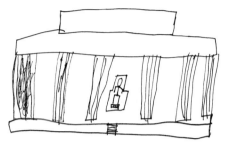

Daily, 24 hours. Closed December 25. Park Service rangers on duty 9:30 a.m.–11:30 p.m.

Metrorail Blue or Orange line (Smithsonian), but this is a long walk for children.

Tourmobile stop.

For information on the annual spring cherry blossom festival,check the website, www.nationalcherryblossomfestival.org.

Korean War Veterans Memorial

A group of 19 stainless-steel statues, created by World War II veteran Frank Gaylord, depicts a squad on patrol and evokes the experience of American ground troops in Korea. Strips of granite and scrubby juniper bushes suggest the rugged Korean terrain, while windblown ponchos recall the harsh weather. The memorial brings together men from diverse backgrounds who served in the Air Force, Army, Navy and Marines. A granite curb on the north side of the statues lists the 22 United Nations countries which sent troops or gave medical support in defense of South Korea. On the south side is a black granite wall displaying etched faces of the American military.

www.nps.gov/kwvm

202-426-6841

Independence Avenue and Chester French Drive, NW, Washington, DC Park during non-rush hours and weekends on Ohio Drive off Independence Avenue or on Constitution Avenue.

Daily, 24 hours. Closed December. 25. Park service rangers on duty from 9:30 a.m.–11:30 p.m.

Tourmobile stop.

Handicapped parking next to the Lincoln Memorial.

Lincoln Memorial

This classical Greek memorial to the Great Emancipator, Abraham Lincoln, is one of the most beautiful sights in Washington. Thirty-six marble columns, representing the states of the Union at the time of Lincoln's death, surround the impressive seated statue of Lincoln. Passages from two of his great speeches, the Second Inaugural Address and the Gettysburg Address, are carved on the walls. At the foot of the memorial is the 2,000-foot-long Reflecting Pool, which mirrors the Washington Monument at its other end. Try to visit the Lincoln Memorial twice—once in the daytime and once at night.

www.nps.gov/linc

202-426-6841

Memorial Circle, between Constitution and Independence Avenues, SW, Washington, DC

Daily, 24 hours. Closed December 25. Park rangers are on duty from 9:30 a.m.–11:30 p.m.

Metrorail Blue or Orange line (Foggy Bottom).

Tourmobile stop.

Handicapped parking next to the Memorial. Special ramp and elevator for wheelchairs.

National Air and Space Museum

This great aerospace center has 26 exhibit areas, an IMAX film theater, flight simulators and planetarium. The central display on "Milestones of Flight" includes: the Wright brothers' Flyer of 1903, the X-1, first plane to break the sound barrier, Lindbergh's Spirit of St. Louis and the command module of the Apollo 11 moon-landing mission. In another section, children can walk through the Skylab orbital workshop and examine the astronauts' living and lab quarters. Each gallery explores a different theme: helicopters, satellites, World War I and II planes and rockets. Many exhibits use videos or a moving display to explain a particular subject.

To avoid crowds, go early on a weekday morning or in winter months when there are fewer tourists. Purchase IMAX film and flight simulator tickets when you arrive, as the day's showing can be sold out quickly.

www.nasm.si.edu

AIR and SPACE MUSEUM

202-633-1000

6th Street and Independence Avenue, SW, Washington, DC

Daily, 10–5:30. Closed December 25.

Metrorail Yellow, Green, Blue, and Orange lines (L'Enfant Plaza, Maryland Avenue exit, and Smithsonian exit).

Tourmobile stop.

Security: Must pass through metal detectors and have bags checked.

Highlight tours daily at 10:30 and 1; no reservations. Tour groups should schedule in advance via email or via phone at 202-633-2563.

Films daily on the museum's five-story IMAX movie screen. Presentation at the museum's Albert Einstein Planetarium. Fee for both.

There are two flight simulators, both with height restrictions.

Wheelchair access through ramps on both sides of building.

Take Note

Kids love the paper airplane contests held several times a day in the "How Things Fly" gallery. The hands-on exhibits let you hop on a scale to learn your weight on Jupiter, make a ball hover in the air, and explore nearly 50 other interactive devices.

National Aquarium, Washington

It's an unlikely spot, but you'll find the oldest aquarium in the United States on the lower level of the U.S. Department of Commerce Building. Among the 1,200 creatures of the deep are rare sea turtles, American alligators and tropical clownfish. Children enjoy the "Touch Tank," where they can hold hermit crabs and horseshoe crabs. A real draw for your child may be the shark feedings on Monday, Wednesday and Saturday at 2 p.m., the piranha feedings, Tuesday, Thursday and Sunday at 2 p.m. or the alligator feeding on Friday at 2 p.m. Even though some tanks are a bit high for the younger ones to peer into by themselves, this small aquarium is fun for all ages.

Take Note

This little gem is not to be confused with the National Aquarium in Baltimore, a much larger facility that can be a day-long outing. The aquarium in Washington is small with a subterranean feel; plan for a short visit.

www.nationalaquarium.com

202-482-2825

U.S. Department of Commerce Building, 14th Street and Constitution Avenue, NW, Washington, DC

Daily, 9–5. Last admission 4:30. Closed December 25 and Thanksgiving.

Adults, $5; children 2–10, $2.50; seniors and military personnel $4; children under 2, free.

Metrorail Blue or Orange line (Federal Triangle).

National Archives

The repository of America's records and documents features three exhibit galleries—the Lawrence F. O'Brien changing exhibit gallery; the Public Vaults permanent exhibit gallery; and the Rotunda for the Charters of Freedom, the home of the Declaration of Independence, the Constitution and the Bill of Rights. A good way to start your tour is by viewing the 11-minute introductory film in the McGowan Theatre. The theater also shows a film about the Charters of Freedom twice a day. A complete tour of the Archives takes about 90 minutes.

The Boeing Learning Center's Learning Lab allows 35 students to work as archivists and researchers in small teams. Reservations are required.

In the Center's ReSource room, students can sign their names to the Declaration of Independence via computer and print a copy before viewing the original, or grab a magnifying glass and examine a copy of a 1783 map. Reservations are not required.

www.archives.gov

202-501-5000 (recording)

Constitution Avenue between 7th and 9th Streets, NW, Washington, DC

Daily, March 15–Labor Day, 10–7; Tuesday after Labor Day–March 14, 10–5:30. Closed December 25 and Thanksgiving. ReSource Room open Monday–Friday 10–4.

Metrorail Yellow or Green line (Archives).

Guided tours, Monday–Friday at 9:45 a.m. Reservations must be made six weeks prior to visit date. Call 202-357-5450 to make a reservation. Reservations are also recommended for self-guided tours. These can be made via email at visitorservices@nara.gov. Visitors without reservations must wait in the general public line for entry.

Wheelchair entrance on Pennsylvania Avenue at 8th Street.

National Gallery of Art

One of the world's great art museums, the National Gallery contains major collections of European and American paintings and sculpture. Among its Renaissance and Dutch paintings are masterpieces by Raphael, Rembrandt and Titian. The gallery hosts major shows on loan from around the world in addition to its own special exhibits.

The West Building's main foyer, with its circular indoor fountain, is huge and awe-inspiring. For the main collection, children do well with an audio tour. For a small fee, recorded tours are also available for most major exhibits.

It's a quick trip on the lower-level "people mover" from West to East buildings and a pleasant place to take a break. Visitors pass a waterfall encased in glass as they travel between the two buildings. This is a scenic, indoor lunch spot. Small children especially enjoy this subterranean fountain, and love to ride the "people mover" back and forth.

The East Building is a feast for the eyes; children love the geometric shapes and unusual visual spaces created by architect I.M. Pei. Look for isosceles triangles in the architecture; they're everywhere. Mostly 20th-century art and special temporary exhibitions are displayed here, along with Henri Matisse's cutouts—the massive Alexander Calder mobile, and the Joan Miro tapestry in the vast open space.

Major special exhibits require a pass for admittance. These passes are distributed free of charge for each day beginning at 10 a.m. Some passes may be reserved in advance or purchased through Ticketmaster, 202-432-SEAT or 800-551-SEAT.

Free concerts are performed in the airy West Garden Court Sunday at 6:30 p.m., and on Wednesday at 12:10 p.m. in the East Building Auditorium. At other times, the court and other open spaces in the West Building offer visitors a peaceful place to rest.

The Micro Gallery, on the main floor at the West Building Mall Entrance, features interactive computers that let visitors create a personal tour. Visitors can choose a subject—horses, waterfalls, ballerinas or knights, for example—and print a map showing the locations of works of art fitting their theme.

Take Note

The 6.1 acre sculpture garden adjacent to the West Building offers benches and shady walkways, featuring 17 works by post-World War II artists. The garden's central plaza encircles a pool with a fountain in the warm months which also serves as an ice-skating rink in the winter. For information about the Sculpture Gardens Ice Rink and Pavilion Café call 202-289-3361. Skate rentals and lockers are available at the rink.

www.nga.gov

202-737-4215

East Building: 4th Street and Constitution Avenue, NW, Washington, DC
West Building: 6th Street and Constitution Avenue, NW, Washington, DC

Open Monday–Saturday, 10–5; Sunday, 11–6. Closed December 25 and January 1.

Metrorail Red line (Judiciary Square, 4th Street exit); Yellow or Green line (Archives).

Tourmobile stop.

Introductory tours: East Building, Monday–Friday, 11:30 and 1:30; Saturday–Sunday, 11:30 and 3:30. See web site for the list of several introductory tours of the West Building offered daily. Group tours may be booked three to four months in advance. A variety of school tours are available.

Parking spaces for handicapped visitors are next to the East Building entrance, located on 4th Street between Madison Drive and Pennsylvania Avenue. Wheelchair access is at both the East Building main entrance and

Take Note

The NGAKids page on the museum's web site offers interactive features for children, and lists many family programs at the museum, including family workshops and children's films.

23

the Constitution Avenue entrance to the West Building. Wheelchairs and strollers are available on a first-come, first-served basis at all entrances.

See Chapter 11, Field Trips, for more information.

National Museum of African Art

Located in the Smithsonian Quadrangle building next to the Arthur M. Sackler Gallery and the Smithsonian Arts and Industries Building, this underground structure is devoted to the collection, study and display of the traditional and contemporary arts of the entire African continent. Its exhibitions are drawn from the museum's collection of 7,000 African art objects in wood, metal, clay, ivory and fiber.

The museum offers ongoing drop-in workshops designed to encourage parent-child interactions as they learn about the arts and cultures of Africa. Each workshop involves exploring in the galleries and a hands-on art activity. These programs are free, require no registration and are intended for children ages 4–8. Check website for current offerings.

www.africa.si.edu

202-633-4600

950 Independence Avenue, SW, Washington, DC

Daily, 10–5:30. Closed December 25.

Metrorail Blue or Orange line (Smithsonian, Mall or Independence Avenue exit).

Wheelchairs are available upon request from the security officer at the Security Desk in the Pavilion.

National Museum of American History

The National Museum of American History is a repository of more than three million artifacts that preserve the history of the United States of America. The museum is closed for renovation and is expected to reopen in the summer of 2008.

More than 150 objects from the museum's historical collections are on view at the National Air and Space Museum while American History is closed. Objects include Dorothy's ruby slippers from "The Wizard of Oz,"

Kermit the Frog, Abraham Lincoln's top hat, Lewis and Clark's compass, Custer's buckskin coat, the Greensboro lunch counter, Thomas Jefferson's Bible and Edison's light bulb.

www.americanhistory.si.edu

202-633-1000

14th Street and Constitution Avenue, NW, Washington, DC

National Museum of Natural History

It's hard to decide where to begin a visit to this incredible Smithsonian center for the study of humans and their natural environment. The Kenneth E. Behring Family Hall of Mammals is spectacular. It contains 274 mammal specimens and nearly a dozen fossils in incredible exhibits with numerous hands-on features. It also has an evolution theater, which tells the dramatic story of mammal evolution over the past 225 million years.

Children are dazzled by the gem and mineral collections that include the world-famous Hope Diamond in the Hall of Geology, Gems and Minerals, and no trip is complete without a visit to the Dinosaurs/Hall of Paleobiology.

For children (and adults) with a buggy curiosity, you won't want to miss the Insect Zoo with its giant centipedes, tiny fruit flies, working anthills and beehives and other insect communities. A museum guide may even let you touch or hold some of the inhabitants. Well-marked exhibits and an enthusiastic staff make this display a highlight for children. The tarantula feedings are always popular, Monday–Friday at 10:30, 11:30 and 1:30, and Saturday and Sunday at 11:30, 12:30 and 1:30.

The museum's entertainment complex features an 80,000 square-foot multi-story Discovery Center, an IMAX Theater with a 3-D screen, an attractive café and great museum shops.

The museum also features a Discovery Room, a unique hands-on educational facility for families and students, where visitors can look at fossils, use a microscope and try on costumes from around the world. It is open from Labor Day–Memorial Day, Tuesday–Friday, noon–2:30, Saturday and Sunday, 10:30–3:30. Closed Mondays and most holidays. Summer hours (Memorial Day–Labor Day): Tuesday–Sunday, 10:30–3:30. Closed Mondays and some holidays.

Consider using the museum's new GO Interactive Audio Tour, a self-paced tour using a hand-held, touch screen computer, which allows visitors to select either a guided tour or a random-access tour. Highlight tours are given Tuesday–Friday at 10:30 and 1:30.

www.mnh.si.edu

202-633-1000

10th Street and Constitution Avenue, NW, Washington, DC

Daily, 10–5:30. Closed December 25.

Metrorail Blue or Orange line (Smithsonian, Mall exit; Federal Triangle, 12th Street exit).

Wheelchair access at Constitution Avenue entrance.

Security: All bags will be searched.

National Museum of the American Indian

The newest of the Smithsonian museums. NMAI a center for ceremonies, performances, and educational programs, as well as an exhibition space for the arts, history, and material culture of the indigenous peoples of the Western hemisphere and Hawaii.

The Lelawi Theater is a 120-seat circular theater where, through a 12-minute multimedia presentation, "Who We Are," visitors are introduced to the themes and messages they will encounter during their visit.

A one-hour highlight tour is offered Monday–Friday at 1:30 and 3 and Saturday and Sunday at 11, 1:30 and 3. During the summer tours are held on Mondays at 1:30 and 3 and Tuesday–Sunday at 11, 1:30 and 3.

The Museum provides a wonderful family guide on its website that suggests questions and activities to consider during a museum visit.

Take Note

Don't miss the Mistitam Café, which offers a welcome change from the food court fare found at many museum restaurants. The menu, based on the Native culinary traditions of the Americas, can feature anything from pumpkin soup and fried plantains to salmon smoked on a wood plank. The menu boasts kid-friendly fare, including buffalo burgers. Kids enjoy the view out the wall of windows to the water-feature landscaping. Open 10–5, full menu available from 11–3.

www.nmai.si.edu

202-633-1000

3rd Street and Independence Avenue, SW, Washington, DC
Next to the National Air and Space Museum on the Mall, across from the National Gallery of Art East Building.

Daily, 10–5:30, except December 25.

Security: All bags are searched.

Metrorail Blue, Orange, Yellow, Green lines (L'Enfant Plaza, Maryland Avenue/Smithsonian Museums exit).

Smithsonian Information Center ("The Castle")

For the visitor who wishes to be introduced to the 14 Smithsonian museums and the National Zoo in Washington, the Castle is the place to start. This aptly named structure was the first of the Smithsonian buildings and was designed by James Renwick, Jr. and completed in 1855. Today, it houses the Smithsonian Information Center. An 18-minute video orientation to the Smithsonian Institutions and two interactive touch screen stations provide information on the Smithsonian in six languages. There is also a scale model of the federal city.

www.smithsonian.org

202-633-1000

1000 Jefferson Drive, SW, Washington, DC

Daily 8:30–5:30. Closed December 25.

Metrorail Blue or Orange line (Smithsonian, Mall exit).

There is a limited number of on-street parking spaces for visitors with disabilities.

Wheelchair access at the northwest entrance. To receive "Smithsonian Access," a guide for visitors with disabilities, write: Information, Smithsonian Institution, Room 153, MRC010, Washington, DC 20560.

Take Note

★ The Smithsonian carousel, located near the Arts and Industries Building and the National Air and Space Museum, provides a pleasant way to take a sightseeing break while visiting the National Mall. Operates daily, year-round (weather-permitting), except Deccember 25. $2 per person.

★ M ♿ Ⓢ **United States Botanic Garden**

The United States Botanic Garden is the oldest botanic garden in North America. The Conservatory is a huge indoor space that allows visitors to experience bird's-eye views of the facility's plants, mosses and bridges by taking the stairs or the elevator to the catwalks two stories up, as well as wandering through the ground level. The Conservatory's "jungle" section also is home to hundreds of tree frogs, geckos and other amphibians and reptiles.

The complex also includes the Frederick Auguste Bartholdi Park with its historic fountain of sea nymphs and monsters, the newly created three-acre site of the National Garden and the DC Village Production Facility—a nursery and greenhouse complex responsible for producing all the Botanic Garden plants as well as many for Capitol Hill. Public programs offered include classes, information on gardening and botany, tours for schoolchildren and special exhibits. "Sprouts" is the Botanic Garden's family program. Check the website for current offerings.

A 45-minute highlight tour is available on some days; check with the information desk for availability. Groups of 10–25 may reserve a highlight tour that takes place Monday–Friday at 10:30 and 1:30 and on weekends if space permits. Reservations should be made at least three weeks in advance at 202-226-4082.

www.usbg.gov

202-225-8333

Independence Avenue and First Street, SW, Washington, DC
The main entrance to the conservatory is on Maryland Avenue, SW.

Conservatory 10–5; Bartholdi Park is open to visitors dawn until dusk.

Metrorail Orange or Blue line (Federal Center).

Sign language interpreters available by advance reservation 202-226-4082.

Restrooms are large and very clean.

★ Ⓜ ♿ ☐ Ⓢ Vietnam Veterans Memorial

This memorial to Vietnam Veterans was dedicated November 13, 1982. The design by Maya Ying Lin, then a 21-year old architecture student, consists of two black granite walls set in the ground in a shallow V. The walls are inscribed with over 58,000 names of the dead. At the entrances, books are available to assist visitors in finding specific names. Frederick Hart's life-sized sculpture of three soldiers and the Vietnam Women's Memorial designed by Glenda Goodace are also part of this memorial.

Set in the peaceful, contemplative surroundings of Constitution Gardens, the Vietnam Veterans Memorial imparts a powerful sense of loss. People touch and make rubbings of the names and leave tokens of every description. Be prepared to answer difficult questions from children about the Vietnam War.

> **Take Note**
>
> During the winter holiday season there is a spectacular model train display. The track winds around the West Orangerie. The trains travel past replicas of the DC monuments, the White House, and the Supreme Court. Everything is made from plant material, such as twigs, acorns and berries. Each year a new monument or two is added. The displays offer jaw-dropping detail, and are fun for children of all ages.

www.nps.gov/vive/home.htm

202-426-6841

Constitution Avenue between Henry Bacon Drive and 23rd Street, NW, Washington, DC
Park during the day on Ohio Drive off Independence Avenue or on Constitution Avenue during non-rush hours and on weekends.

> **Take Note**
>
> The Wall, by Eve Bunting and illustrated by Ronald Himler (Clarion, 1992), provides an excellent introduction for children ages 5–12 visiting the Vietnam Veterans Memorial.

Daily, 24 hours. Park Service rangers on duty 9:30 a.m.–11:30 p.m.

Metrorail Blue or Orange line (Foggy Bottom).

Wheelchair-accessible parking on Constitution Avenue between 20th and 21st streets, during non-rush hour times and on weekends. Additional handicapped parking is off of Independence Avenue and Ohio Drive on the Lincoln Memorial Circle near French Drive.

Facilities include bookstore, restrooms and concessions.

Washington Monument

This impressive obelisk rising 555 feet is our nation's memorial to our first president. A 70-second elevator ride takes visitors to the 500-foot level for a magnificent view of the city.

The stairwell inside the monument is closed to the public, but the elevator slows and the opaque elevator doors become clear, so that visitors can see some of the commemorative stones at several points on the way down.

www.nps.gov/wamo

202-426-6841

15th Street near Constitution Avenue, NW, Washington, DC

Daily 9–5, except December 25 and July 4. Last tour starts at 4:45.

Free timed tickets are handed out at the Washington Monument kiosk at 8:30 a.m. A maximum of 6 tickets will be given out per person in line. To reserve tickets in advance ($1.50/ticket fee) call 877-444-6777 or go to www.reservation.gov (24 hours to five months in advance). For advance group tickets call 877-559-6777. Pick up tickets at the "will call" window at the kiosk on the day of the tour.

Metrorail Blue or Orange line (Smithsonian, Mall exit).

Tourmobile stop.

Wheelchair ramp and elevator. Strollers must be parked before going up in the monument.

Security: Heightened security restrictions include no food or drink (open and unopened), and no suitcases or large backpacks. Allow up to 30 minutes prior to ticket time to go through security.

The White House and the White House Visitor Center

The White House has been the home of the American President since John Adams moved from Philadelphia in 1800. The private family quarters are not open to the public, but a visit to the handsome state rooms is always rewarding. Visitors should contact their Senator or Representative for information about tours of the Executive Residence.

Public tours of the White House are available for groups of 10 or more, and requests must be submitted through one's Member of Congress up to six months in advance. These self-guided tours take place between 7:30 a.m. and 12:30 p.m. Tuesday–Saturday, excluding federal holidays. Spots are available on a first-come, first-served basis, but tours are subject to last-minute cancellation. There is a 24-hour tour phone line to check the status of a tour: 202-456-7041. Please check the website for security procedures. The only items permitted in the White House are wallets, car keys, cell phones and umbrellas. (Note that purses are prohibited.) There are no storage facilities for personal items; do not bring them with you.

Take Note

A great website for kids to learn about the White House: www.whitehousekids.gov.

www.whitehouse.gov

202-456-7041-tours

1600 Pennsylvania Avenue, NW, Washington, DC (White House)

1450 Pennsylvania Avenue, NW, Washington, DC (Visitor Center)

The White House Visitor Center, located at the southeast corner of 15th and E streets, is open daily, 7:30–4, except for Thanksgiving, December 25 and January 1.

Metrorail Blue or Orange line (McPherson Square, Federal Triangle, or Metro Center); Red line (Metro Center).

The White House Visitor Center offers a 30-minute video and provides information.

Tourmobile stop on the Ellipse.

Restrooms and telephones are located at the Visitor Center. The public is not permitted to use the restrooms or telephones in the White House.

Wheelchair access at northeast gate. Strollers are not permitted in the White House. A stroller parking area is outside the visitors' east gate.

Special activities include the annual Easter Egg Roll festivities held on the White House lawn and the Ellipse on the Monday after Easter (open to children under age 7 accompanied by an adult).

Tours of the gardens are offered annually in the spring and fall. Tickets are required and can be obtained through the National Park Service. Call 202-208-1631 for more information or check the website.

The House is decorated for Christmas in early December. The National Christmas Tree Lighting and Pageant of Peace take place each December at the Ellipse across from the White House, at which the President lights the national Christmas tree and officially opens the holiday season.

ON CAPITOL HILL

The Capitol

The Capitol Guide Service offers a 45-minute guided tour of the U.S. Capitol. See all the areas in the Capitol open to the public: the Rotunda, Statuary Hall, original Capitol, Old Senate Chamber, Old Supreme Court Chamber, crypt area and beautifully decorated Brumidi and Cox corridors. The Whispering Gallery is fun for children. To visit the House and Senate Galleries, you must obtain a pass from your Representative or Senator. International visitors are issued passes by the Capitol Guide Service Personnel inside the South Screening Facility.

Tours begin at the Rotunda, daily, 9–4:30, Monday through Saturday, except Thanksgiving and December 25. First come, first served ticket distribution begins at 9 daily. One ticket per person in line—including children of any age. Tickets are not available in advance. Tickets are distributed at the Capitol Guide Service Kiosk near the intersection of 1st Street, SW and Independence Avenue. Ticket holders are then directed to the South Visitor Receiving Facility. Visit your Member's website for information on tours conducted by staff.

www.aoc.gov; www.house.gov; www.senate.gov

202-225-6827; 202-224-3121

East end of the Mall on Capitol Hill, Washington, DC

Open on federal holidays. Closed Thanksgiving and December 25.

Metrorail Red line (Union Station); Blue or Orange line (Capitol South).

The United States Capitol Historical Society conducts exterior walking tours of the Capitol every Monday at 10:00. The tour is two hours long. Call 202-543-8919 x17 or email tours@uschs.org for reservations. The cost of the tour is $10; $5 for children 6–10; free for children under 6. For more information check the website www.uschs.org.

Senate and House open only when in session and by advance reservations with your Congressional representative.

Wheelchair access on east side; elevators inside. Special areas in both galleries for wheelchairs.

Security: Call 202-225-6827 to check security concerns. No cans, bottles, aerosols, liquids, backpacks or large bags allowed, and entry is prohibited for visitors with these items. Check the website for up-to-date security information.

Take Note

Out-of-town school groups (or individuals) should write or call their Senators or Representatives before coming to Washington. Elected officials will sometimes meet with their young constituents and even have a picture taken with the group on the steps of the Capitol, but you must arrange this before your trip. If you are planning to visit in the busy spring season, be sure to make arrangements six months prior to your visit.

Eastern Market

This farmers' market, originally built in 1873, is still a lively produce market. Children enjoy the outdoor event on Saturdays; there is much to look at and much to buy. Vendors sell an array of fruits, vegetables, and flowers; other colorful stalls are crowded with jewelry, cotton clothing, wooden toys, African-American art and pottery.

www.easternmarket.net

202-546-2698

7th and North Carolina Streets, SE, Washington, DC

Metrorail Blue or Orange line (Eastern Market), walk north on 7th Street until you see the market.

Limited wheelchair access. Strollers are allowed, but the market is crowded during the summer and on Saturdays.

Folger Shakespeare Library

The largest Shakespeare collection in the world, the Folger Shakespeare Library houses a unique collection of rare books and manuscripts relating to the humanities of the Renaissance and focusing on Shakespeare. Don't miss the Elizabethan Theater, used throughout the year for plays, lectures, concerts and poetry readings.

www.folger.edu

202-544-4600

201 East Capitol Street, SE, Washington, DC
Capital Beltway (I-495) to the Baltimore-Washington Parkway (Rt. I-295). Turn left onto 6th Street. Turn left on Pennsylvania and then right on 3rd Street. The Folger is the second building on the left. To reach the front of the building, turn left on East Capitol Street. Located one block from the US Capitol, between 2nd and 3rd Streets on East Capitol Street SE.

Open Monday–Saturday, 10–4. Closed Sunday and federal holidays.

Metrorail Blue or Orange line (Capitol South) or Red line (Union Station).

Walk-in tours, 11 a.m., Monday–Saturday, and an additional 1 p.m. tour on Saturdays. Children's guides to the exhibition are available at the visitors' desk at no cost.

Wheelchair access in rear of building, between 2nd and 3rd Streets. Enter behind the Folger and ring bell at the entrance to notify security staff.

Special activities include a series of Saturday Family Programs for children 8–12, and 12+ and their parents, with activities ranging from paper-making to fencing; Shakespeare's Birthday Open House in April features food, games, balloons and free performances for kids of all ages, including demonstrations of stage combat and swordplay. This is the one day of the year when the reading rooms are open to the general public allowing the public to view the "Famed Seven Ages of Man" stained glass window.

Library of Congress

The Library of Congress is the oldest cultural institution in the United States and the largest literary treasure house in the world. Home to an astonishing collection of nearly 135 million items, as well as beautifully organized digital collections and online resources for scholars of all ages, its three impressive buildings are named after U.S. Presidents who contributed to the development of Congress's library.

Thomas Jefferson's personal collection of nearly 6,500 books became the foundation for the Library's collection after the British burned the Capitol and the first Library in 1814. The building named for him was built in 1897, and its magnificent Main Reading Room with its 160 foot high domed ceiling is not to be missed. Though the entrance is through the Visitors Center, take a look outside at the three decorative bronze doorways depicting Tradition, Writing and Printing. Look for Minerva (shown as both a Goddess of War and of Peace) and her owl in the statues along the ceiling of the marble Great Hall. One of the three perfect copies of the Gutenberg Bible is displayed in the East Corridor.

A stellar series of chamber concerts, poetry readings and film programs are offered in the Library throughout the year. Most events are free, though the concerts require tickets that carry a small service charge.

www.loc.gov

202-707-8000

101 Independence Ave, SE Washington, DC
The Visitors Center is located inside the west front entrance of the Thomas Jefferson Building, Ground Level. The entrance is open to the general public from 10 a.m.–5 p.m., Monday–Saturday.

Metrorail Orange or Blue line (Capitol South)

Monday–Saturday, 10–5; closed Sundays and federal holidays.

National Children's Museum

The National Children's Museum, founded on the 30-year legacy of the former Capital Children's Museum, is scheduled to open in National Harbor in 2012.

www.ncm.museum

202-675-4120

National Postal Museum

Housed in an historic 1914 Beaux-Arts building, the National Postal Museum is the perfect place to engage school children in a trip through history. They'll see the railway postal car where 600 pieces of mail were sorted in an hour, early mail planes hanging from the ceiling in the central court area, the unusual homemade mailboxes from rural America and around the world and vehicles used in mail delivery—a stagecoach, a mail truck on a sled and a Model T with wild snow tires.

Many interactive kiosks are available, including one allowing children to use a computer to address a postcard and receive information about the postcard's destination. The visitor inserts the postcard into a high tech postage meter in order to find out the postcard route.

The final highlight of the National Postal Museum is a state-of-the-art interactive exhibit of three-dimensional holograms. Make your own personal ID card, which records your photograph, personal preferences and tastes, as you travel through the gallery to learn about direct mail. Adults enjoy the ZIP code database where they can punch in a ZIP code and learn about the people in that area. A final memento as you leave includes a discount coupon at the museum store.

www.postalmuseum.si.edu

202-633-5555

2 Massachusetts Avenue, NE, Washington, DC
Next to Union Station.

Daily, 10–5:30. Closed December 25.

Metrorail Red line (Union Station, Massachusetts Ave exit).

To schedule a guided tour, call 202-633-5534.

United States Supreme Court

This dazzling white marble building dates from 1935 and houses the highest Court in the land. It is a powerful symbol of the third branch of our democratic government. The spectacle of the Court in session is most impressive. Note the bronze doors at the west entrance, depicting scenes in the historic development of law, and the Great Hall with the marble busts of all the former Chief Justices.

www.supremecourtus.gov

202-479-3211

1st Street and Maryland Avenue, NE, Washington, DC
Located at One First Street, NE, across from the US Capitol and the
Library of Congress.

Weekdays, 9–4:30. Closed weekends and federal holidays.

*Seating for oral arguments is on a first come, first seated basis. Lines
form on the plaza in front of the building. There are two lines: one to
listen to the entire argument, for which seating begins at 9:30, and one
for a three-minute viewing, for which seating begins at 10.*

Metrorail Red line (Union Station); Blue or Orange line (Capitol South).

Tourmobile stop.

*Free lectures offered every hour on the half-hour, 9:30–3:30, except dur-
ing court sessions. Visitors informationline, 202-479-3211, provides current court sitting information.*

Wheelchair access at Maryland Avenue entrance.

*Security: Supreme Court Police Officers are on duty and there are two
security checkpoints. Security is very tight.*

No infants or small children are allowed in the court.

AROUND TOWN

The African-American Civil War Memorial Freedom Foundation and Museum

The memorial design features low semi-circular walls bearing plaques with over 209,000 names of members of the United States Colored Troops as well as the names of the white officers that led them. These walls surround a bronze sculpture depicting soldiers from the various armed forces along with a family of women, children and elders. The sculpture serves as a reminder of the efforts of African-American Civil War soldiers to free their families from slavery. The museum, two blocks away at 12th and U Streets, contains prints, photographs, newspaper articles and replicas of period clothing, uniforms and weaponry.

www.afroamcivilwar.org

202-667-2667

10th and U Streets, NW, Washington, DC

Metrorail Green or Yellow line (U Street-Cardozo).

Special activities include First Saturday drills and Civil War Reenactments, Founder's Day, Martin Luther King, Jr. Day, Black History Month, Veterans Day and "Drummer Jackson" tours for children (available on request).

Anacostia Community Museum and Center for African American History and Culture

This museum, run by the Smithsonian Institution, documents the experiences, culture and heritage of African Americans and people of African descent through paintings, sculpture and historical documents. Films, slides and touchable artifacts often accompany exhibits and make for a stimulating museum experience for all. Exhibitions change frequently and include a variety of projects and activities that stress participation from preschool to adult groups. Guided tours are available on Saturdays by reservation. Pre-tour materials are provided for scheduled groups, and teaching kits are available to educators.

www.si.edu/anacostia

202-287-2060 recording, 202-287-3306 main office

1901 Fort Place, SE, Washington, DC
Capital Beltway (I-495) to I-395 north over the 14th Street Bridge. Stay in the right lane to cross over the Case Bridge, stay to the left and proceed on I-395 (Southeast/Southwest Freeway) and cross over the 11th Street Bridge. Follow signs to Martin Luther King, Jr. Avenue exit to Morris Road, which becomes Erie Street and then Fort Place. Stay to the right at Fort Place; the museum is on the right.

Daily, 10–5. Closed December 25.

Metrorail Green line (Anacostia). Take the LOCAL exit and turn left to the W2/W3 bus stop on Howard Road. The W2 and W3 buses stop in front of the museum.

Special activities include film programs, lectures and history discussions.

Bureau of Engraving and Printing

Millions of dollars are printed here daily. The Bureau also prints stamps and other official government financial papers. Visitors watch all the processes involved in producing currency—printing and cutting sheets of special papers and, most impressive, stacking and counting the bills. A recording gives explanations and background information.

Take Note

The "BEP for Kids!" section of the website presents many entertaining "Money Facts," including anti-counterfeiting features of our currency.

www.moneyfactory.gov

202-874-2330

14th and C Streets, SW, Washington, DC

Call the Tour Office, 202-874-2330 or toll free 866-874-2330, for updates on public tours and visitor hours.

In peak season (March–August) free tickets are required; the ticket booth is at Raoul Wallenberg Place (formerly 15th Street).

Metrorail Orange or Blue line (Smithsonian).

Tourmobile stop.

Some wheelchairs available. Strollers are not permitted on tour route.

Security: Photo I.D. required. No backpacks or sharp objects allowed.

Corcoran Gallery of Art

The Corcoran Gallery is the oldest and largest private museum of art in the nation's capital. Founded in 1869 by William Wilson Corcoran, the museum is dedicated to encouraging American excellence in the fine arts.

Spacious entrance atriums and a grand staircase welcome visitors to this museum, famous for its American art collection with outstanding examples from the Colonial period to present times. Gilbert Stuart's famous portrait of George Washington, well-known landscapes of the Hudson River School and monumental historical paintings are familiar to many children. In the European galleries, look for the fine selection of French Impressionist paintings. The museum is also known for its extensive collection of modern photography.

The Corcoran School of Art and Continuing Education Program offers children and adults a variety of classes on drawing, painting, sculpture and American crafts.

www.corcoran.org

202-639-1700, 202-639-1786 cafe

500 17th Street, NW, Washington, DC
Located at 17th Street and New York Avenue, NW.

Sunday, Monday and Wednesday, 10–6; Thursday, 10–9, Friday and Saturday 10–5. Closed Tuesdays, December 25, and January 1.

The café is open for lunch Wednesday–Saturday, dinner on Thursday and Sunday Gospel Music brunch.

Admission to the permanent collection: $6, children under 6 are free. Admission fees for special exhibits vary. Check website for details and prices.

Metrorail Orange or Blue line (Farragut West, 17th Street exit); Red line (Farragut North, K Street exit).

Walk-in tours daily at noon (except Tuesdays), 7:30 p.m. on Thursday; and Saturday–Sunday at 2:30. Special tours for children's groups can be arranged by calling 202-639-1730.

Wheelchair access on E Street; call prior to visit.

Special activities include exhibitions emphasizing contemporary art, photography and Washington regional art. Special events, dance performances, concerts, and storytelling are frequently scheduled in conjunction with these exhibitions. The Sunday Tradition program encourages families with children ages 5–12 to investigate the various styles of art represented in the galleries. Contact the Office of Education, 202-639-1727, for specific information or email familyprograms@corcoran.org.

Daughters of the American Revolution Museum

The museum, located in DAR headquarters, features two galleries with changing exhibitions of American decorative arts and 31 period rooms. Visit the New Hampshire Attic, where dolls, toys and children's furniture from the 18th and 19th centuries are displayed. Then visit the parlors, kitchen and dining rooms, all furnished with fine period objects.

www.dar.org/museum

202-628-1776

1776 D Street, NW, Washington, DC.

Gallery open 9:30–4, Monday–Friday; 9–5 Saturday. Period rooms open weekdays, 10–2:30 and Saturdays 9:30–4:30. Closed Sundays and federal holidays.

Metrorail Red line (Farragut North); Blue or Orange line (Farragut West).

Special school program tours are offered for elementary school classes. Teachers should call 202-879-3240 at least two weeks in advance to schedule a visit.

Wheelchair access on C Street; call prior to visit.

Special activities include "Colonial Adventure," offered the first and third Saturdays from September to May for children age 5–7 years; call 202-879-3240 for reservations.

Decatur House Museum

This elegant, Federal-style townhouse faces Lafayette Square across from the White House. It was designed by Benjamin Henry Latrobe for Commodore Stephen Decatur, an early American naval hero. Decatur and his wife moved into this home in 1819, but they lived here only 14 months before the Commodore was mortally wounded in a duel. There followed a succession of distinguished residents. In 1871 General Edward Fitzgerald Beale and his wife moved into the house and introduced a number of Victorian features. The first floor, in the Federal style, is furnished as it might have been during the Decaturs' residency.

The second floor is furnished in the Victorian manner and includes parquet flooring in the drawing room.

www.decaturhouse.org

202-842-0920

748 Jackson Place, NW, Washington, DC
Capital Beltway (I-495) to Connecticut Avenue south. Follow several miles into downtown Washington. Turn right on 17th street. Turn left onto H Street. The museum is on the right at the corner of H Street and Jackson Place.

Open Tuesday–Saturday, 10–5; Sunday, noon–4. Closed Thanksgiving, December 25, and January 1.

Call to make reservations for groups larger than 10 people and for school and children's programs; 202-842-0920.

Metrorail Red line (Farragut North, K Street exit); Blue or Orange line (Farragut West, 17th Street exit).

Partial wheelchair access.

Special activities include three open houses, walking tours, family programs, lectures, workshops and holiday events throughout December and January. Interactive programs and tours are available for groups of children and schools.

Discovery Creek Children's Museum of Washington

Discovery Creek is a living laboratory for science, history and art exploration, committed to helping children experience, appreciate and become stewards of the natural environment. Discovery Creek has four environmental education centers and one mobile site, but most programs are planned around the 12-acre wilderness of the Potomac Palisades Parkway. The museum offers high-quality science workshops for children. The staff is knowledgeable and excellent at teaching large groups of children. The workshops and classes incorporate live animals, art projects and a guided walk in the woods.

Discovery Creek offers wildlife, craft activities, hikes, summer and winter camps, adventure programs, birthday parties and family field trips at the Glen Echo Stable. Special exhibits change every few months.

Take Note

The outdoor play area features a large sandbox, and a small bridge in a natural setting that's perfect for playing "The Three Billy Goats Gruff." Children like to trip-trop across the bridge as goats and hide underneath as trolls.

www.discoverycreek.org

202-337-5111

4954 MacArthur Boulevard, NW, Washington, DC

Open to families on weekends: Saturdays and Sundays from 10–3.

Ages 2–64, $5; seniors, $3; members and infants under 2, free.

Group visits for 10 or more can be booked Tuesday–Friday.

Climbing wall available the first weekend each month.

Dumbarton Oaks Gardens and Museum

Dumbarton Oaks Gardens, an oasis in bustling Georgetown, is spectacular in the spring, beautiful in the fall and pleasant in the winter. The estate's ten acres of terraced hillsides, formal and informal plantings, and curving footpaths are artfully landscaped, expertly maintained and enjoyed by children and adults. After viewing the gardens, follow Lover's Lane (on the east border of the gardens) to Dumbarton Oaks Park, a 27-acre wooded, natural area best known for its pools, waterfalls and spring wildflowers.

The museum features Pre-Columbian and Byzantine art. The Byzantine Gallery presents the luxury arts of the Roman Empire with a few choice objects from the western Medieval and Islamic traditions, while the Pre-Columbian Collection displays some of the finest artistic achievements of the native peoples of the New World.

www.doaks.org

202-339-6401

3101 R Street, NW, Washington, DC
Museum entrance at 1703 32nd Street, NW.

Museum is open Tuesday–Sunday, 2–5. Closed Monday and federal holidays. Suggested $1 donation at museum.

Gardens open daily, 2–5, except for Mondays, holidays and inclement weather. Gardens open until 6 from March 15–October 31.

Admission to gardens March 15–October 31: adults and children over 12, $8; senior citizens and children, $5. No admission charge to gardens from November–March 15.

Nearby Montrose Park (see p. 176) has many pleasant picnic spots.

Tours available by appointment for groups of 12 or more.

Visitors with disabilities should call 202-339-6409 in advance of a visit for accessibility information.

Ⓜ Ford's Theatre, Lincoln Museum, Petersen House

The museum, located in the basement of the theater, provides a self-guided tour that follows Lincoln's career as a lawyer, campaigner, president and, finally, as the victim of an assassin's bullet. Among the memorabilia on display are the clothes Lincoln wore that fatal night. Talks by Park Service rangers describe the events that led up to the assassination.

To complete the story, visit the Petersen House directly across the street at 516 10th Street, NW, 202-426-6830. The wounded president was carried into the bedroom of the house, where he died the next morning. The theater and museum are scheduled to be under construction. Petersen House remains open during this period.

www.fordstheatre.org

202-426-6924

511 10th Street, NW, Washington, DC
Capital Beltway (I-495) to I-395 north toward Washington DC, over the 14th Street Bridge past the National Mall. At F Street turn right and then right onto 10th Street. The theater is located between E and F Streets.

Daily, 9–5. Closed December 25. Theater closed to visitors during matinee performances (Thursday, Saturday, Sunday). Call to verify museum hours on matinee days.

Self-guided tours when no performance is in progress. Call 202-426-6924 to check times.

Metrorail Red, Blue or Orange line (Metro Center, 11th Street exit); Yellow or Green line (Gallery Place, G Street exit).

Talks are held 15 minutes past each hour from 9–5 by National Park Service rangers in the orchestra of the theater. When the theater is closed, talks are held in the museum.

Wheelchair access to theater and museum, but not to balcony or Petersen House. Strollers permitted, but must be carried up and down stairs.

M Franciscan Monastery

The Mount St. Sepulchre Franciscan Monastery is an unusual church, located in a 44-acre woodland a short drive from the Basilica. The grounds include one of the largest rose gardens in the country. Along the garden walks are the 14 Stations of the Cross with replicas of shrines in Bethlehem and Lourdes. Children like the catacombs beneath the church.

www.myfranciscan.org

202-526-6800

14th and Quincy Streets, NE, Washington, DC
Capital Beltway (I-495) to I-395 north to 12th Street exit. Turn right onto Constitution Avenue. Turn left onto Louisiana Avenue and then left onto North Capitol Street to Michigan Avenue; go east (right) on Michigan Avenue, past Catholic University; right on Quincy Street. Monastery is at the top of the hill. Parking across the street on 14th and Quincy.

Daily, 1–5.

Metrorail Red line (Brookland/Catholic University), then take the H2/H4 bus to 14th and Quincy Street NE.

Free tours of the Monastery, including the catacombs, at 10,11,1,2,3 (Monday–Saturday) and 1,2,3 Sunday.

Wheelchair accessible everywhere but catacombs.

Frederick Douglass Home (Cedar Hill)

The noted orator and anti-slavery editor Frederick Douglass spent the later years of his life at Cedar Hill. The character of the fervent abolitionist is reflected in the furnishings of the house and in information given on regular tours, which cover 14 of 21 rooms. One point of interest is the "Growlery," a small, one-room structure, separate from the house, to which Douglass often retreated. Most of the furniture and artwork is original to the house and is typical of that found in any upper-middle-class white or African-American home of the late 19th century. The handsome brick house with its commanding view of the Federal City is spacious and comfortable by the standards of the late 19th century.

www.nps.gov/frdo

202-426-5961, 877-444-6777; reservations required

1411 W Street, SE, Washington, DC
South Capitol Street from the Capitol to the Southeast Freeway; then cross the 11th Street Bridge; go south on Martin Luther King, Jr. Avenue; east on W Street. Parking available on site.

Daily, 9–4; from mid-April to mid-October, 9–5. Closed Thanksgiving, December 25 and January 1.

$1.50/person.

Metrorail Green Line (Anacostia). Connect to a B-2 (Mt. Rainer) bus; there is a bus stop directly in front of the home. Continue down W Street to 15th Street; the Visitor Center is a half-block from the stop on the right.

Films about Douglass's life are shown on the hour, followed by National Park Service guided tours of grounds and home. All tours begin at the Visitor Center.

Wheelchair accessibility is limited.

Special activities include an annual Christmas open house in December, events commemorating Frederick Douglass's birthday and Black History Month in February. The Annual Oratorical Contest for area students is held in mid-January.

Hillwood Estate, Museum and Garden

The home of American businesswoman and cereal heiress Marjorie Merriweather Post boasts among its treasures 90 jeweled items crafted by Fabergé. The 25-acre estate in the middle of Washington DC is home to one of the world's most remarkable collections of 18th- and 19th-century Russian imperial art outside of Russia, a fascinating collection of French decorative arts and an impressive house and gardens. A film about Mrs. Post's life precedes the tour and is an excellent introduction to the founder's life and her collections of art.

www.hillwoodmuseum.org

202-686-5807

4155 Linnean Avenue, NW, Washington, DC
Tilden Street east from Connecticut Avenue to second left onto Linnean Avenue. The entrance gate is on the right.

Tuesday through Saturday, 10–5. Closed January and on national holidays.

Self-guided tours and docent-led tours available daily. Young person's audio tour of the Russian collection available.

Free parking available.

20-minute walk from the Van Ness/UDC Metro station.

Suggested donation: Adults $12, seniors $10, college students $7, children $5.

Café open 11–4:30 for lunch and tea. Reservations for lunch are recommended; call 202-243-3920.

Special activities include the Fabergé Egg Family Festival held the weekend of Palm Sunday, and the Russian Winter Festival held the middle weekend of December. Both programs feature hands-on art activities, family tours and Russian music.

Interior Department Museum

The breadth of the Interior Department's activities is evident in the variety of the exhibits here. Native-American artwork, dioramas and natural history specimens help to tell the Department's story. National parks, mining, geological research and pottery are among the topics explored in the museum's well-crafted displays. Exhibits, featuring hundreds of photographs and historic and contemporary artifacts, present an overview of the Department's past and current activities.

www.doi.gov/interiormuseum

202-208-4743

1849 C Street NW, between 18th and 19th Streets, NW, Washington, DC Capital Beltway (I-495) to I-66 East. Go to the Constitution Avenue exit, go north two blocks on 18th Street, NW, turn left on C Street to the entrance on the right.

Weekdays, 8:30–4:30 and on the third Saturday of each month from 1–4. Closed on federal holidays.

Reservations for guided tours and appointments to view the New Deal murals must be made two weeks in advance by calling 202-208-4743.

Metrorail Blue or Orange line (Farragut West, 18th Street exit).

Stroller and Wheelchair access at E Street entrance.

Security: Photo I.D. required.

International Spy Museum

The International Spy Museum has a fantastic collection of espionage artifacts from around the world and provides an educational and entertaining look at the role that spies play in current and historical events. The "School for Spies" exhibit looks at the motivation and skill required for a career in espionage, along with a chance for visitors to try out their proficiency in observation and analysis. In the "Spies Among Us" exhibit, visitors may be intrigued to find chef Julia Child along with singer Josephine Baker and movie director John Ford.

www.spymuseum.org

202-393-7798, 866-779-6873 toll-free

800 F Street, NW, Washington, DC
Between 8th and 9th Streets, across from the National Portrait Gallery.

Daily from 10 a.m. (9 in the summer) except Thanksgiving, December 25 and January 1. Closing times vary; check the website.

Adults (12–64), $16; seniors, active duty military, and the Intelligence community, $15; children 5–11, $13; children under five free. Tickets are available until one hour before closing and may be purchased in advance; this is recommended April through Labor Day, especially on weekends and holidays. Self-guided tours are available at special rates for student and youth groups grades five and above. There are various membership packages.

Metrorail Red, Yellow or Green line (Gallery Place/Chinatown and National Archives).

No strollers.

Ⓜ Islamic Center

This mosque is one of the largest and most ornate in the United States. Guides explain the religious service and point out the rich decorations of the building—the rugs, mosaics and art objects are outstanding examples of Islamic design and craftsmanship. Prayers are held five times daily.

www.islamiccenterdc.com

202-332-8343

2551 Massachusetts Avenue, NW, Washington, DC

Open for individual visits 10 a.m.–10 p.m.

Guided tours are available for groups, by prior reservation, 10:30–4:30, every day except Tuesday.

Shoes must be removed; female visitors must cover themselves except for face, hands and feet.

Metrorail Red line (Dupont Circle).

Katzen Arts Center/American University Museum

Permanent exhibitions at the Museum are the University's memorial Watkins collection of modern art and the collection of representative works in Pop Art (Roy Lichtenstein), Washington art (Gene Davis and Sam Gilliam) and glass sculpture donated to American University by Dr. Cyrus and Myrtle Katzen.

www.american.edu/museum

202-885-3634

4400 Massachusetts Avenue NW, Washington DC
Ward Circle at the intersection of Massachusetts and Nebraska Avenues NW

Tuesday Sunday, 11–4.

"Kids@TheKatzen" series offers hands-on art activities for children ages 5 and up.

Performances at the Katzen Arts Center's Studio Theatre include music and drama.

John F. Kennedy Center

Performances of music, opera, dance, theater and film from the United States and abroad are presented on the stages of the Kennedy Center. There are five main theaters: the Concert Hall, Opera House, Eisenhower Theater, Terrace Theater and Theater Lab. The first three of these theaters is separated by two great parallel halls, one decorated with the flags of the 50 states, and the other with the flags of the nations of the world. Children enjoy these impressive displays and enjoy the outdoor terrace overlooking the Potomac. The center has been decorated with a dazzling array of gifts from many nations.

www.kennedy-center.org

202-467-4600

2700 F Street, NW, Washington, DC
Capital Beltway (I-495) to I-66 east across the Roosevelt Bridge. Bear right to exit to Independence Avenue. Go under Roosevelt Bridge and Kennedy Center is the second entrance on the right. Parking garage on site.

Building open daily. Business hours are 10–6; open to the public from 10 a.m.–midnight.

Metrorail Orange or Blue line (Foggy Bottom), about a seven-minute walk. Shuttle service provided from Foggy Bottom.

Tourmobile stop.

Free tours by Friends of the Kennedy Center, Monday–Friday, 10–5 and Saturday–Sunday, 10–1 every 15–20 minutes. Tours start at Parking Level A.

Tours in Spanish, German, French and Japanese upon request. Print and online tour guides are available in 11 languages. For special tour arrangements, call 202-416-8340.

Call 202-416-8340 to arrange for a wheelchair. Free listening system for the hearing-impaired in theaters.

Take Note

Don't miss seeing the renowned bronze sculpture of President John F. Kennedy in the Grand Foyer and the view from the rooftop terrace; these are worth a trip even if you don't see a show. Also free performances are offered most evenings at 6 on the Millennium Stage. (See p. 213.)

Special activities include performances for children and families throughout the year (Kennedy Center Performances for Young Audiences feature ticket prices as low as $15 per ticket) and an annual open house in September.

10+ Koshland Science Museum

The Marian Koshland Science Museum of the National Academy of Sciences engages the public in many of the most important scientific issues of our time. Interactive displays based on findings of the National Academy of Sciences illustrate the role of science in informing national policy and people's daily lives. Recent exhibits have included DNA, global warming, infectious diseases and the wonders of science. The museum hosts several special events per month, including educational activities for groups, teachers and school district coordinators.

www.koshland-science-museum.org

202-334-1201 or 888-KOSHLAND

6th and E Streets, NW, Washington, DC

Daily, 10–6, except Tuesdays. Last admission, 5 pm. Closed Thanksgiving and December 25.

Metrorail Red, Green or Yellow line (Gallery Place/Chinatown or Judiciary Square)

Adults, 18–65, $5; Seniors, children, students active duty military, $3; Groups of 20 or more $2.

Recommended for children 13+

Wheelchair accessible.

Field trips are available for middle school, high school and undergraduate classes and are free to student groups from the Washington area.

 ### The Kreeger Museum

The Kreeger Museum, located at the former residence of Carmen and the late David Kreeger, contains an impressive collection of 19th- and 20th-century paintings and sculptures by such artists as Picasso, Van Gogh, Monet, Kandinsky, Miro, Rodin, Stella and Moore, as well as has a broad range of African art and sculpture. The setting alone is worth the visit!

www.kreegermuseum.org

202-338-3552 (for reservations), **202-337-3050** (office)

2401 Foxhall Road, NW, Washington, DC. Free limited parking.

90-minute docent-led tours Tuesday–Friday, 10:30 and 1:30, and Saturday, 10:30. Reservations are required for weekday visits. Closed some holidays

$8; seniors and students, $5.

Children over 12 are welcome for weekday tours. All ages welcome during Saturday open hours. With prior arrangements, school groups (sixth grade and above) are welcome.

Wheelchairs available for access to main floor only. No strollers or child carriers.

Recommended for children age ten and older.

Special activities include story times for ages 3–5, and art workshops for children aged 8–12.

Lincoln Cottage/President Lincoln and Soldiers' Home National Monument

Note: The cottage is expected to open to the public in February 2008.

During the Civil War, Lincoln resided seasonally on the grounds of the federally owned Soldiers' Home. Each year from 1862 to 1864, Lincoln commuted daily by horseback or carriage from the Soldiers' Home to the White House from June through November. During his first summer in residence, Lincoln developed his emancipation policy. Today, the Soldiers' Home still commands spectacular views of the city.

www.lincolncottage.org

202-829-0436

Located on the grounds of the Armed Services Retirement Home, Upshur Street and Rock Creek Church Road, NW, Washington, DC

M Madame Tussauds Washington DC

The newest addition to this London institution's chain, Madame Tussauds Washington, DC features this town's local celebrities—politicians. Former DC Mayor Marion Barry and *Washington Post* reporter Bob Woodward, of Watergate fame, join Hillary Clinton, George W. Bush and Richard Nixon, among other local luminaries. The museum uses touch-screens and recordings to bring to life historic celebrities such as Abraham Lincoln and Rosa Parks.

www.madametussaudsdc.com

888-929-4632

1025 F Street, NW, Washington, DC

Open daily 10–6.

Adults, $25; children $18; $10 for all ages Friday and Saturday.

Metrorail Red, Yellow or Green line (Gallery Place).

National Building Museum

As soon as you step off the Metrorail escalator, you will be awed by this massive and beautiful brick structure. Adapted from palace plans of the Italian Renaissance, it was designed in 1881 to be a modern office building for the Pension Bureau. Now it serves as a museum celebrating American achievements in building. As you approach the museum, look up at the buff-colored terra cotta frieze. It shows six Civil War military units encircling the building on an endless march. Inside, children love the Great Hall, a space large enough to enclose a 15-story building, and the frequent, family-friendly special events. Exhibition galleries are in interconnecting rooms off the Great Hall and upstairs.

The permanent exhibit "Washington: Symbol and City" is located on the first floor. The touchable, large-scale models and objects of the Capitol, White House, Washington Monument and Lincoln Memorial have hands-on appeal for families. Exhibit games ask questions that are answered by pushing a button.

Other permanent and temporary exhibits focus on the building trades, urban planning, architecture, engineering and historic preservation.

www.nbm.org

202-272-2448

401 F Street, NW, Washington, DC

Daily, 10–5; Sunday, 11–5. Closed Thanksgiving, December 25 and January 1.

Metrorail Red line (Judiciary Square, F Street exit).

45-minute tours, Monday–Wednesday, 12:30; Thursday–Sunday, 11:30, 12:30 and 1:30. No reservations required for groups fewer than 10. Call ahead to schedule a group tour.

Wheelchair access, G Street entrance. Wheelchairs are available upon request at the Information Desk.

Special activities include summer camps, workshops, photography and architecture displays and demonstrations. Check out the "Family Tool Kits," the "Treasure Hunt Activity Booklet," or the "Adventures in Architecture Scavenger Hunt," available daily at the museum. Families love the special festivals for exploring science, engineering, and the building arts, which feature hands-on activities such as making marshmallow molecules or building a brick wall; see web site for dates.

Take Note

The National Building Museum offers free family walk-in workshops on bridges and structures on weekends. Bridging the Gap is offered at 10:30 on Saturdays and Arches and Trusses is offered at 11:30 on Sunday. Additional hands-on family programs occur two to three times per month, including model airplane flying in the Great Hall.

National Geographic Society Explorers Hall

Explorers Hall houses a wide variety of interactive traveling exhibits, installations that include the society's famous photography and a National Geographic store.

www.nationalgeographic.com/explorer

202-857-7000, 202-857-7588, recording

17th and M Streets, NW, Washington, DC

Open Monday–Saturday, 9–5; Sunday, 10–5. Closed December 25.

Metrorail Red line (Farragut North); Metrorail Blue or Orange line (Farragut West).

National Museum of Health and Medicine of the Armed Forces

Originally established during the Civil War as the Army Medical Museum, this is one of the few places where you can learn about medical history, the human body and disease by actually seeing real specimens. Some are graphic and may not be appropriate for all ages or for those who are squeamish. The museum has five main displays: Civil War Medicine, Battlefield Surgery 101, From A Single Cell, Human Body/Human Being and Evolution of the Microscope. For older children and teens interested in nursing or medicine as a career, this museum is worth a visit. You can compare a smoker's lung to a coal miner's lung, or view a real human hairball and a brain still attached to the spinal cord.

www.nmhm.washingtondc.museum

202-782-2200

Walter Reed Army Medical Center, 6900 Georgia Avenue, NW, Bldg. 54, Washington, DC
Capital Beltway (I-495) to Georgia Avenue (Rt. 97) / Wheaton exit south; drive past the junction with East-West Highway (Rt. 410). Turn right onto Elder Street, NW onto the Walter Reed Army Medical Center campus. Turn right at the first stop sign and follow the winding road past the hospital/garage complexes onto Dahlia Street to the museum entrance on the right.

Daily, 10–5:30. Closed December 25.

On weekdays, free parking with a pass from the museum's information desk. On weekends, parking is free and passes are not required.

The museum is a short bus ride from the Silver Spring or Takoma Park stops on the Metrorail's Red Line. Take Metrobus 70 or 71 from the Silver Spring Metro station to the Dahlia Street bus stop. Take Metrobus 52, 53, or 54 from the Takoma Park Metro station to Butternut Street gate, or the K2 Metrobus to the Dahlia Street gate.

Guided tours available for grades five and up.

Special activities include the free "National Health Awareness Kickoff" program on the first Saturday of each month. Each month a new topic is highlighted. Call 202-782-2200 to make reservations.

National Museum of Women in the Arts

This is a comfortably small museum housing art by women from the 16th century to the present day. Included are works by Mary Cassatt, photographs by Louise Dahl-Wolfe, and sculpture by Camille Claudel. Special exhibits present international women's accomplishments. The galleries in which works are displayed are not too large, so children can wander through them without feeling lost.

During the school year, the museum's Education Department offers Sunday children's programs relating to the current exhibition or aspects of the permanent collection. Special tours geared to children ages 6–12 are offered and often are followed by a related hands-on experience. Call for details.

The Museum offers a variety of programs for children and families, including Family Programs, Family Festivals and Role Model Workshops. These are designed to foster creativity and celebrate art.

www.nmwa.org

202-783-5000

1250 New York Avenue, NW, Washington, DC

Daily, 10–5; Sunday, noon–5. Closed Thanksgiving, December 25 and January 1.

Adults, $10; senior citizens and students, $8; youth 18 and under, free.

Metrorail Red, Blue or Orange line (Metro Center, 13th and G Streets exit).

Walk-in tours conducted if a docent is available.

A limited number of wheelchairs is available on site.

Special activities including: the exploration of art in the galleries; art projects guided by museum staff; multicultural performances by local musicians, dancers and singers; and hands-on workshops.

National Portrait Gallery

The National Portrait Gallery examines American history by focusing on the individuals who have aided in the development of our nation. The collection includes paintings, sculptures, prints, drawings and photographs of prominent American statesmen, artists, writers, scientists, Native Americans and explorers. It includes the famous "Landsdowne" portrait of George Washington, as well as portraits of notable Americans such as Pocahontas, Marilyn Monroe and Shaquille O'Neal. The museum shares a building with the Smithsonian American Art Museum at the Donald W. Reynolds Center for American Art and Portraiture.

npg.si.edu; www.reynoldscenter.org

202-357-2700

8th and F Streets, NW, Washington, DC

Daily 11:30–7, except December 25. (Note that opening time is later than most DC museums.)

Metrorail Red, Green or Yellow line (Gallery Place, 9th Street exit).

National Shrine of the Immaculate Conception

This is the largest Roman Catholic Church in the Western Hemisphere. It is an ideal location to introduce children to the majesty and elegance of religious art.

www.nationalshrine.com

202-526-8300

4th Street and Michigan Avenue, NE, Washington, DC
The shrine is adjacent to Catholic University.

Daily Monday–Saturday, 9–11 and 1–3; Sunday 1:30–4.

Group tours (45 minutes long) by special arrangement.

Metrorail Red line (Brookland/Catholic University).

Security guards on duty.

Special activities include seasonal displays, summer organ recital series and periodic free concerts.

National Zoo

The 163-acre National Zoo has long been acclaimed as one of the best and most attractive facilities of its kind in the country. Particularly impressive are the free-ranging Golden Lion Tamarins, which explore the trees in the zoo's Beaver Valley; the many baby animals; and, of course, the giant pandas from China. The feeding and waking times for animals vary according to the season, so refer to an Information Station for a listing of the day's events. The Wetlands Exhibit around the Birdhouse and the prairie dogs across from the outdoor giraffe yard are treats for younger children. Other favorites include the giraffes, lions and tigers, hippos and elephants. Older children and teens will enjoy learning about intelligence in the Think Tank exhibit, while everyone marvels at orangutans crossing overhead on the O-Line between the Great Ape House and Think Tank.

The Amazonia exhibit, housed in its own building, brings the humidity of Washington summers indoors. A translucent domed roof covers the mahogany, kapok, and balsa trees from which sloths hang upside down and singing tanagers dart. Amazonia is a good introduction to tropical rain forests and their interdependent river ecosystems. Children enjoy spotting the hidden animals and watching the water flow through the exhibit.

The new Asia Trail features sloth bears, clouded leopards and the giant pandas. The Kids' Farm features a petting zoo and a giant pizza play area, and is especially popular with small children.

www.natzoo.si.edu

202-673-4717

3001 Connecticut Avenue, NW, Washington, DC
Rock Creek Park entrance at Adams Mill Road and Beach Drive.

Daily except December 25. April 1–October 31: grounds, 6–8; buildings, 10–6. November 1–March 31: grounds, 6–6; buildings, 10–4:30.

Parking fees: $4 for the first hour, $12 for 2–3 hours, and $16 for more than three hours. Parking is free for FONZ (Friends of the National Zoo) members.

Metrorail Red line (Woodley Park-Zoo, a 7-minute, uphill walk) or (Cleveland Park, a 6-minute, level walk).

Strollers are available for rent. $4 per single stroller, $11 per double.

Schedule group tours online, or call 202-673-4989 or send email to grouptours@fonz.org.

How Do You Zoo? is an interactive exhibit for grades K through 5 focused on careers at the zoo. Visit it Saturdays and Sundays from 10–4.

A limited number of wheelchairs are available. Handicapped parking is available in Lot A, near Connecticut Ave. entrance, in Lot B, near the Elephant House, and in Lot D near the lower duck ponds. All exhibits are wheelchair-accessible. However, be aware that the zoo is located on hilly terrain in Rock Creek Park.

Special activities include lectures, Sunset Serenades concert series in the summer (see p. 224), Seal Days in March, African-American Family Celebration in April, Panda Anniversary Celebration, Guppy Gala in May, and Boo at the Zoo in October.

Take Note

The Zoo is crowded on weekends and holidays during good weather, and the parking lots fill up fast. Try to go early in the day during the week, or go later in the day and stay for a picnic dinner. Public transportation is highly recommended, but if little ones are along, remember to conserve energy for the long climb back up the hill and the walk to the Metrorail stop at the end of your visit.

Navy Art Gallery

Spend an intriguing afternoon at the Navy Art Gallery and view some of its over 15,000 paintings, prints, drawings and sculpture. The Navy Art collection contains depictions of ships, personnel and action from all eras of the U.S. naval history, with World War II, the Korean War, the Vietnam War and Desert Shield/Storm particularly well represented.

www.history.navy.mil/branches/nhcorg6.htm

202-433-3815

822 Sicard Street, SE, Washington Navy Yard, Washington, DC

Monday–Friday, 9–3:30. Closed Saturday, Sunday and federal holidays.

Recommended for older children.

The Navy Museum

Explore ship to shore at the US Navy Museum and "sea" what you've been missing. Hands-on permanent exhibits are devoted to the history of the US Navy from the Revolutionary War, through the polar explorations of Admiral Richard Byrd and Finn Ronne, to the Navy's role in the Korean War. Spin the ship's wheel of the USS Hartford in the museum's Civil War exhibit, maneuver the 40mm anti-aircraft guns in the WWII exhibit, and check out the interactive "Dive, Dive" exhibit, featuring working periscopes. Additional exhibits chronicle the Navy's achievements in exploration, diplomacy and scientific development. When you've finished exploring the museum, climb aboard destroyer *Barry* and experience life at sea during the Cold War.

www.history.navy.mil

202-433-4882

805 Kidder Breese SE, Washington Navy Yard, Building 76, Washington, DC

Open Monday–Friday, 9–5; weekends and holidays 10–5.

Reservations are required for visitors without military identification.

Special activities include performances by Navy bands and ensembles, family programs and hands-on educational programs for children. All events are free and open to the public. Please call 202-433-6897 for reservations and additional information.

 Newseum

Exhibits in the Newseum's seven floors offer multiple ways to understand the history, technology and power of reporting. Interactive ways of looking at photographic, print and electronic journalism allow visitors to go behind the scenes to look at the decision making process in developing news stories and at the importance of the First Amendment in keeping us informed.

Pulitzer-prize winning photographs, editorial cartoons and comprehensive looks at the coverage of history-making events, such as the fall of the Berlin Wall and September 11, 2001, are among the permanent exhibits.

www.newseum.org

888-NEWSEUM (639-7386)

555 Pennsylvania Avenue, NW, Washington, DC

Metrorail Green or Yellow line (Archives or Gallery Place); Blue or Orange line (Smithsonian); Red line (Gallery Place)

The Octagon

The Octagon was built by Colonel John Tayloe III between 1799 and 1801 to serve as his winter townhouse. During the War of 1812, the building served as the temporary White House for President and Mrs. Madison, and the Treaty of Ghent was signed here on February 17, 1815, ending that war.

The Octagon served as the headquarters for the American Institute of Architects between 1889 and 1949 and is currently owned by the American Architectural Foundation. Trained docents discuss the early history of Washington, DC, the Tayloe family, the architecture of the house and its decorative arts furnishings and regale visitors with ghost stories. There are changing architectural exhibitions in the second floor galleries.

www.archfoundation.org/octagon

202-638-3221

1799 New York Avenue, NW, Washington, DC
New York Avenue at 18th Street, NW.

The Octagon is currently open only to groups of 10–25 people with advance reservations. Walk-in visitors cannot be accommodated at this time. Adults, $5; senior citizens and children, $3. Call 202-638-3221 for reservations.

Metrorail Blue or Orange line (Farragut West, 18th and I Streets exit); Red line (Farragut North, K Street exit).

Wheelchair access at garden entrance. Strollers are not permitted.

Old Post Office Pavilion

The Old Post Office was restored and rededicated in 1983. Its large interior courtyard houses a wide and lively variety of shops and specialty kiosks and is the setting for concerts and arts programs. Take a free tour of the 315-foot tall clock tower, which offers a breathtaking view of Washington from the 270-foot observation deck and is home to the bells of the U.S. Congress.

www.nps.gov/opot; www.oldpostofficedc.com

202-289-4224

1100 Pennsylvania Avenue, NW, Washington, DC
Capital Beltway (I-495) to I-395 toward DC to 12th street exit.

Pavilion open daily: Labor Day through Memorial Day.

Metrorail Blue or Orange line (Federal Triangle) or Red line (Metro Center).

Tours to Congress Bells and the Old Post Office Tower are available daily and begin approximately every 5 minutes.

Strollers should be left outside or in the lobby.

Security: All visitors must pass through security including metal detectors.

Special activities include live entertainment daily, international cuisine, shopping and seasonal special events such as Family Fun Days. Bell ringing demonstrations are occasionally held for the public.

Take Note

Many locals consider going to the top of the Old Post Office Tour a good alternative to touring the Washington Monument, as there are seldom long lines, no advance tickets are necessary and the view is excellent.

Old Stone House

The Old Stone House is the oldest and only surviving pre-Revolutionary building in Washington. This was the modest home and shop of a Colonial cabinet-maker and is representative of a middle-class dwelling of the period. Its small size makes it seem cozy and comfortable to children. Older children may be intrigued by the rumors of a resident ghost (see p. 118 for more information on Rock Creek Park). This is a good place to stop for a picnic lunch.

www.nps.gov/olst

202-895-6070

3051 M Street, NW, Washington, DC
Capital Beltway (I-495) to exit 34 onto Rockville Pike (Rt. 355) south for 8 miles. (Rockville Pike will become Wisconsin Avenue.) At the intersection of Wisconsin Avenue, NW and M Street, NW in Georgetown, turn left and go 1.5 blocks. The Old Stone House is on your left, across from Jefferson Street, NW.

Open Wednesday–Sunday, noon–5. Closed January 1, July 4, Thanksgiving and December 25.

Metrorail Orange or Blue line (Foggy Bottom). It is a fairly long walk from the Metro.

Ranger-led talks and group programs by reservation.

Wheelchair access limited to ground floor. Strollers permitted in the garden, but not in the house.

Special activities include historical programs and demonstrations of period crafts. There is also a Christmas candlelight program in December.

Phillips Collection

The Phillips Collection, America's first museum of modern art, is a lovely and comfortable place to introduce children to art. This outstanding collection of mainly 19th- and 20th-century European and American painting and sculpture, with a sprinkling of old masters, is tastefully displayed in the former home of the Phillips family. Youngsters like the small rooms and connecting passageways that create a less formal atmosphere than a big museum, and with chairs in each room, children have a place to rest. Try to plan your visit around one of the family tours sometimes available for special exhibits. Don't miss Renoir's "Luncheon of the Boating Party" or other fine paintings by such artists as Bonnard, Braque, Daumier, Cezanne or Klee.

www.phillipscollection.org

202-387-2151

1600 21st Street, NW, Washington, DC
One-half block off Massachusetts Avenue on 21st Street, NW between Q and R streets.

"Family Fun Packs," designed to facilitate visits with children to the permanent collection and special exhibitions, are available upon request. (Please call in advance.) Saturday morning teacher programs provide teachers with approaches for helping students interpret art forms.

Open Tuesday–Saturday, 10–5; Sunday, 11–6; Thursday, 10–8:30. Closed Monday and all major holidays. Regular tours Wednesday and Saturday at 2; call to arrange special tours for children or adults.

Metrorail Red line (Dupont Circle, Q Street exit).

Strollers and front-facing baby carriers are permitted in galleries; backpacks, including back baby carriers, are not.

All galleries are wheelchair accessible. A limited number of wheelchairs is available at the coat check.

Special activities include a Family Free Day with many children's activities, the first Saturday of June; chamber music concerts (free with museum admission) performed in the gallery on Sundays (held October–May) at; and occasional family workshops.

Renwick Gallery

Designed in 1859 by architect James Renwick, Jr. to house the collection of William Corcoran, this building was Washington's first private art museum. Due to the growth in his collection, Corcoran moved his paintings and sculpture to the Corcoran Gallery of Art, and the Renwick became a showcase for American crafts and decorative arts.

 www.americanart.si.edu

 202-633-2850

Pennsylvania Avenue and 17th Street, NW, Washington, DC
Across from the Old Executive Office Building, near the White House.

Daily, 10–5:30. Closed December 25.

Metrorail Red line (Farragut North); Blue or Orange line (Farragut West and Farragut Square exit).

Call 202-633-8550 to arrange group tours.

Wheelchair access, corner of Pennsylvania Avenue and 17th Street. Wheelchairs are available.

Smithsonian American Art Museum

Formerly the National Museum of American Art, the Smithsonian American Art Museum is dedicated to American crafts from the 19th century to the present. More than 7,000 American artists are represented in the collection, including John Singer Sargent, Winslow Homer, Mary Cassatt, Georgia O'Keeffe and Jacob Lawrence. The museum shares a building with the National Portrait Gallery in the Donald W. Reynolds Center.

The museum includes folk, contemporary and pop art that's often off-beat. Children especially enjoy the Lincoln Gallery with its contemporary art, including Nam June Paik's *Electronic Superhighway: Continental U.S., Alaska, Hawaii,* a multimedia floor-to-ceiling map of the U.S. that features simultaneous film clips representing every state. The museum includes lifelike statues of ordinary people doing ordinary things, such as the woman in the Lincoln Gallery eating an ice cream sundae. *Preamble,* by Mike Wilkins, uses 51 vanity license plates to spell out (approximately) the Preamble to the U.S. Constitution, located on the first floor, north wing.

Take Note

Visit the museum's website for "Meet Me at Midnight" and numerous other interactive art rooms for children; and "Ask Joan of Art," a fascinating online reference service.

www.americanart.si.edu, www.reynoldscenter.org

202-633-7970

8th and F Streets, NW, Washington, DC

Daily 11:30–7, except December 25. (Note that opening time is later than that of most DC museums.)

Metrorail Red, Green or Yellow line (Gallery Place, 9th Street exit).

Textile Museum

The Textile Museum is devoted exclusively to the handmade textile arts with a collection of more than 17,000 rugs and textiles. The museum presents several changing exhibitions each year which range from Oriental carpets to contemporary fiber art, giving visitors a unique sampling of the richness and diversity of the textile arts. Of special interest to children is the "Textile Learning Center," comprised of two galleries: The Activity Gallery and the Collections Gallery. The Activity Gallery is a hands-on exhibition where visitors can learn about spinning, dyeing and weaving. The Collections Gallery is devoted to three rotating themes: How are Textiles Made?, Who Makes Textiles?, and Why are Textiles Important?

www.textilemuseum.org

202-667-0441

2320 S Street, NW, Washington, DC
Capital Beltway (I-495) to Connecticut Avenue south to S Street in the Kalorama neighborhood. Turn right on S Street and proceed two blocks to the museum on the left.

421 7th Street, NW, Washington, DC
Second location added in 2008.

Open Monday–Saturday, 10–5; and Sunday, 1–5. Closed federal holidays and December 24.

Metrorail Red line (Dupont Circle, Q Street exit).

Garden area available for picnics; no seating provided.

Stroller and wheelchair accessible; call in advance for information.

Special activities include Family First Saturdays, the first Saturday of every month. Activities are free; reservations are not required. Celebration of Textiles held the first weekend in June features hands-on textile art activities and demonstrations.

8+ Tudor Place

History buffs from third grade up find Tudor Place with its many relics from George Washington's home a logical complement to a visit to Mount Vernon (see p. 106). Located in the heart of Georgetown on five fragrant landscaped acres, Tudor Place was built for Martha Custis Peter, granddaughter of Martha and George Washington. Purchased for $8,000 and designed by Dr. William Thornton, architect of the U.S. Capitol, Tudor Place remained in the Peter family for 180 years. The household objects, sculpture and manuscripts provide insight into America's history and culture in a setting once frequented by Henry Clay, Daniel Webster, John C. Calhoun and General Robert E. Lee. A children's "look and find" pamphlet helps focus young visitors' attention.

www.tudorplace.org

202-965-0400

1644 31st Street, NW, Washington, DC
Capital Beltway (I-495) to Wisconsin Avenue/Rt. 355 south for about
6 miles past the National Cathedral. Turn left onto Q Street. Stay on Q
Street for two blocks and turn left onto 31st Street. Look for the large
gate and tour entrance on the left.

*Open Tuesday–Friday with docent-led tours at 10, 11:30, 1, and 2:30.
Saturday tours are every hour on the hour from 10–3. Sunday tours are
every hour on the hour from 12–3.*

Gardens are open Monday–Saturday, 10–4 and Sunday from 12–4.

Admission for the house tour is: adults, $6; seniors, $5; students, $3; children 6–12, $2; children under 6, free.

Admission for the self-guided garden tour is $2.

Partially wheelchair accessible. Strollers permitted in the gardens only.

*Special activities include Fall Garden Day in October, a day dedicated
to family-oriented activities, candlelight tours at Christmas, Celebrate
George on Presidents Day and summer programs where children become history detectives for a week.*

U.S. Holocaust Memorial Museum

The Holocaust Museum is one of the most visited and talked about museums in Washington. People are drawn from all over the world to try
to understand the history and the deeper meaning of this global tragedy. From the top floor of the building, visitors guide themselves down
through four levels, tracking the Holocaust's progression from Hitler's
rise to power to the liberation of the camps in 1945. Interspersed within
the time line are many opportunities to read, watch and hear personal
accounts of individuals who experienced the Holocaust.

One of the most moving parts of the museum is "Remember the Children: Daniel's Story," geared for younger children. In "Daniel's Story,"
children and their parents can trace the life of a young boy and his
family as they struggled to survive Nazi persecution. As visitors move
through the maze of rooms that represent the various places Daniel's
family lived during the war, they can see the war's impact on even the
most mundane level of life. At the end of the exhibit, children are encouraged to draw a picture or to write about their feelings.

www.ushmm.org

202-488-0400

100 Raoul Wallenberg Place, SW, Washington, DC
14th Street and Independence Avenue.

Daily, 10–5:30. The museum is open until 7:50 p.m. on Tuesdays and Thursdays, April through mid-June.

Timed tickets are required to enter the permanent exhibition. Reserve advance tickets (with service fee) through www.tickets.com or 800-400-9373. A limited number of same-day tickets are available at the 14th Street entrance beginning at 10.

Closed on Yom Kippur and December 25.

No passes are needed for the special exhibits and the interactive Wexner Learning Center.

Metrorail Blue or Orange line (Smithsonian, Independence Avenue exit).

Most museum programs do not require tickets.

To schedule groups larger than 21 people, contact Group Scheduling at 202-488-0419 or group_visit@ushmm.org about six months in advance.

Union Station

Just minutes from the Capitol, Union Station contains over 125 stores, an immense food court, and a nine-screen movie complex. The restored 1907 Beaux-Arts structure still serves as Washington's primary train station, and was once the largest in the world. Its classic lines in white granite set the stage for many of the early 20th-century buildings and monuments of Washington including the Lincoln and Jefferson Memorials and the Supreme Court building.

Take Note

The food court downstairs offers a wide array of options, while the family-friendly restaurants on the main floor offer excellent people-watching as travelers and tourists bustle through the impressive, high-ceilinged interior.

www.unionstationdc.com

202-371-9411

50 Massachusetts Avenue, NE, Washington, DC
Massachusetts Avenue between 1st and 2nd Streets, NE.
Adjacent parking garage with entry on H Street, NE (many shops in Union Station will validate parking tickets).

Stores: Monday–Saturday, 10–9; Sunday 12–6.

Metrorail Red line (Union Station).

Tourmobile stop.

U.S. Navy Memorial and Naval Heritage Center

Discover a beautiful 100-foot diameter world map in granite, visit the Lone Sailor Statue—one of the most photographed statues in America—participate in Navy ceremonies, visit the U.S. Presidents Room and enjoy evening spring concerts by the U.S. Navy Band. A highlight is the 35-minute film explaining life on an aircraft carrier. Viewers young and old are absorbed by the demonstrations and explanations of the way jet pilots take off and land safely on a ship's moving flight deck.

www.navymemorial.org

202-737-2300, ext. 713 or 733

701 Pennsylvania Avenue, NW, Suite 123, Washington, DC
Between 7th and 9th streets.

Open Monday–Saturday, 9:30–5. Closed Mondays, November–February.

Movie "At Sea" shown at 9:45, 12:45 and 3:30. "A Day in the Life of the Blue Angels" airs at noon.

Metrorail Yellow or Green line (Archives/Navy Memorial).

Special activities include outdoor concerts on the plaza with the U.S. Navy Band, Memorial Day through Labor Day. Call 202-737-2300, ext. 768, for the special events hotline.

WVSA ARTiculate Gallery

Washington DC's only youth-run art gallery, ARTiculate Gallery opens eight original shows each year. These events primarily showcase the remarkable artwork of the artist apprentices in the ARTiculate Employment Training Program studios adjacent to the gallery. ARTiculate Gallery also occasionally features other youth or community artists.

www.wvsarts.org

202-261-0204

1100 16th Street, NW, Washington, DC
At L Street, NW.

Monday–Friday, 10–6.

Metrorail Red line (Dupont Circle, South) or Blue or Orange line (Farragut West).

M **◻** Washington National Cathedral

This splendid Episcopal 14th-century–style Gothic cathedral, begun in 1907 and completed in 1990, is the sixth largest in the world. The tour of the main cathedral, small chapels and crypts is especially informative. Children are impressed by the stained glass and stonework in the Children's Chapel. A visit to the Pilgrim Observation Gallery is also exciting, beginning with an elevator ride to the enclosed gallery at the roof level of the cathedral. The gallery affords an excellent view of Washington as well as the gargoyles, flying buttresses and gardens of the cathedral. Don't miss the gardens and the herb cottage.

The Cathedral Medieval Workshop, open to the public on Saturday from 10–2, is a hands-on workshop where parents and children can work with stones to see how cathedrals are built. This workshop is appropriate for ages five and up. There is a materials fee. Please call 202-537-2934 for more information.

There are also hands-on demonstrations of the other art forms involved in the "Family Saturday," where children are introduced to the wonder and majesty of the Cathedral with storytelling, Cathedral exploration, and art projects. Reservations are accepted up to one month in advance.

Be sure to bring your binoculars and walking shoes for the Gargoyle tours. These tours feature stories about the Cathedral gargoyles, and give you a chance to see these funny and surprising creatures. A fee does apply. The tour is available between April and October (on the fourth Sunday of the month at 2) and between May and July (on the fourth Thursday of the month at 6:30) Reservations are not required. The tour is open for children 10 and older.

www.cathedral.org/cathedral

202-537-6200

Massachusetts and Wisconsin Avenues, NW, Washington, DC
Capital Beltway (I-495) to Wisconsin Avenue South for about six miles. The Cathedral is on the left at the corner of Wisconsin and Massachusetts.

Weekdays, 10–5:30; Saturdays, 10–4:30; Sundays, 8–6:30.

Guided tours, adults, $3; senior citizens, $2; children, $1. Audio tour $5 per person. Tours last approximately 30 minutes and are held on Monday–Friday, 10–11:30 and 12:45– 4; Saturday, 10–11:30 and 12:45–3:15;

and Sunday, 12:45–2:30. No tours during services or special events. Maps for self-guided tours are available.

Metrorail Red line to Tenleytown/AU. Obtain a bus transfer while in the Metro for discount bus fare, then take any "30" series bus south for about 1 mile to the Cathedral.

A limited number of wheelchairs are available on loan. Most of the nave and some crypt chapels are accessible with ramp entrances.

Security: No strollers, bags or packages may be left unattended. Bags are subject to search at some events.

Special activities include the annual Open House, usually held the last Saturday of September. Featured are craft demonstrations and hands-on crafts; musical performances; games; and special activities. The "Cathedral's Flower Mart," usually held the first Friday and Saturday in May, features an antique carousel, hands-on crafts, and an excellent selection of herbs and plants to purchase for your garden. For more information regarding seasonal events please call 202-537-6200.

Washington Navy Yard

The Washington Navy Yard is the Navy's oldest shore establishment, home to the Naval Historical Center, which comprises Navy Art Gallery (see p. 59), the Navy Museum (see p. 60), and the display ship *Barry*, a decommissioned destroyer open to the public for self-guided tours.

www.history.navy.mil

202-433-2218

Main entrance to complex at 9th and M Streets, SE, Washington, DC

The U.S. Navy Museum and display ship Barry *are open Monday–Friday from 9–5 and on weekends and holidays from 10–5.*

The Navy Museum is free to the public. Visitors must use the 11th and O streets Gate on weekdays. On weekends, use the entrance at 6th and M Streets, SE. Reservations are required to visit the museum on weekends, and for all visitors without military I.D. Call 202-433-6897. Reservations must be made by noon on the preceding Friday.

M **Woodrow Wilson House**

Immediately following the inauguration ceremonies for President Harding, Woodrow Wilson and his wife moved from the White House to this stately townhouse, where he lived until his death. The only house of a former president open to the public in Washington, it still reflects the presence of this scholarly and idealistic man; the drawing room and library contain souvenirs from all over the world. Children might also be interested in the well-stocked kitchen of the 1920s, the 1915 elevator and the graphoscope and an early film projector.

www.woodrowwilsonhouse.org

202-387-4062

2340 S Street, NW, Washington, DC
From Dupont Circle, travel north on Massachusetts Avenue for five blocks, turn right onto 24th Street, then right onto S Street, and proceed to 2340 S Street.

Tuesday–Sunday, 10–4; closed major holidays.

Adults, $7.50; senior citizens, $6.50; students, $3; children under 7, free. Free to National Trust Members.

Advance reservations preferred. Fill out the form on the website. Non-reserved tours available as space permits.

Metrorail Red line (Dupont Circle). Go west to 24th and S Street.

Special tours and outreach programs for elementary and secondary classes are available. Call for details.

Limited wheelchair access. Strollers should be parked downstairs.

Special activities include Preservation Garden party in May; Museum Walk Weekend the first weekend in June; Kalorama House and Embassy Tour the third Sunday in September; Christmas on S Street in December; and school programs and exhibitions held throughout the year.

3

MAIN SIGHTS IN MARYLAND

African Art Museum of Maryland

10+

This museum displays African art and offers hands-on art experiences for children. The building, called the Historic Oakland, dates to 1811.

www.africanartmuseum.org

410-730-7106

5430 Vantage Point Road, Columbia, MD
Rt. 29 to Columbia; exit at Rt. 175 (Town Center) to Vantage Point Road; proceed to Historic Oakland, which houses the museum.

Open by appointment only. Call for information.

Adults, $2; children and seniors, $1; members, free.

Available for rental by calling the Columbia Association at 310-730-4801.

Limited wheelchair accessibility.

Special activities include programs for children age 6–12.

American Indian Cultural Center/Piscataway Indian Museum

The Piscataway Indian Museum offers a vision of Native American life in Maryland before European settlers. A major exhibit of the museum is the full scale, re-constructed "longhouse," the type of home lived in by the Piscataways at the time of their first contact with the early settlers. Docents dressed in traditional clothing greet students and teach history through a presentation involving a series of hands-on, participatory activities. These activities teach students about diversity and help to break down stereotypical images associated with the term "American Indians." A learning/resource room and a Trading Post also are housed in the building.

www.piscatawayindians.org/museum.html

301-372-1932

16816 Country Lane, Waldorf, MD
Capital Beltway (I-495) to Branch Avenue (Rt. 5) south (east toward Waldorf for ten miles). Turn left onto Cedarville Road and follow for one and a half miles. Turn right onto Country Lane; the entrance to the museum is on the left.

Sunday, 11–4, and by appointment.

Admission, $3.

Special tours by appointment for grades K–12.

Special activities include a Native American Indian Festival in June and a fall festival in September. Additional events posted on website.

Beall-Dawson House and Stonestreet Museum of 19th Century Medicine

This 19th-century home teaches children of all ages about the history of Montgomery County, including lots of clues about rural life in the 1800s. Children discover unusual period furniture, 19th-century alternatives to plumbing, and subtle ways (by today's standards) that Upton Beall displayed his wealth.

The Stonestreet Museum of 19th Century Medicine is located on the grounds of the Beall-Dawson House. It is the original one-room office used by Dr. Edward Elijah Stonestreet from 1852–1903. This unique museum displays exhibits of medical, surgical, dental and apothecary equipment. Children are delighted by the real skeleton, the Civil War amputation kit and bleeding instruments. A hands-on reproduction of an 1850s stethoscope shows how difficult it was for a 19th-century doctor to diagnose illnesses.

www.montgomeryhistory.org

301-340-2825

Montgomery County Historical Society, 111 West Montgomery Avenue, Rockville, MD
Capital Beltway (I-495) to I-270 north to Rt. 28 exit east toward Rockville; turn left on Montgomery Avenue (Rt. 28); go one block, entrance on left. Free parking behind house on Middle Lane.

Open Tuesday–Sunday, noon–4; closed major holidays.

Adults, $3; students and seniors, $2. Members, children 5 and under, free.

Metrorail Red line (Rockville).

No wheelchair access. Strollers are permitted.

Special educational programs available for Brownies and Girl Scouts.

Special activities include "Dr. Stonestreet Holds Office Hours" the second Sunday of every month; Heritage Days, a county-wide event with history sites throughout the county, held the last full weekend in June; Summer History Camp for grades 5–7, held in July and August; an annual Happy Birthday, Montgomery County community celebration the Sunday after Labor Day; In Search of Ghosts, a Halloween ghost tour (best suited for children 9 and up), the Friday before Halloween; Santa arrives at the Water House in a horse-drawn wagon the first Sunday in December, followed by a tree lighting; Holiday Decorations Tour including hot cider and cookies during December. Groups should call ahead for all programs.

Belair Mansion

The Belair Mansion, a Georgian plantation house built in about 1745 by the provincial governor of Maryland, Samuel Ogle, is filled with 18th-century paintings, furniture and silver.

www.cityofbowie.org/museum

301-809-3089

12207 Tulip Grove Drive, Bowie, MD

Capital Beltway (I-495) to Rt. 50 east (toward Annapolis) travel about 7 miles to Exit 11 (Rt. 197) for 1 mile; turn right on Tulip Grove Drive; turn right at the stoplight. Proceed 0.5 miles down Tulip Grove Drive. The Mansion is at the top of the hill, and the library and stable are further down the street where Tulip Grove Drive terminates at Belair Drive. Parking available.

Take Note

The City of Bowie operates the Belair Mansion, the Belair Stable Museum and the Bowie Railroad Station and Old Town Bowie Welcome Center and Childrens Heritage Center, their collections and exhibits. The City joins with the Radio History Society to present the Radio and Television Museum. Call 301-809-3088 for information.

Wednesday–Sunday, 12–4, except federal holidays.

Group tours for 10 or more by appointment.

Metrorail Orange line (New Carrollton). Transfer to Metrobus B24.

Mansion available for rental for up to 75 people; call 301-575-2488.

Check website for special family events.

Belair Stable

The Belair Stable was built in 1907 and produced some of the greatest American thoroughbred race-horses. The small museum, soon to undergo a substantial renovation, is on the grounds of the beautiful Belair Mansion. Groups of children can tour the estate with a docent and imagine what life might have been like on an 18th-century tobacco farm.

www.cityofbowie.org/museum

301-809-3089

2835 Belair Drive, Bowie, MD

Wednesday–Sunday, 12–4, except federal holidays.

Bowie Train Station and Old Town Bowie
Welcome Center and Childrens Heritage Center

Children will particularly enjoy the railroad museum located at the site of the junction of the old Baltimore and Potomac Railroads founded in 1872. They can climb the tower at the depot and get a bird's eye view of trains as they fly by the station. Inside, they can send an imaginary message via telegraph and get an idea of communication in the pre-email era.

www.cityofbowie.org/museum

301-809-3089

8614 Chestnut Avenue, Old Bowie, MD

Capital Beltway (I-495) to Rt. 50 east (toward Annapolis) travel about 7 miles to Exit 11 (Rt. 197) Collington Road/Bowie north, drive 4 miles. Left onto route 564 for 1 mile into Old Bowie. Rt. 564 makes a right and goes over the bridge crossing the railroad; however, continue straight on 11th Street, turn right onto Chestnut Street, and go to the end of the block alongside the tracks. Parking available.

Tuesday–Sunday, 10–4, except federal holidays.

Boyds Negro School House

The one-room, unheated public school house was the only Boyds area school for African-Americans from 1895 to 1936. Today, the Boyds Historical Society preserves this site.

www.boydshistory.org

19510 White Ground Road, Boyds, MD

Clara Barton National Historic Site

Visit the home of Clara Barton, who founded the American Red Cross in 1881. This house was not only her home from 1897–1912, but also the headquarters of the American Red Cross from 1897–1904. The Clara Barton National Historic Site, established in 1975 to commemorate both Miss Barton and the early American Red Cross, offers educational tours for children (grades K–6) stressing the role volunteers played.

www.nps.gov/clba

301-320-1410

5801 Oxford Road, Glen Echo, MD
Located off MacArthur Boulevard, adjacent to Glen Echo Park. Parking available.

House shown by guided tour on the hour, 10–4. Closed January 1, Thanksgiving and December 25.

Adults, $4; seniors and groups, $3; children, $2.

Ride-On bus #29 from Friendship Heights.

Reservations required for groups larger than ten.

First floor is wheelchair accessible.

Junior Ranger two-day summer camps in conjunction with Glen Echo Park, free of charge.

New interactive website activities and certificates for grades 2–4, and grades 5 and up.

Walking distance to Glen Echo Park.

Special activities include spring and fall evening open house programs. Heritage Day is celebrated the last Saturday in April in conjunction with Glen Echo Park.

College Park Aviation Museum

The College Park Airport was founded in 1909 by the Wright Brothers and is the oldest continuously operating airport in the world. It serves as the general aviation airport for small privately-owned aircraft and is the site of many famous "first in flight" accomplishments including the first army flying school and the first commercial airmail service.

The College Park Aviation Museum commemorates the historic importance of the airport. This interactive, hands-on museum has exhibits and year-round programs including an animatronic Wilbur Wright, vintage aircraft and museum-quality replicas of early airplanes. Family-oriented programs and special activities include model-making and kite-building workshops, lectures, film series and children's events.

www.pgparks.com/places/historic/cpam

301-864-6029

1985 Corporal Frank Scott Drive, College Park, MD
Capital Beltway (I-495) to Kenilworth Avenue south toward Bladensburg; turn right on Paint Branch Parkway; then right at the second traffic light on Corporal Frank Scott Drive (sign will say College Park Airport); continue to the airport and museum. Parking on site.

Daily, 10–5. Closed most major holidays.

Adults, $4; seniors and groups, $3; children, $2.

Metrorail Green line (College Park).

Group tours for 10 or more available by appointment.

Dennis and Philip Ratner Museum

The Dennis and Phillip Ratner Museum was established "to foster love of the Bible through the graphic arts." The museum's three buildings include a Resource Center, with a library, conference space, and children's art and literature museum. The Resource Center contains an Ark, Eternal Light, Menorah and Torah. The main building houses the museum. The third building is Philip Ratner's studio.

www.ratnermuseum.com

301-897-1518

10001 Old Georgetown Road, Bethesda, MD
Capital Beltway (I-495), exit onto Old Georgetown Road. Go north
toward Rockville for approximately 0.25 miles. Turn right on Lone Oak
Drive (east) and immediately left into the first driveway. Proceed to
the smaller building in back.

Sunday, 10–4:30; Monday–Thursday, 12–4.

Groups free by reservation only (Sunday–Thursday).

Available for rental.

★ ⚶ Glen Echo Park (and Carousel)

Glen Echo Park was originally the site of a National Chautauqua Assembly, and later a well-known amusement park. The National Park Service in partnership with the Glen Echo Partnership for Arts and Culture and Montgomery County now manage this park as an arts center with over 500 art classes per year, covering the visual and performing arts, as well as classes in history and the environment. Summer camp sessions are an additional offering. The park houses artists-in-residence who often are available to discuss their work with the public. Glen Echo Park is also known for the Spanish Ballroom with its exquisite dance floor, Bumper Car Pavilion, and yurts housing craft workshops.

The Dentzel Carousel is a special treat. Riding the multi-colored, hand-carved animals to the rhythm of the 1926 Wurlitzer band organ is pure joy for children. When Glen Echo Park closed and the carousel was about to be shipped to California, a group of concerned citizens raised money, bought it back, and presented it to the National Park Service. Because the carousel is covered, it operates rain or shine, and it is the best one in the area.

www.nps.gov/glec

301-634-2255

MacArthur Boulevard at Goldsboro Road, Glen Echo, MD
Capital Beltway (I-495) to Exit 40 and follow signs to Glen Echo Park, about 3 miles from exit. Capital Beltway (I-495) to Exit 41, Clara Barton Parkway east for 2–3 miles; then follow signs to park. From Washington, DC, Massachusetts Avenue until it ends at Goldsboro Road. Turn left; go to MacArthur Boulevard; follow signs to park.

The park is open year-round. The Dentzel carousel ($1 per ride) operates May–September. (4/28–6/30, Wednesday and Thursday 10–2, Saturday/ Sunday 12–6; 7/1–8/31, Wednesday, Thursday, Friday 10–2, Saturday/ Sunday 12–6; 9/1–9/30 Saturday/Sunday12–6.)

The park houses two children's theaters: The Puppet Company Playhouse (see p. 220) and Adventure Theatre (see p. 204).

Family square dances sponsored by the Folklore Society of Greater Washington (www.fsgw.org), second Sunday of every month, 3–5.

Clara Barton National Historic Site is next to the park (see p. 78).

The Discovery Creek Museum's "Stable at Glen Echo Park" is on the premises (see p. 42).

Take Montgomery County Ride-On bus #29, operating daily from the Friendship Heights Metro station on the Red Line.

A small playground, picnic area and snack bar on site.

Appropriate for preschool and elementary school age children.

Special activities include "Family Day" celebrating the opening of the carousel, (weekend nearest May 1st); "Glen Echo Then and Wow" park history and fun day, (last Saturday before July 4th); the Washington Folk Festival (first weekend in June); "Fall Frolic" (last Saturday in October); "Winter Wonderland" (second Saturday in December.)

Greenbelt Museum

Greenbelt is one of three "green towns" built by the U.S. government in an effort to provide jobs during the Great Depression. As one of America's earliest and most successful planned towns, Greenbelt is a National Historic Landmark. The Greenbelt Museum is located in an original home, half of a duplex building, constructed by the federal government. The home appears much as it did in 1937 when the first residents were selected by the government to move into the town of the future. The collection includes early photographs of the town, Art Deco pieces and furniture.

The home is adjacent to many of the revolutionary planning features of the town: inner walkways, a pedestrian underpass and a town center. The nearby Greenbelt Community Center is considered one of the best examples of Art Deco architecture in the area. The Museum has an exhibition room in the Greenbelt Community Center at 15 Crescent Road, next to the Greenbelt Library.

The historic section of Greenbelt has more than 20 playgrounds, most of which are connected by pedestrian paths, including the walking path around the lake.

www.greenbeltmuseum.org

301-507-6582

Museum: 10–B Crescent Road, Greenbelt, MD
Community Center: 15 Crescent Road, Greenbelt MD
Capital Beltway (I-495) to Kenilworth Avenue north; at second light turn right on Crescent Road and turn right into the parking lot that is shared by the Greenbelt Community Center and Library.

House: Sunday, 1–5, and by appointment. Community Center: daily, 9–9.

Playground and lake nearby.

Wheelchair access to the home is limited. Strollers permitted, but the house is very small, and it is best to leave them outside.

John Poole House

The oldest building in Poolesville, this log house was built in 1793 by John Poole Jr. as a trading post for merchants and families of surrounding farms and plantations. It also served as a post office and was a stimulus to growth in the area. The original one-room log store contains articles sold from 1793–1820, when it was in operation, including leaf tobacco, sheepskins, leather hides, slabs of bacon, tools and hand spun yarns. The room behind the store, the kitchen/living area for the storekeeper and his family, has been restored to include original fabrics, paint and furniture.

www.johnpoolehouse.com/

301-972-8588

19923 Fisher Avenue, Rt. 107, Poolesville, MD
Capital Beltway (I-495) to I-270 to Rt. 28 west. Bear left on Rt. 107 to Poolesville. House will be on right before the four-way stop sign.

Open year-round, Friday–Sunday, 12–5, and by appointment.

First floor of house and arboretum are wheelchair accessible.

Marietta House Museum

Gabriel Duvall, a Justice of the U.S. Supreme Court, built this Federal-style country home between 1812 and 1813. The home is the current headquarters of the Prince George's County Historical Society and the Society's library. Furnishings reflect the three generations of Duvalls who lived in the house from 1815 to 1902. The land surrounding Marietta was a working farm where the Duvall family raised tobacco and grain crops. Walk around the grounds to see a root cellar, the judge's law office, a smokehouse and a cemetery with family gravestones.

www.pgparks.com/places/eleganthistoric/marietta_intro.html

301-464-5291, 301-699-2544 TTY

5626 Bell Station Road, Glenn Dale, MD
Capital Beltway (I-495) to Exit 10A Lanham Annapolis Road east (Rt. 450); follow 450 East for 4 miles, left on Rt. 193 West; first left on Bell Station Road. Marietta is the first driveway on the left.

Friday, 11–3; Saturday and Sunday, noon–4. Closed January and February.

Adults, $3; students (5–18 years), $1; seniors/groups, $2; children 4 and under, free.

Wheelchair access basement and 1st floor only; no strollers.

Special events: Mad Hatter's Tea Party in March, Marching Through Time-Multi Period Living History in April, Roman Days in June, History Weekend in July, Family Summer Fun in July and August, Campfire and Storytelling in June and October, Roman Legion Encampment in September, Victorian Scrap Booking (10 years and up) in November, Traditional Irish Celtic Music in November, Holiday Candlelight Tours in December.

Montpelier Mansion

Completed in the 1780s, Montpelier is a masterpiece of Georgian architecture. The expansive grounds (75 acres) include a boxwood maze and one of the two remaining 18th-century gazebos in the nation that is still on its original site. The property is atop a high bluff overlooking the Patuxent River, one of the most beautiful views in the state. Children enjoy seeing the Quaker classroom and secret staircase.

The Montpelier Cultural Arts Center is located in a modern barn on the property. It is open seven days a week from 10–5 (except holidays). The Arts Center features artists in residence, art galleries, and classes. Exhibits range from paintings to pottery. For information on Arts Center programs, call 301-953-1993.

www.montpeliermansion@pgparks.com

301-953-1376

9401 Montpelier Drive, Laurel, MD
Baltimore-Washington Parkway (Rt. 295) to Rt. 197 (Laurel-Bowie Road). Turn west onto Rt. 197. Turn left onto Muirkirk Road. Make first right into Montpelier grounds.

Adults, $3; children, $1; seniors, $2.

Tours by guides in period costumes: March–November, Sunday–Thursday, 12–3 on the hour. Last tour begins at 3 pm. December–February, Sundays, 1 and 2.

Weekday tours for large groups (10 or more) by appointment.

Take Note

Mansion Tours are led by guides in period costume.

Wheelchair access to the first floor only; please call in advance for assistance.

No strollers.

Special activities include Christmas candlelight tours in December, George Washington musicale, Herb, Bread and Tea Festival in the spring and the Traditional American Trails Fair in the fall.

NASA Goddard Space Flight Center

NASA Goddard's visitor center provides an opportunity for self-guided strolls through a sampling of NASA's historic satellites, spacecraft and rocketry. Exhibits include interactive displays of the "New Views of the Universe," astronomical discoveries of the Hubble Space Telescope, satellite imagery, and "piloting," a mockup of the Gemini Spacecraft.

www.nasa.gov/centers/goddard/home/index.html

301-286-9041

8800 Greenbelt Road, Greenbelt, MD
Capital Beltway (I-495) to exit 22A, Greenbelt Road east (Rt. 193) for about 2 miles. Pass the GSFC main gate on the left. Follow signs to Visitor Center.

September 1–June 30, Tuesday–Friday, 10–3; Saturday and Sunday, 12–4. July 1–August 31, Tuesday–Friday, 10–5; Saturday, 12–4. Closed federal holidays.

Currently, security regulations do not permit "drop-in" tours by the general public. All tour participants must be United States citizens.

Model Rocket Launches, first Sunday of every month, 1 pm. Reservations required.

Earth and Space Film Series, Saturdays and Sundays, 2 pm.

Science on a Sphere, a suspended 6-foot sphere that displays 3D animated data of the planets, moons and our earth, can be viewed and is the subject of "Footprints," a movie that shows on the half hour, every hour.

🛉 National Capital Trolley Museum

The highlight of this small museum is a 20-minute ride on an old-time trolley through the surrounding woods; the staff relates history and anecdotes about the cars. Try to schedule your visit for one of the occasional open houses when all of the museum's collection will be on display. On weekends, only one trolley runs at a time.

www.dctrolley.org

301-384-6088

1313 Bonifant Road, Colesville, MD
Capital Beltway (I-495) to Georgia Avenue north (Rt. 97); turn right on Layhill Road (Rt. 182); after two miles, turn right on Bonifant Road.

January–November Saturday–Sunday, noon–5. March 15–May 15 and October 1–November 30, Thursday–Friday, 10–2; weekend hours 12–5. June 15–August 15, Thursday–Friday, 11–3; weekend hours 12–5. Memorial Day, July 4, and Labor Day, noon–5.

Trolley fares for adults, $4; children, 2–17; seniors 65+, $3; children under two, free.

Tours can be arranged for preschool and elementary school children.

Summer children's program from June 15–August 15, Thursdays and Fridays, 11–3 offering stories and crafts on Thursdays and films on Fridays.

Special activities include Holly Trolley Feast every weekend in December 5–9 p.m.; parade days in April when all the trolley cars are brought out for display or use; an annual Open House in September along with monthly special events.

National Cryptologic Museum and National Vigilance Park

The National Cryptologic Museum, created by the National Security Agency, is the first and only public museum in the U.S. government intelligence community. Exhibits examine the breaking of the Enigma codes and a look at the Navajo Code Talkers, along with other dramatic historical moments in American code making and code breaking, and machines, devices and techniques employed by defense cryptologists. The adjacent National Vigilance Park showcases two reconnaissance aircraft used for secret missions.

www.nsa.gov/museum

301-688-5849

Fort George G. Meade, Fort Meade MD
MD 295 (Baltimore/Washington Parkway) North OR I-95 North to Rt. 32 East/Ft Meade. Exit onto Canine Road. Turn left at the light onto Colony Seven Road. Follow past the aircraft into Museum parking lot.

Monday–Friday, 9–4: first and third Saturdays, 10–2. Closed Sundays and federal holidays.

 Radio and Television Museum

 Enter the 1906 Harmel House country store and explore the history of radio. Learn about the history of radio from Marconi's earliest wireless telegraph to the primitive crystal sets of the 1920s, through Depression-era cathedrals and the post-War plastic portable radios, and, finally, to the development of radio with pictures, called television.

The museum is operated in a joint effort by they City of Bowie and the Radio History Society.

www.cityofbowie.org/museum

301-390-1020

2608 Mitchellville Road, Bowie, MD
Capital Beltway (I-495) to Rt. 50 east (toward Annapolis) travel about 7 miles to Exit 11 (Rt. 197) Collington Road/Bowie, bear right following Collington Road (Rt. 192 S), turn right at Mitchellville Road.

Friday, 10–5; Saturday and Sunday, 1–5.

Partially accessible for people with disabilities.

Sandy Spring Museum

Sandy Spring Museum is a non-profit community museum, established in 1980, whose mission is to bring local history to life by "time traveling" to the era of our founding fathers and exploring the world of the early settlers at work, play, school and home. Their story is brought vividly to life with a rich assortment of artifacts, visual images, hands-on objects and oral presentations. The museum's on-site and outreach programs are designed to complement classroom lessons in social studies. The museum has a collection of old-fashioned toys that children may play with during or after the tour.

www.sandyspringmuseum.org

301-774-0022

17901 Bentley Road, Sandy Spring, MD
Capital Beltway (I-495) to New Hampshire Avenue north toward Ashton. At Rt. 108 turn left. Continue less than a mile past Sherwood High School to Bentley Road on the right. Turn on Bentley and into museum parking lot.

Monday, Wednesday and Thursday, 9–4; Saturday and Sunday, 12–4; additional hours by appointment.

Adults, $3; members and children under 12, free.

Concert series.

Special activities include a Summer Heritage and Craft Camp for first-through fifth-graders; Strawberry Festival, the first Saturday in June; Montgomery County History Tour; Family Fun Day; Presidents Day; Historic Homes tour. Special programs and tours for student groups are available with an appointment. Special events may include demonstrations of blacksmithing, hearth cooking, basket weaving, yarn spinning, woodcarving and rope making.

Surratt House Museum

This two-story frame house was a tavern, post office, polling place and the home of the first woman executed by the U.S. government, Mary Surratt. In July 1865, she was hung for her alleged role in the assassination of President Abraham Lincoln. John Wilkes Booth stopped briefly at the house the evening of April 14, 1865, as he tried to escape after shooting the President. Today, costumed docents give visitors tours of the home and discuss the question of whether or not Mary Surratt was a co-conspirator in the assassination plot.

The home is a typical middle class home of the Victorian period. The displays include Victorian furniture, rugs, lace curtains, clothing and kitchen implements.

www.surratt.org

301-868-1121, 301-868-1020

9118 Brandywine Road, Clinton, MD
Capital Beltway (I-495) to Branch Avenue/Rt. 5 exit; go south for three and a half miles to right exit on Woodard Road (Rt. 223 west); continue one mile to left turn on Brandywine Road; house is on the left, immediately after the turn. Ample free parking at visitors center.

Open mid-January to mid-December, Thursday and Friday, 11–3; Saturday and Sunday, noon–4.

Adults, $3; senior citizens, $2; children 5–18, $1.

Tours approximately every half hour, with last tour 30 minutes before closing. Group tours Wednesday, by appointment.

John Wilkes Booth Escape Route Tour, a 12-hour bus tour, is available by reservation. These tours are offered in April and September and sell out quickly.

Visitors Center with exhibits and electric map display.

Wheelchair access on first floor only; no strollers.

Special activities include an exhibit which focuses on 19th-century life and an exhibit of 19th-century valentines and crafts in February. Spring and Fall Open Houses offer free tours and special activities.

Uncle Tom's Cabin (Riley House/Josiah Henson's Cabin)

This 13-by-17-foot 18th-century cabin is the former home of slave Josiah Henson, whose autobiography The Life of Josiah Henson, Formerly a Slave was the model for Harriet Beecher Stowe's novel Uncle Tom's Cabin. Josiah Henson was born in 1789 in Charles County, Maryland. Before he escaped to Canada on the Underground Railroad Henson was sold to, worked and lived on the Montgomery County plantation owned by Isaac Riley.

www.mc-mncppc.org

11420 Old Georgetown Road (Old Georgetown Road and Tilden Road), Rockville, MD

Washington Temple Visitors' Center (also known as the "Mormon Temple")

The Washington DC Mormon Temple, dedicated in 1974, is one of the largest in the world. It is an extraordinary edifice covered in 173,000 feet of white marble, and situated on 57 acres in Kensington, Maryland. The International Visitors' Center is open to the public, and offers films and exhibits describing the temple's construction and programs of the church.

www.lds.org/placestovisit

301-587-0144

9900 Stoneybrook Drive, Kensington, MD
Capital Beltway (I-495) to Connecticut Avenue north, exit 33 toward Kensington; turn right on Beach Drive and follow to the end; turn left on Stoneybrook drive. The Visitors' Center is one-quarter of a mile on the left. Free parking available at the Visitors' Center.

Visitors' Center and gardens open daily, 10–9. No access to the Temple.

Special activities include the Festival of Lights, which has a live nativity scene, 450,000 Christmas lights covering trees and bushes on the grounds and nightly concerts. Exhibit and holiday entertainment continue from December until the first week of January. Concerts are offered on weekends throughout the year.

White's Ferry

A 24-car ferry crosses the Potomac River to connect with Route 15, two miles from Leesburg on the Virginia side. The ferry is the only cable-guided fresh water ferry on the east coast, and is the last operating ferry across the Potomac River. The store sells hot and cold food and live bait. The fishing is reputedly good in the area because a Pepco plant upstream in Dickerson warms the river. Canoeing groups of four or more are taken to Point-of-Rocks, about ten miles upstream. Depending on weather conditions, the trip downstream will take about six hours, during which you can fish, float or socialize. Canoe trips as far as Harpers Ferry can be arranged. You might also plan a hike on the C&O Canal.

www.historicwhitesferry.com

301-349-5200

24801 White's Ferry Road, Dickerson, MD
Capital Beltway (I-495) to I-270 north; exit at Rt. 28 west toward Dawsonville; west on Rt. 107 until it becomes White's Ferry Road.

Ferry operates daily, 5 a.m.–11 p.m.

Fees per car: $6 round-trip and $4 one-way. Bicycles: $1. No credit cards. No charge for groups of children, such as scout troops, on foot, but advance notice is required.

Rowboat and canoe rentals.

Pavilion Rental for groups up to 100 available with advance notice. Includes volleyball, horse shoes, electricity and gas.

Alexandria Archaeology Museum

10+

The Alexandria Archaeology Museum was formed to preserve and interpret archaeological information from the diverse city of Alexandria and to involve the public in archaeological preservation. At the museum's lab, children can observe volunteers working with artifacts, cleaning and cataloging. Visitors also see a life-size model of an archaeologist at work. The organization encourages participation in field trips to archaeological digs when possible.

www.AlexandriaArchaeology.org

703-838-4399

105 North Union Street, Studio 327, Alexandria, VA
In the Torpedo Factory Art Center (see p. 112).

Tuesday–Friday, 10–3; Saturday, 10–5; Sunday, 1–5. Closed Easter, July 4, Thanksgiving, December 25 and January 1.

School groups can arrange to visit the lab/museum for a 45-minute hands-on Alexandria Archaeology Adventure Lesson. Programs are directed for groups with at least 20 children in grades 3–12. Reservations are required.

Picnic in the two parks located on either side of the Torpedo Factory. There is a food court behind the Torpedo Factory.

Virginia TimeTravelers site.

Special activities include Archaeology Summer Camp in July, Public Dig Days, Art Safari, Historic Hauntings, Ornament Decorative Workshop and seasonal site tours. Public and family events are scheduled throughout the year.

Alexandria Black History Resource Center

The Center includes the Museum, the Watson Reading Room and the Alexandria African American Heritage Park. The museum, devoted to exhibiting local and regional history, is housed in the Robert H. Robinson Library, originally constructed in 1940 following a peaceful sit-in at the segregated Alexandria Library.

The Watson Reading Room is a non-circulating research library with a focus on African-American history and culture.

The nine-acre park adjacent to the Center offers a place for celebration, a preserved one-acre 19th-century African-American cemetery and a natural wetlands habitat.

oha.alexandriava.gov/bhrc

703-838-4356

638 N. Alfred Street (Old Town), Alexandria, VA
Capital Beltway (I-495) to George Washington Parkway south into Alexandria. The parkway becomes Washington Street. Turn right on Wythe Street. The Center is on the next corner, at Wythe and N. Alfred streets. Park on Wythe Street.

Tuesday–Saturday, 10–4. Closed January 1, Easter, July 4, Thanksgiving and December 25.

Metrorail Yellow or Blue line (Braddock Road). Walk across the parking lot and bear right; at West and Wythe streets, follow Wythe five blocks east. The Center is on Wythe and Alfred streets.

Arlington House, the Robert E. Lee Memorial

Robert E. Lee courted and wed Mary Custis in this hilltop mansion. They lived here for 30 years, from 1831-1861, and raised seven children here. It has been restored with some of the original furnishings and similar pieces of the 1850s. Don't miss the magnificent view of the Washington skyline from the front portico, which Lafayette described as the "finest view in the world." Show the children the upstairs children's room and playroom. The house is staffed by park rangers.

www.nps.gov/arho

703-235-1530

Arlington National Cemetery, Arlington, VA
Walk from Arlington Cemetery Visitors Center
parking lot or ride the Tourmobile.

*Though the Memorial is scheduled to be under
construction through 2010, the site will be open
with very few exceptions. Call ahead to make
sure.*

*Daily, 9:30–4:30. Closed December 25 and
January 1.*

*Grounds open April 1–September 30, 8–7, and
October 1–March 31, 8–5.*

Metrorail Blue line (Arlington Cemetery).

Tourmobile stop.

Take Note

*Students can take advantage
of free or discounted admission
to Virginia TimeTravelers sites.
Visit www.timetravelers.org
to download a TimeTravelers
Passport, honored at over 350
participating TimeTravelers sites
of interest and special events
throughout Virginia. Each year,
students are challenged to get
passports stamped at six sites
to earn a signed certificate
from the governor and a
patch representing the annual
TimeTravelers theme.*

*Wheelchair lift to the first floor; tours for the visually- and hearing-
impaired can be arranged by calling ahead.*

*Special activities include a special tour for African-American History
Month during February; St. Patrick's Day open house in March; a candlelight open house in October; Robert E. Lee Wedding Day Open House in
June; and a Christmas open house featuring mid–19th-century decorations in December.*

Ⓜ Arlington National Cemetery

There is no better place than Arlington National Cemetery for both
children and adults to bgin to understand the human scale of war.
The sheer expanse of the cemetery, 612 acres, with its vast number of
graves spanning the time period from the American Revolution to the
present, brings a sense of the finality and devastation of our wars. At
the Information Center, one can obtain the location of the burial site
for any individual buried here. In addition to soldiers' graves, sections
of the cemetery are dedicated to veterans who were astronauts, chap-
lains and nurses.

Children enjoy the hike up the hill to the Kennedy gravesites, where
they can see a panoramic view of Washington with airplanes flying
overhead. (Even if you plan to walk through part of the cemetery, it is
advisable to buy a ticket at the Tourmobile booth at the Visitors Center
so that you can board a bus at any of the Tourmobile stops.) At the
Tomb of the Unknowns, the Changing of the Guard is fascinating because of the breath-taking precision of each step and maneuver made

by the Tomb Guards. Across from the Tomb of the Unknowns is the actual mast of the U.S.S. Maine (the sinking of the Maine began the Spanish American War).

Tourmobile guides provide fascinating tidbits of information. Travelers have learned of Mary Custis (Mrs. Robert E.) Lee's failure to pay taxes of $92.07 on her 1100-acre property, and the government's subsequent takeover of Arlington Estate to use as headquarters for the Army of the Potomac; or Colonel Robert E. Lee's leaving the Union for the Confederacy, and General Meigs's decision to use Lee's home as a Union cemetery. Even young children can follow the history of the cemetery on a Tourmobile ride: older parts of the cemetery have various sizes of headstones, pointed headstones designate soldiers from the Confederate armies, and the more recent gravestones are arranged to look like soldiers standing at attention. (See also Arlington House, p. 92.)

www.arlingtoncemetery.org

703-607-8052, 202-979-0690, group tours

Arlington, VA
Directly across from the Lincoln Memorial Bridge. Parking lot.

Daily, October–March, 8–5; April–September, 8–7.

Metrorail Blue line (Arlington Cemetery).

Tourmobile stop. Stops at Kennedy gravesites, Tomb of the Unknowns, and Arlington House. Without disembarking to visit the sites, the ride takes approximately 40 minutes. (See Tourmobile Information in Chapter 1, "Starting Out," p. 5.)

Changing of the Guard: April–September, every half hour; October–March, every hour on the hour. Over 20 funeral services occur each day.

Special activities include services held in the amphitheater for Easter, Memorial Day and Veterans Day.

M

10+

Carlyle House Historic Park

This English country-style mansion was built by Scottish merchant John Carlyle in 1753. The home was a social and political center and the site of a historic governors conference at the outset of the French and Indian War. The Carlyle House is on the National Register of Historic Places and is Alexandria's only stone 18th-century Palladian-style house.

www.carlylehouse.org

703-549-2997

121 N. Fairfax Street, Old Town, Alexandria, VA
In Old Town Alexandria, across from Alexandria's City Hall.

Tuesday–Saturday, 10–4; Sunday, noon–4:30; closed Monday.

Adults, $4; Students 11–17, $2; 10 and younger, free.

Metrorail Blue or Yellow line (King Street).

School programs and tours are offered.

VA TimeTravelers site.

Special activities include Candlelight Tours of the house decorated with Christmas decorations of the 1700s and living history events throughout the year.

Christ Church

This lovely colonial Georgian church, in continual use since its completion in 1773, is the oldest in Alexandria and one of the oldest on the East Coast. Visitors can sit in the boxed-in pew belonging to George Washington. Look for the little brass tablet that marks where Robert E. Lee knelt at the altar rail to be confirmed. Franklin Roosevelt and Winston Churchill attended services on the World Day of Prayer for Peace, January 1, 1942.

Children find the greatest fascination, however, in the adjacent graveyard, where searching tombstones for dates and inscriptions is an adventure in this peaceful setting.

www.historicchristchurch.org

703-549-1450

118 North Washington Street, Alexandria, VA
Located on North Washington Street between King and Cameron
streets in Old Town Alexandria.

*Open Monday–Saturday, 9–4; Sunday, 2–4. A docent greets visitors at
the door. Because this is an active church, visitors should plan for unexpected closings for weddings, funerals and special church services.*

Sunday Services at 8, 9, 11:15 a.m. and 5 p.m.

Wheelchair access (1-step barrier; assistance is provided).

*Special activities include The Blessing of the Pets in October, when
people bring their pets to be blessed.*

Colvin Run Mill Historic Site

Colvin Run Mill, built in the early 1800s, is a working grist-mill that
produces whole grain products to sell in the on-site general store. The
huge grinding stones, the wooden gears and the outside water wheel
fascinates children of all ages.

The historic site also includes the original miller's house, with hands-on
exhibits such as a grain elevator that can be manipulated, the original
general store, and a re-created dairy barn with typical period farming
equipment of the community and a scale model of the mill.

703-759-2771

10017 Colvin Run Road, Great Falls, VA
Capital Beltway (I-495); exit Rt. 7 west (Tysons Corner); Colvin Run Mill
is seven miles west of Tysons Corner and 15 miles east of Leesburg.

*March–December, Wednesday–Monday, 11–5; January–February,
Wednesday–Monday, 11–4. Closed Tuesdays.*

*Free admission to grounds. Tours of the mill and the miller's house: adults,
$6; children 5–15 and seniors, $4; students 16 and older with I.D., $5.*

*Tours of the mill and the miller's house are given every hour on the hour;
last tour, one hour before closing.*

Conditions permitting, grinding takes place on Sundays from noon–3.

Puppet show for preschoolers, Thursdays at 1. Admission is $3 for children; adults, free.

Limited wheelchair access.

Special activities include Country Christmas, the third weekend in December, with Victorian decorations, Santa Claus and family crafts. Admission is charged for this event.

Drug Enforcement Administration Museum and Visitors Center

This provocative museum intended for teens and adults attempts to show the stark realities of drug use in America. Drug paraphernalia and grisly photos are displayed along with a history of intoxication and drug use over the course of the last century, along with a look at the historical, global influences of drug trafficking from the ancient Silk Road to the present.

www.deamuseum.org

202-307-3463

700 Army-Navy Drive, DEA Headquarters, Arlington, VA
Capital Beltway (I-495) to I-395 North to Rt. 1 (8C). The museum is at the end of the off-ramp.

Metrorail Blue or Yellow line (Pentagon City).

Tuesday–Friday, 10–4.

Fort Ward Museum and Historic Site

Of special interest to Civil War buffs, this museum exhibits weapons, uniforms, musical instruments and period memorabilia. Children can learn about the everyday life of Civil War soldiers and civilians. In addition to the museum building, there is a Civil War fort and an officers' hut within the adjacent Fort Ward Park (see p. 149).

www.fortward.org

703-838-4848

4301 West Braddock Road, Alexandria, VA
I-395 to Seminary Road east; after approximately one mile, turn left onto N. Howard Street, then right onto West Braddock Road; the museum entrance in on the left. Parking on-site.

Open April–October, Tuesday–Saturday, 9–5; Sunday, noon–5. November–March, Tuesday–Saturday, 10–5; Sunday noon–5. Closed all Mondays, Thanksgiving, December 25 and January 1.

Metrorail Blue or Yellow line (King Street) to DASH bus #5.

VA TimeTravelers site.

Wheelchair accessible except for library upstairs. Restrooms in separate building.

Special activities include A Christmas in Camp Open House in December, A Civil War Camp Day in June and "living history" programs throughout the year. Film and lectures series are also offered.

Friendship Firehouse

The Friendship Fire Company was established in 1774 and was the first volunteer fire company in Alexandria. The company moved to this house in the 1850s. The first-floor Engine Room features historic firefighting apparatus, including hand-drawn fire engines, buckets, axes and hoses, along with replicas that children can handle. Call for updates on special events and educational programs.

oha.alexandriava.gov/friendship/ff-museum.html

703-838-3891, 703-838-4994

107 S. Alfred Street, Alexandria, VA
In Old Town Alexandria on South Alfred Street, between King and Prince streets.

Friday–Saturday, 10–4; Sunday, 1–4. Closed December 25 and January 1.

Annual Friendship firehouse Street Festival, first Saturday in August.

Metrorail Blue or Yellow line (King Street).

10+ Gadsby's Tavern Museum

Gadsby's Tavern museum offers an exciting look into the operations of an eighteenth-century tavern. The museum consists of the 1770 City Tavern and the 1792 City Hotel, named after John Gadsby, the Englishman who operated them between 1796 and 1808. The tour covers architectural highlights, a display of period objects and furnishings and the ballroom where George Washington danced to celebrate his birthday in 1798 and 1799.

www.gadsbystavern.org

703-838-4242

134 North Royal Street, Alexandria, VA
Capital Beltway (I-495) exit onto Rt. 1 North, right on King Street and then left on Royal Street. On the corner of North Royal and Cameron street.

Open November–March, Wednesday–Saturday, 11–4, Sunday, 1–4. Open April–October, Tuesday–Saturday, 10–5, Sunday 1–5. Closed on Thanksgiving, December 25, January 1 and July 4.

Adults, $4; children ages 11–17, $2; children age ten and under, free with paying adult. Group rates are available on request. $1 off for AAA membership.

Gadsby's Tavern Restaurant is open for lunch and dinner.

Tours start 15 minutes before and after each hour, and last about 30 minutes. Last tour begins 15 minutes before closing.

Limited wheelchair access. Strollers are not permitted above the first floor. A video shown in the first floor reception room offers an alternate tour of the site for persons unable to go up the steps.

VA TimeTravelers site.

Special activities include Time Travels, a first-person interpretive tour; a Young Ladies' Tea for girls and their dolls; and a summer camp program.

Ⓜ George Washington Masonic National Memorial

This memorial to George Washington towers over the Alexandria skyline, affording a good view of the area. Displays include George Washington's Bible and a clock that was stopped at the time of his death. Children enjoy the animatronic George Washington and the large mechanical model of a Shriners parade, complete with platoons of brightly clad nobles marching to recorded band music.

www.gwmemorial.org

703-683-2007

101 Callahan Drive, Alexandria, VA
North Washington Street to King Street west; turn left on Callahan Street. Memorial is on Callahan between King Street and Duke Street. Free parking.

Daily, 10–4. Closed Thanksgiving, December 25, January 1 and some federal holidays.

Tours daily at 10, 11:30, 1:30 and 3.

Metrorail Yellow or Blue line (King Street).

Call about wheelchair access.

VA TimeTravelers site.

George Washington Memorial Parkway

The "G.W. Parkway," as Washington-area residents call it, has two main sections: the 25-mile Virginia section, from Mount Vernon south of Alexandria along the Potomac River to the Capital Beltway (I-495); and in Maryland, the Clara Barton Parkway, which begins at the Great Falls and parallels the Potomac River for seven miles.

Work on the national park that became the G.W. Parkway began in 1932. The Parkway as it is today was completed in 1970. The park incorporates sites that connect our nation's history from George Washington through the Civil War and into the 20th century. It is also a major route connecting Maryland, Washington, DC and Virginia. The park is made up of 7,600 acres, which protects the natural habitat and landscape along the Potomac shoreline. It includes more than 25 sites associated with George Washington. There are many more sites that honor our history, our military and the natural habitat of the area. There are also numerous fun, recreational sites. Properly describing the sites and history of the George Washington Memorial Parkway would require a guide book of its own. Below are listed *some* of the many sites, trails and memorials that can be found along the beautiful Parkway (a number of which are detailed in this guide).

www.nps.gov/gwmp/

703-289-2500

Arlington House: The Robert E. Lee Memorial
Belle Haven Park and Marina
Clara Barton National Historic Site
Collingwood Park
Columbia Island Marina
Daingerfield Island
Dyke Marsh Wildlife Preserve
Fort Hunt Park
Fort Marcy
Glen Echo Park
Gravelly Point
Great Falls Park
Lady Bird Johnson Park
Lyndon Baines Johnson Memorial Grove-on-the-Potomac
Memorial Avenue
Mount Vernon Trail
Netherlands Carillon
Potomac Heritage Trail
Riverside Park
Roaches Run Wildlife Sanctuary
Theodore Roosevelt Island
Turkey Run Park
U.S. Marine Corps War Memorial
Washington Sailing Marina

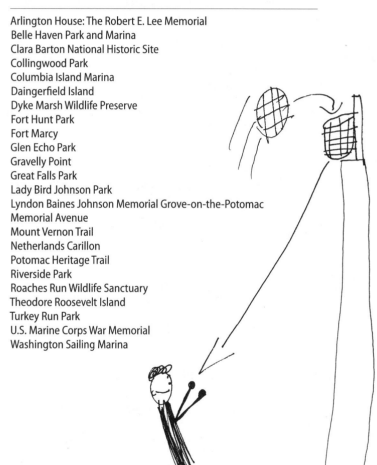

Gunston Hall Plantation

This Colonial plantation is one of the finest homes in the area, with its tasteful interior and spacious grounds overlooking the Potomac River. Gunston Hall was the home of George Mason, an author of Virginia's Declaration of Rights. The 18th-century furnishings and the intricately carved woodwork are outstanding. The children's rooms and nursery contain simple, small-scale furniture of the period. A museum features mementos from the Mason family, and a diorama shows how the plantation worked. Outbuildings include the kitchen, dairy, smokehouse, schoolhouse and laundry.

www.gunstonhall.org

703-550-9220

Gunston Road (Rt. 242), Mason Neck, VA
Capital Beltway (I-495) to Rt. 1 south from Alexandria for 14 miles; then go east on Rt. 242 for four miles to Gunston Hall. From I-95 south, exit 163 toward Lorton. Follow signs to Gunston Hall.

Daily, 9:30–5. Closed Thanksgiving, December 25 and January 1.

Adults, $8; children grades 1–12, $4; seniors, $7; children under six and Friends of Gunston Hall, free. Call in advance for group tours and rates.

A marked trail wanders through the woods to the river.

Wheelchair access can be arranged.

VA TimeTravelers site.

Special activities include a kite festival and picnic in March; Plantation Sleuths during the summer months; Nature walk in September; Archeology Day in October; Military reenactment in November; Plantation Christmas in December.

Iwo Jima Memorial

The United States Marine Corps War Memorial stands as a symbol of this grateful Nation's esteem for the honored dead of the U.S. Marine corps. The statue depicts one of the most famous incidents of World War II, the raising of the American flag on Mt. Suribachi in February 1945. The photographer Joe Rosenthal won a Pulitzer Prize for his photograph of the flag-raising, and sculptor Felix W. deWeldon captured that image in the bronze sculpture at the memorial. The memorial is dedicated to all Marines who have given their lives in the defense of the United States since 1775.

At the memorial, the Marine Drum and Bugle Corps and the Marine Corps Silent Drill Platoon continue a Marine Corps Tradition begun in 1954, the Sunset Parade, a 75-minute performance of music and marching on Tuesday evenings during the summer. The memorial is open year-round.

ww.nps.gov/gwmp/usmc.htm

703-289-2500

George Washington Memorial Parkway, Rosslyn, VA
Capital Beltway (I-495) to the George Washington Memorial Parkway south; Rt. 50 West exit; next right (Rosslyn) then left at stop sign onto Ft Myer Drive. Turn left onto Marshall and then a left into the park.

Sunset Parade and concert held Tuesdays, 7 p.m., May–August.

Lee-Fendall House Museum

Built in 1785 by Robert E. Lee's uncle, Philip Fendall, and steeped in Civil War history, this house has been restored to reflect its early Victorian period. This child-friendly house offers hands-on items and specialized educational programs. Advance reservations are recommended.

www.leefendallhouse.org

703-548-1789

614 Oronoco Street, Alexandria, VA
Capital Beltway (I-495) south to US Highway 1 north. Continue north past Duke, Prince and King Streets and turn right onto Queen Street. Turn left onto Washington Street. Go two blocks and turn right onto Oronoco Street.

Tuesday–Saturday, 10–4; Sunday, 1–4. (On weekends call to check for closings due to special functions.)

Adults, $4; Students age 11–17, $2. Children 10 and younger, free.

Special tours can be arranged for school and youth groups.

Metrorail Yellow or Blue line (King Street/Braddock Road), 10-minute walk.

Special event attendees may use the city employee parking lot located at the corner of Oronoco Street and North Pitt Street (two blocks east of the Lee-Fendall House) on weekends, holiday, and weekdays after 5.

VA TimeTravelers site

Facilities rentals for celebrations, parties and conferences.

Special activities include summer programs for children.

The Lyceum, Alexandria's History Museum

An impressive example of Greek Revival architecture, the Lyceum was built in 1839 as a cultural center. Since 1985, it has been Alexandria's History Museum.

oha.alexandriava.gov/lyceum

703-838-4994

201 South Washington Street, Alexandria, VA
Capital Beltway (I-495), exit Rt. 1 north (Alexandria). Right on Prince Street, right on S. Washington Street. Limited, on-site free parking.

Open Monday–Saturday, 10–5; Sunday, 1–5. Closed Thanksgiving, December 24, December 25 and January 1.

Metrorail Blue or Yellow line (King Street).

VA TimeTravelers site.

Special activities include concerts, interactive exhibitions and public programs.

Market Square/Alexandria City Hall

During the original 1749 survey of Alexandria, two half-acre lots were set aside for a market place and town hall. Over the town's history, the sites have held schools, jails, whipping posts and a town courthouse. On Saturday mornings, year-round, from 6–10:30 a.m., it is the home of the oldest continuously operating farmer's market in the country.

www.funsside.com

703-838-4200

300 block of King Street, Alexandria, VA

Monday–Friday, 8–4:30

Free parking for Farmers Market in the garage.

Summer concert series.

Special activities include weekday lunchtime concerts in spring and summer and an annual Christmas lighting ceremony in December. For a calendar of events, call the Alexandria Convention and Visitors Bureau, 703-838-4200.

Morven Park

This 1,200-acre estate is operated as a memorial to Westmoreland Davis, former Governor of Virginia. Children tend to be most interested in the extensive vehicle collection. In the old carriage house and Carriage Museum, there are coaches, breaks, and gigs driven by turn-of-the-century American Society members, plus everyday phaetons, surreys, carts, sleighs, a funeral hearse and a charcoal-burning fire engine. The mansion on the estate is closed for renovation through 2009.

www.morvenpark.com

703-777-2414

17263 Southern Planter Lane, Leesburg, VA
From Virginia, Capital Beltway (I-495) to exit at Rt. 7 west (Tysons Corner); continue through the town of Leesburg; then right to Morven Park Road; left to Old Waterford Road (Rt. 698); then right to main entrance.
From Maryland, Capital Beltway (I-495) to Rt. 192, Georgetown Pike; at Rt. 7, turn right, heading west several miles, through the town of Leesburg; then follow above directions.

The carriage house is open for tours April–November. Tours are given Friday–Monday from 11–4. Tours can be made at other times by appointment.

Wheelchair access to the carriage museum. Strollers are permitted in the carriage museum.

The gardens are open during the renovation during touring hours.

Special activities include an arts and crafts festival in June, steeplechase races in October and May and a special Christmas tour in December. There are two reproduction civil war huts from which occasional reenactments are staged. Call or check website for dates and times.

★ Mount Vernon Estate and Gardens
(George Washington's Home)

✕ This elegant and stately 40-acre estate and plantation was George Washington's home. Today the site provides an education in the economic and social life of the South in the 18th century.

Walk through the mansion, painted in bright, historically accurate colors and furnished with original heirlooms. Share Washington's views of the Potomac. More than a dozen outbuildings are meticulously restored, including a large greenhouse, stables, slave quarters and kitchen. History abounds with fascinating exhibits in the refurbished George Washington Museum, the Archaeology and Restoration Museum, active archaeological dig, the slave Memorial and burial ground and the family tomb where Washington is buried.

A visit to Mount Vernon begins at the Ford Orientation Center. A 20-minute action-adventure movie, "We Fight to Be Free," is shown in a pair of luxury theaters. Although the film depicts a heroic and charismatic Washington at pivotal moments in his life, the realistic portrayal can be too intense for some young children

After visiting the Ford Orientation Center and before arriving at the mansion, families should visit the new Donald Reynolds Museum and Education Center, a fascinating destination in its own right. Forensic anthropologists helped create life-sized statues of Washington. A video offers an intriguing debate on whether Washington should have been a stronger abolitionist and freed his slaves while he was alive rather than waiting until his death to free them through his will. Don't miss the interactive movie about the Battle of Yorktown, which features seat-shaking cannon blasts, fog and artificial snow that falls on the audience. A hands-on room offers dress-up clothes, Colonial toys and an archaeological puzzle for kids to piece together colonial pottery using replicas of pieces discovered on the estate grounds. The museum and education center make history come alive, and there's lots of outdoor space for kids to stretch their legs and learn about pioneer farming. Be sure to ask for the free Adventure Map at the Orientation Center. It has a map of the estate on one side to help find the nine puzzle places listed on the other, all providing "fill in the blank" clues to help solve the final puzzle. The Orientation Center also features a 1/12-scale replica of Mt. Vernon, with beautifully reproduced interiors. Note how low the ceilings are on the second floor compared to the first. Washington was 6'2" and always had to stoop to enter his bedroom. A food court attached to the museum has several vendors and two attractive eating areas: a glass-enclosed pavilion and an open-air terrace. Be sure to bring cash; the food court does not accept credit cards.

Children love the *George Washington: Pioneer Farmer* exhibition, a four-acre demonstration farm that features a recreation of Washington's 16-sided treading barn. The "Hands-on History Exhibit," presented Memorial Day to Labor Day, is full of interactive games and activities for children of all ages.

www.mountvernon.org

703-780-2000

Mount Vernon Memorial Highway, Mount Vernon, VA
George Washington Memorial Parkway south; Parkway becomes the Mount Vernon Memorial Highway. Mount Vernon is located eight miles south of Alexandria. Free parking.

Mount Vernon is open seven days a week, every day of the year, including holidays and Christmas.

April–August, 8–5; March, September, and October, 9–5; November through February, 9–4.

Adults $13; children ages 6–11, $6; seniors, age 62 and above $12; children 5 and under, free. Children's fare includes a free Adventure Map of the Mansion.

Tourmobile stop.

Picnicking is not permitted on the plantation grounds, but good riverside spots are located along the Parkway.

Mount Vernon welcomes dogs on leashes during daytime hours. The gate attendants provide a bowl of water for your pet.

Mount Vernon is home to many farm animals.

The Mount Vernon Inn, 703-780-0011, is just outside the main gate.

Stroller and wheelchair access to museums and the mansion's first floor.

VA TimeTravelers site

Special activities include seasonal riverboat cruises, "Colonial Days at Mt. Vernon," with demonstrations by blacksmiths and paper makers; an 18th-century crafts fair; a costumed actor dressed as George Washington greets guests and gives performances on special occasions.

M National Firearms Museum

The NRA (National Rifle Association) has a collection of 3,500 historically significant firearms from 1450 to the present day.

www.nrahq.org/museum

703-267-1600

11250 Waples Mill Road, Fairfax, VA
Capital Beltway (I-495) to I-66 west to Exit 57-A onto U.S. Rt. 50 east
toward Fairfax. On Rt. 50, turn left at the first traffic light, onto Waples
Mill Road. The blue and white NRA Headquarters building will be on
your right. The National Firearms Museum is located on the 1st floor
south tower.

Daily, 10–4. Closed on all federal holidays.

Metrorail Orange line (Vienna/Fairfax-GMU).

Oatlands Plantation

This hunt-country estate dates from the early 1800s. Decorative and
unusual features, such as the octagonal drawing room and a flanking
pair of staircases, make for a worthwhile visit, especially for those interested in architecture. There is a terraced, four-acre, formal English
garden, considered one of the finest examples of early Virginia landscape design, a tea house and a reflecting pool. Children may be especially interested in the one room schoolhouse on the property which is
open to the public March 30–December 30.

www.oatlands.org

703-777-3174

20850 Oatlands Plantation Lane, Leesburg, VA
Capital Beltway (I-495) to Dulles Toll Road (Rt. 267) to the Dulles
Greenway; right onto Rt. 15 south for approximately 5 miles.

Monday–Saturday, 10–5; Sunday, 1–5.

House tours on the hour; the last tour of the mansion begins at 4 p.m.

Property and gates close at 5:30.

*Adults, $10; seniors (60+)/students (6–16), $9; garden and grounds only,
$7. National Trust members, $5. Friends of Oatlands and children younger than 5, free (except during selected special events such as Christmas
at Oatlands).*

*Groups: Reduced rates for 20 or more for tours of the house, gardens and
plantation. Closed Thanksgiving, December 24–25.*

Closed January–March except for selected programs and activities.

VA TimeTravelers site.

Self-guided tours available.

Special activities include point-to-point races in April; July–August Art Show. During November and December, the mansion is decorated with traditional greenery and ornaments.

 ## Stabler-Leadbeater Apothecary Shop and Museum

George Washington, Robert E. Lee, Daniel Webster were among those who used this actual drugstore. When the Depression forced the shop's closing in 1933, the doors were simply locked, preserving its contents for history. Most of the original herbs, potions and paper labels remain in their drawers and over 8,000 objects, such as pill rollers, mortars and pestles, drug mills, medical glassware and furnishings are still in place. Original prescription books and a sampling of pharmaceutical equipment are on display. A recording relates the shop's history.

www.apothecarymuseum.org

703-838-3852

105 and 107 South Fairfax Street, Alexandria, VA
Capital Beltway (I-495) and exit onto Rt. 1 north. Go 6 blocks, turn right on King Street and proceed for seven blocks. Turn right on S. Fairfax

Open April–October, Tuesday–Saturday, 10–5; Sunday–Monday, 1–5.
Open November–March, Wednesday–Saturday, 11–4; Sunday, 1–4.
Closed Thanksgiving, December 25 and January 1.

Adults, $4; Children 11–17, $2; children under 12, free.

Tours 15 minutes before and after the hour. Last tour, 4:45.

Wheelchair accessible on the downstairs floor of the museum.

Metrorail Blue or Yellow line (King Street and Braddock).

VA TimeTravelers site.

Steven F. Udvar-Hazy Center

The Steven F. Udvar-Hazy Center near Washington Dulles International Airport is the companion facility to the Air and Space Museum on the National Mall. In combination the two sites display the largest collection of aviation and space artifacts in the world. The Udvar-Hazy center, named for its largest donor, is comprised of two display areas, the Boeing Aviation Hangar and the James S. McDonnell Space Hangar, the Donald D. Engen Observation Tower, an IMAX Theater, space simulators, museum store and kiosks, a café offering basic fare and multimedia classrooms/learning labs. Highlights of the museum include the Lockheed SR-71 Blackbird, the fastest jet in the world, some of the tiniest aircraft in the world and the Space Shuttle Enterprise. On display in this exciting space are 141 aircraft, more than 145 large space artifacts and over 1,500 smaller items.

www.nasm.si.edu/museum/udvarhazy/

202-633-1000

14390 Air and Space Museum Parkway, Chantilly, VA
South of Washington Dulles International Airport along route 28, a half-mile north of the intersection of routes 28 and 50. Parking available.

Daily, 10–5:30. Closed December 25.

Public parking, $12. Annual passes available.

Public transportation via Virginia Regional Transit (VRTA). Check VRTA website (www.vatransit. org) for details.

Free docent tours twice daily.

Sully Historic Site

Programs at the Sully Historic Site emphasize the enslaved African American community, and show what life was like throughout the 18th and 19th centuries. One of several restored Lee family houses in Virginia, Sully Historic Site was built in 1794 for Richard B. Lee, first Congressman of Northern Virginia and uncle of General Robert E. Lee.

For school groups, there are special programs on textiles, food preparation, school life and slavery. Students learn spinning and weaving, make beaten biscuits from an old Lee recipe and try old-fashioned slates and quill pens. These programs run October-winter break and March through the end of the school year. Advance reservations required.

www.fairfaxcounty.gov/parks/sully

703-437-1794

3601 Sully Road (Rt. 28), Chantilly, VA
Capital Beltway (I-495) to I-66 west; then Rt. 50 west to right turn on Rt. 28 north, Sully Road, and right at the next stop light. Sully is 0.25 miles from the intersection of Rt. s 50 and 28.

Open Wednesday–Monday, 11–4; closed Tuesday, some holidays and part of December–February.

Adults, $6; students,$5; seniors and children 5–15, $4. Guided tours on the hour. Admission to the grounds is free.

Limited wheelchair access.

Strollers not permitted in the house, but they can be stored at the door.

VA TimeTravelers site.

Special activities include Antique car show in June, WWII life demonstration in July, Civil War life encampment in August, Quilt Show with hands-on activities in September, Lantern Tours in October, candlelight tours and holiday concerts in December and rotating spring programs. Weekend programs feature living history activities.

Torpedo Factory Art Center

Located on the Potomac riverfront in historic Old Town Alexandria, the Torpedo Factory Art Center has 82 studios and six galleries housing more than 165 working artist and craftsmen working, exhibiting and selling their art in this renovated World War I munitions plant.

www.torpedofactory.org

703-838-4565

105 North Union Street, Alexandria, VA
Capital Beltway (I-495) and exit onto Rt. 1 north. Go six blocks, turn right on King Street to the river, and turn left on Union Street; Art Center is in the first block on the right.

Daily, 10–5. Closed Easter, July 4, Thanksgiving, December 25, and January 1.

Metrorail Yellow line (King Street), then Alexandria DASH Bus to King and Fairfax Streets, and walk two blocks east on King Street to Union Street.

Second Thursday of each month the Torpedo Factory is open free to the public from 6–9 p.m. as part of gallery tours in Old Town Alexandria.

Visitor guides available in six languages.

Special activities include Annual Alexandria Arts Safari on a Saturday in early October, a family oriented day of art activities offering artists' demonstrations in clay, painting and enamel, as well as hands-on activities for young children in various media.

U.S. Geological Survey National Visitors Center

Visitors to the U.S. Geological Survey will find a wealth of information and activities. In addition to watching films on a variety of subjects, groups may take guided tours and sightsee along the woodland trail. On the tour, children can place their feet in actual dinosaur footprints in stone taken from a quarry in Stevensburg, VA, and visit the hands-on room for activities related to biology, geology, geography and hydrology. They will also see a seismic station where earthquakes are recorded.

www.usgs.gov/visitors/index.html

703-648-4748

12201 Sunrise Valley Drive, Reston, VA
Capital Beltway (I-495) to Dulles Toll Road, to exit 12 at Reston Parkway south; turn right at third light on South Lakes Drive; go 0.5 miles
to USGS on the right. Parking in visitor area.

Weekdays, 8–4, except federal holidays.

Free, self-guided and guided tours are available October–May.

Hiking.

*Special activities include different monthly displays of artwork, and two-
week summer camp sessions.*

⛱ Woodlawn Plantation/Frank Lloyd Wright Pope-Leighey House

George Washington gave part of his Mount Vernon estate to Mrs. Washington's granddaughter, Nelly Custis, and his nephew, Lawrence Lewis,
as a wedding present. Woodlawn Mansion, designed by Dr. William
Thorton, architect of the U.S. Capitol, was built here. Adults will appreciate the elegant living room, dining room and parlor. Youngsters like
the children's bedrooms and the collection of stuffed birds acquired by
Nelly Custis's son Lorenzo. A restored garden features roses and boxwood plantings. As a plantation site, Woodlawn was also home to over
90 slaves, as well as free hired workers, black and white.

The Pope-Leighey house is a "Usonian" home designed by Frank Lloyd
Wright. The house reflects Wright's belief that people of moderate
means are entitled to well-designed homes. Originally built in Falls
Church, the Pope-Leighey House was moved to the Woodlawn property in the early 1960s. Visitors can pick up a discovery packet to compare this 20th-century home to the earlier plantation home.

www.nationaltrust.org/woodlawn/index.html

703-780-4000

9000 Richmond Highway, Alexandria, VA
Capital Beltway (I-495) to Rt. 1 south; located at the junction of Rt. 1
and Rt. 235 (Mount Vernon Memorial Highway). Parking available
on-site.

*Tuesday–Sunday, 10–5. Closed January–February, Thanksgiving, De-
cember 25.*

Adults, $7.50; students (grades K–12), $3; children under five, free. Group rates (for 15 or more). Combination ticket for Woodlawn Plantation and the Pope-Leighey House: adults, $13; students (grades K–12), $5; under 5, free.

Special hands-on tours and slide presentation for school groups by appointment.

Nature trails wind through the woods.

Wheelchair access to the first floor only.

Security: Strollers, backpacks and shopping bags must be kept in reception area.

Special activities include a needlework exhibit during March; monthly in-depth tour of Pope Leighey House; a children's needlework workshop in early August; ghostly tours around Halloween; and a holiday exhibit in December. (Reservations are required for some events.)

THE GREAT OUTDOORS

Explore history by visiting battlefields and historic farms; learn about plants, animals and the night sky; get out and play: Washington has many open-air opportunities for fun and many ways to connect with the great outdoors. Before you plan your trip, make sure to call or check websites for hours and directions.

HIKING, FISHING, BIKING
AND BOATING IN WASHINGTON, DC

 Anacostia Park

This large area along the east bank of the Anacostia River has playing fields for football and baseball, picnic spots, playgrounds, basketball and tennis courts, an outdoor swimming pool, and an outdoor pavilion for roller-skating and community gatherings. One section of the park has been designated as a bird sanctuary where you might see a variety of marshland birds, such as herons, egrets, ducks and geese. Kenilworth Park and Aquatic Gardens, part of Anacostia Park, is the only National Park Service site devoted to the propagation and display of aquatic plants. The 77-acre Kenilworth marsh is the Capital's last tidal marsh. For a close-up view of plants and wildlife, bring your own canoe and paddle along the banks of the river and its inlets.

www.nps.gov/anac

202-472-3883

1900 Anacostia Drive, SE, Washington, DC
Along the Anacostia River between South Capitol Street and Benning Road, SE. On-site parking.

Open 9:30–5:30 daily except Thanksgiving, December 25 and January 1.

Newly renovated tennis and basketball facilities; public boat ramp.

Langston Golf Course offers an 18-hole course and driving range.

Supervised roller skating, June–September.

Outdoor swimming pool (managed by the DC Department of Parks and Recreation 202-671-0335).

Athletic fields, boating, fishing, picnicking, playgrounds, skating, swimming, roller skating, walking and jogging trails, basketball, tennis, environmental education programs.

Battery-Kemble Park

Without leaving the city, you can enjoy an afternoon picnic and a nature walk in this fine, hilly, woodsy park. Historically a part of the circle of Civil War Defenses of Washington DC, Battery-Kemble is one of the best area locations for sledding and cross-country skiing, and is ideal for kite flying.

www.nps.gov/archive/rocr/ftcircle/kemble.htm

202-282-1063

Chain Bridge Road, NW, below Loughboro Road, Washington, DC
The park is bounded by Chain Bridge Road, MacArthur Boulevard, 49th Street and Nebraska Avenue.

Daily, dawn–dusk.

Hiking.

Capital Crescent Trail

The Capital Crescent Trail is an approximately 11-mile long hiker-biker trail running from Silver Spring to Georgetown along the former B&O Railroad line. The trail crosses four historic bridges and runs through two historic tunnels and provides a look at the Potomac River through some of the prettiest woodlands in Washington. The trail connects with both the C&O towpath and with the Rock Creek Trail. The entrance to the trail in Bethesda is at the corner of Bethesda and Woodmont avenues, next to the public parking lot.

www.cctrail.org

202-234-4874

Excellent maps and descriptions also are available at: www.bikewashington.org/trails.

Biking, hiking.

 ## Glover-Archbold Park

Leave the hustle and bustle of the city behind as you enter this serene, heavily wooded park to wander its nature trails, bird watch or daydream. This section of Rock Creek Park runs from MacArthur Boulevard and Canal Road, NW to just south of Van Ness Street and Wisconsin Avenue, between 42nd and 44th Streets. Look for community gardens, planted and tended by local residents, in the section of the park closest to Whitehaven Park.

www.nps.gov/rocr

202-895-6000

Daily, dawn–dusk.

Hiking.

🄰 Rock Creek Park

Rock Creek is a wooded 1,754-acre park, about four miles long and one mile wide, that runs through northwest Washington from the Potomac River into Montgomery County. Picnic groves with tables, fireplaces, and shelters are abundant. A 1.5-mile exercise course begins near Calvert Street and Connecticut Avenue, NW, and another begins at 16th and Kennedy Streets, NW. The park's many resources include the Rock Creek Nature Center and Planetarium (see p. 191) and the Carter Barron Amphitheatre.

Bikers and walkers should note that Beach Drive, between Military and Broad Branch roads, NW, is closed to cars on weekends and holidays. A marked bike trail, much of which is paved, runs from the Lincoln Memorial to Maryland and from the Memorial Bridge to the Mount Vernon Trail in Virginia.

Hiking trails are maintained by the Potomac Appalachian Trails Club. Check at the Nature Center (202-895-6070) for information on hiking trails.

www.nps.gov/rocr

202-895-6000; Rock Creek Park Activity Line 202-895-6239

The park includes areas on both sides of Rock Creek Parkway, NW, and connects with other parkland throughout the city.

Daily, dawn–dusk.

Visitors centers are at the Nature Center, 5200 Glover Road, NW, Wednesday–Sunday, 9–5; Pierce Barn on Tilden and Beach Drive Saturday–Sunday, 12–5; the Old Stone House, 3051 M Street, NW, Wednesday–Sunday, 9–5.

Maps are available at the visitor centers.

To reserve picnic areas, reservations must be made in person at the DC Department of Parks and Recreation, 3149 16th Street, NW. For more information, call 202-673-7646.

Tennis courts at 16th and Kennedy Streets, NW are open year round. Tennis courts at Park Road, NW, east of Pierce Mill, open Memorial Day–Labor Day by reservation only. Reserve and pay fees through Guest Services 202-722-5949.

The 18-hole golf course at 16th and Rittenhouse Streets, NW, 202-882-7332, is open daily, dawn to dusk. Closed December 25. Clubs and carts can be rented.

Rock Creek Park Horse Center, Inc., off Military on Glover Road, NW, 202-362-0117, is the only riding facility in Washington, DC The Center offers barn tours, a summer camp, lessons for all ages and trail rides.

Rent bikes, canoes, kayaks, small sailboats, rowing shells and rowboats at Thompson's Boat House, 202-333-9543, opposite the entrance to Rock Creek Parkway at Virginia Avenue, NW (near the Watergate). www.thompsonboatcenter.com.

Pierce Barn (Tilden Street and Beach Drive): Weekends noon–4. Public nature and historical programs 202-895-6070.

Old Stone House, 3051 M Street, NW 202-426-6851. *(See p. 62.)*

Ranger-led programs are free and open to the public (202-895-6239).

Biking, boating, hiking, roller blading, equestrian and cross-country skiing trails, sledding, and tennis.

Special activities include Rock Creek Park Day in late September.

HIKING, FISHING, BIKING AND BOATING IN MARYLAND

Black Hill Regional Park

This park is located on 1,854 acres, including Little Seneca Lake with 16 miles of shoreline. The two challenging playgrounds are favorites of younger children. There is also a picnic area (call to reserve shelters, 301-495-2480), a Visitor Center, a half-acre dog park, paved hiker/biker trail, ten miles of hiking and equestrian trails, horseshoe pits, volleyball courts, boat launching, canoe and rowboat rentals and fishing.

www.mc-mncppc.org/parks/facilities/directory

301-972-3476, Visitor Center

20926 Lake Ridge Drive, Boyds, MD
Capital Beltway (I-495) to I-270 north to Father Hurley Boulevard; exit left on Rt. 355 to West Old Baltimore Road; continue for one mile to park entrance on the left. Parking available.

Open March–October, 6 a.m.–sunset; November–February, 7 a.m.–sunset.

"Nutshell News," a newsletter published by the parks commission, provides a schedule of events, other news and security information.

Biking, boating, fishing and hiking.

Special activities include a variety of nature programs (star search, hawk watch, family hikes, cornhusk basketry); Twilight Concerts, Summer Stage and canoe and kayak classes throughout the year.

Calvert Cliffs State Park

On the western side of the Chesapeake Bay, the Cliffs of Calvert dominate the shoreline for thirty miles along the shores of Calvert County. They are nearly as impressive a sight today as they were when Captain John Smith came upon them in his exploration of the Bay in 1608. The cliffs were formed over 15 million years ago when all of southern Maryland was covered by a warm shallow sea. These ancient sea floors can now be seen carved into the cliffs.

The park offers 13 miles of marked foot trails for hiking, including a 1.8 mile hike to a 100-yard stretch of the beach where you can go fossil hunting and search for shark's teeth and shells. Visitors may keep what they find. However, because of the constant erosion of the cliffs, access to the cliffs is no longer permitted. The trail to the beach winds through forest and marshland—great for bird watching. There is a one-acre fishing pond containing bass, bluegill and catfish. (A Maryland freshwater fishing license is required for persons 16 years and older.) Fishing from the beach is also permitted. (A Maryland sport fishing license is required to fish in the Chesapeake Bay.)

www.dnr.state.md.us/publiclands/southern/calvertcliffs

301-743-7613

500 H.G. Truman Parkway, Lusby, MD
14 miles south of Prince Frederick on Maryland Rt. s 2 and 4. Capital Beltway (I-495), exit Rt. 4 south to Lusby.

Daily, sunrise–sunset.

Admission: $5 per vehicle.

Swimming is at your own risk.

Pets are not allowed in the park area, but are permitted on hiking trails from Hunter parking lot.

Camping is available for youth groups only. (Reservation service 888-432-2267.)

Cliff area and beach are not wheelchair or stroller accessible.

Fishing, hiking, playgrounds and fossil hunting.

Bring sturdy shoes for the hike and sandals for the beach area.

🏕 Catoctin Mountain Park

This park offers campsites, hiking trails, rock climbing, fishing streams (fly fishing allowed, catch and release only), picnic tables and grills. In winter, when there may be up to 12 inches of snow, there is ample cross-country skiing, snow shoeing and sledding. A variety of special events for children and adults, including campfire programs and nature walks, make this park an ideal retreat for the whole family.

www.nps.gov/cato

301-663-9330

6602 Foxville Road, Thurmont, MD
Capital Beltway (I-495) to I-270 north to Frederick; Rt. 15 north to second Thurmont exit (Rt. 77 west); continue for three miles to park entrance on right.

Daily year-round, dawn to dusk. Seasonal road closures in the winter months, so be sure to check the website for information.

Visitor center open Monday–Thursday, 10–4:30; Fri. 10–5; Saturday– Sunday, 8:30–5. Closed federal holidays.

Camping: Owens Creek Campground is open April 15–late November ($20 per night per site). Camp Misty Mount (cabin rental, $55 per night) is open April 25–end October. Two-day minimum required on weekends. Call 301-271-3140 for reservations.

Wheelchair access to some areas. Call for specific information.

Camping, fishing, hiking, rock climbing.

Cedarville State Forest

This forest was once the winter home to southern Maryland's Piscataway Indians, who lived near Zekiah Swamp, a freshwater swamp where wildlife was abundant. The forest contains 50 different species of trees and rare carnivorous plants that catch and eat insects. The forest features 19 miles of marked trails for hiking, biking and horseback riding, a stocked pond for fishing, nature walks and campfire programs. Some of the trails may be extremely wet at times. Hikers using designated trails during hunting season should wear fluorescent orange.

www.dnr.state.md.us/publiclands/southern/cedarville

301-888-1410

10201 Bee Oak Road, Brandywine, MD
Capital Beltway (I-495) to Rt. 5 south (toward Waldorf) until it ends at Rt. 301. Follow 301 south and turn left on Cedarville Road. Continue on Cedarville to Bee Oak Road (on your right), the main entrance to the forest.

Daily, sunrise–sunset. Limited access on Thanksgiving and December 25.

Entrance fee $3 per vehicle, $4 per out-of-state vehicle (honor system).

Hiking trails are color coded. The Green Trail is the shortest (two miles) and passes through the headwaters of the Zekiah Swamp. May be extremely wet, especially during springtime.

Family and Youth Group Camping available late April to late October. Check website www.reservations.dnr.state.md.us or call 888-432-2267 for reservations. Two-night minimum required Memorial Day–Labor Day.

Hiking, biking and equestrian trials, horseback riding, archery, fishing, grilling (charcoal only, no wood fires are permitted).

Chesapeake and Ohio (C&O) Canal Historical Park and Great Falls, MD

The Great Falls of the Potomac River are one of the most impressive natural sights in the area. Here the river drops more than 70 feet over spectacular rock formations and proceeds downstream through rapids and river islands to its junction with the tidal estuary at Little Falls (Chain Bridge). Be prepared to walk about half a mile from the parking lot along the canal towpath and across two footbridges to Olmsted Island lookout.

The canal towpath is a pleasant place to walk and ride bikes. You will see many of the original locks and lockhouses of the historic C&O Canal, where mule-drawn barges used to travel between Cumberland, MD and Old Georgetown in Washington, DC. Older children will enjoy the Billy Goat Trail, a vigorous three-mile, round-trip hike that provides stunning views of the Potomac River and Mather Gorge. Directions for this and less strenuous hikes are available at the Great Falls Tavern Visitors Center.

The Canal Clipper Boat and the James F. Mercer, authentic replicas of 19th-century mule-drawn boats, operate on the canal from mid-April to October, Wednesday–Sunday at 11, 1:30 and 3 starting from Great Falls Tavern or Georgetown. The ride lasts about an hour and costs $7 for adults, and $5 for seniors and children, ages 5–15 (Life jackets are provided.) Children can bring fruit or carrots to feed the mules. For more information and group rentals, call the Georgetown Canal Information Center (202-653-5190).

The three-room Canal Museum in the Great Falls Tavern features exhibits such as a lock model, artifacts from the days when the canal was used as a busy transportation route, historic photographs and short films explaining the colorful history of the canal and of the Tavern.

www.nps.gov/choh

301-767-3714

11710 MacArthur Boulevard, Potomac, MD
The park follows the Potomac River from Georgetown in Washington to Cumberland, MD. Capital Beltway (I-495) to exit 41, Clara Barton Parkway. Past Falls Road, turn left onto the MacArthur Boulevard entrance to Great Falls Park.

The Georgetown Canal Information Center is in the Foundry Mall, between 30th and Thomas Jefferson Streets, NW, Washington, DC.

Daily, dawn–dusk. The Great Falls Tavern Visitor Center is open daily 9–4:45. Closed Thanksgiving, December 25, and January 1.

Entrance fee at Great Falls National Park: $5 per vehicle for a three-day pass; $3 per person arriving by foot or bike.

Warning: *Stay on the trail and off slippery rocks and cliff faces. Do not wade in the water or climb on rocks in restricted areas. The current here is exceptionally (and deceptively) powerful. Sadly, a number of people who disregard the warning signs drown each year.*

Take Note

Gold was mined near Great Falls in the late 1800s.

Snack bar at Great Falls Visitors Center is open April–October.

Wheelchair access to Great Falls Tavern Visitors Center and the Georgetown boat ride.

Biking, boating, fishing, hiking.

Special activities include Civil War Encampment during the last weekend in September; and Living History Boat Charters for school groups, April–June and September–October, for which park rangers dress in period clothing and transport students back in time to the 1870s.

Cosca Regional Park

With 690 acres of rolling and wooded terrain and a 15-acre lake, Cosca Regional Park offers a variety of recreation for the outdoor enthusiast, and is home to the Clearwater Nature Center (see p. 184). The park features equestrian and hiking trails, lighted athletic fields, picnic grounds and play areas and indoor and outdoor tennis courts (for schedule and fees for indoor courts, call 301-868-6462). Campers have access to 23 tent and trailer campsites with bathhouses, toilets, water hook-ups and electricity.

www.pgpks.com.places/parks/cosca.html

301-868-1397

11000 Thrift Road, Clinton, MD
Capital Beltway (I-495) to Branch Avenue (Rt. 5 toward Waldorf), turn right on Woodyard, left on Brandywine Road, right on Thrift Road to the park.

Daily, 7:30 a.m.–dusk; ball fields and tennis courts are open from 7 a.m.–11 p.m.

Non-residents of Prince George's or Montgomery Counties must pay a $5 parking fee. Miniature train is $0.75 a ride or $2 for three.

Boating, camping, fishing, hiking, tennis.

Cunningham Falls State Park

Named for the splendid 78-foot waterfall, the 4,446-acre park offers great nature walks, camping, picnicking (tables, grills and one shelter) and hiking. The 43-acre sandy-bottomed lake features boat launching, canoe rental, fishing and swimming. Lifeguards are on duty at the lake during daylight. Be sure to take the half-mile hike from the lake across the boardwalk to the beautiful, cascading falls. Kids will enjoy the playground built by volunteers from 3,000 recycled tires. In winter, this is a great place for cross-country skiing and sledding.

www.dnr.state.md.us/publiclands/western/cunninghamfalls.html

301-271-7574

14039 Catoctin Hollow Road, Thurmont, MD
I-270 north to Frederick; follow Rt. 15 north from Frederick to entrance to **Manor Area,** adjacent to Catoctin Mountain National Park. To reach the **William Houck Area,** continue north on Rt. 15 to second Thurmont exit (Rt. 77 west); continue to park entrance on Catoctin Hollow Road.

Admission for Manor Area year-round: $3 per vehicle, $7 for out-of-state vehicles; for William Houck area, summer rates: $4 per person, weekends and holidays; $3 per person, weekdays; $3/vehicle all other times.

Canoe rentals, Memorial Day–Labor Day.

Family camping available at campsites and camper cabins (equipped with a double bed and a bunk bed). Two-night minimum required between Memorial Day and Labor Day. Reservations can be made up to one year in advance at www.reservations.dnr.state.md.us or by calling 888-432-2267.

Wheelchair access includes picnic areas, campsites, fishing pier and boardwalk to falls.

Boating, camping, fishing, hiking, playgrounds, swimming.

Special events: In mid-March, visit the annual Maple Syrup Heritage Festival in the William Houck Area of the park. Tree tapping, maple syrup making demonstrations, pancakes and local crafts ($2/person donation requested).

Dickerson Conservation Park

Also known as the Cherrington Cooperative Wildlife Management Area, this lush 304-acre property is preserved for conservation purposes. The park (which feels more like a forest) is located along the Potomac River and the C&O Canal, south of the Montgomery/Frederick County border. Home to white-tailed deer, wild turkeys, squirrels and songbirds, it is a peaceful enclave ideal for bird watching, nature hikes and fishing. Kids will enjoy wading in the small trickling streams (Be sure to bring some boots or extra shoes.) A well-paved towpath loops around the park, making it a great place to stroll, bike, or have a leisurely picnic.

www.mc-mncppc.org/parks

301-495-2595

20700 Martinsburg Road, Dickerson, MD
Capital Beltway (I-495) to I-270 North; exit at Sam Eig Highway, turn left on Muddy Branch Road, right on Frederick (Rt. 28); continue 15.5 miles to Martinsburg Road; turn left and continue 2 miles to the Conservation Area.

Daily, sunrise–sunset.

No cars are allowed inside, but ample parking is available off of Martinsburg Road.

Hiking, biking, bird watching, warm water fishing, nature photography.

 ### Greenbelt Park

Greenbelt Park is part of the National Park Service and has 174 woodland campsites for tents, recreational vehicles and trailers up to 30 feet long. Restrooms, picnic tables, fireplaces, showers and water are available, but there are no utility hook-ups. The 1,100-acres features four marked nature trails. Park rangers lead campfire programs and nature walks in the summer, and offer a Junior Ranger Program for children 8–12 years old. (Two 4-day programs limited to ten children; no fee charged, but children must apply in advance and write an essay).

www.nps.gov/gree

301-344-3944

6565 Greenbelt Road, Greenbelt, MD
Capital Beltway (I-495) to Kenilworth Avenue (Rt. 193); turn left on
Greenbelt Road, continue 0.5 miles to park entrance.

*Daily, sunrise to sunset. Campgrounds are accessible 24 hours, picnic
areas from 8–8.*

*Family and group camping. Reservations required May through October,
www.recreation.gov or call 800-365-2267, 10a.m.–midnight. Fee is $16
per night, per site.*

Three picnic areas with restrooms, water, tables and charcoal fireplaces.

*Special activities include invasive plant removal days on the first Sat-
urday of each month. Participants meet at the Sweetgum Picnic Area
where volunteer leaders teach participants how to recognize and re-
move invasive plants.*

Jug Bay Natural Area, Patuxent River State Park

If you are planning a visit to this scenic 2,000-acre natural area, you
will need to plan ahead. Much of the parkland is open to the public,
though visitors need special permits and groups need reservations. To
the east side of the Patuxent River is the Jug Bay Wetlands Sanctuary
and to the west side of the river is the Patuxent River Park. The Jug Bay
Natural Area is the headquarters for the Patuxent River Park properties.
Outdoor recreation activities include primitive camping, fishing, hunting, canoeing (canoes can be rented at Jug Bay by advance reservation) and boating. Horse owners may use the park's trails. The park also
offers the following natural attractions:

Chesapeake Bay Critical Area Driving Tour is a four-mile, self-guided,
one-way drive connecting the Pautuxent River Park with the Merkle
Wildlife Sanctuary. A drive along the Patuxent River shoreline may
reveal osprey, Canadian geese or bald eagles. The tour includes educational displays, observation towers, and a 1,000-foot bridge across
Mattaponi Creek. The drive is open daily for hiking and bicycling and
open Sundays for vehicles.

At the heart of Jug Bay, children will enjoy the McCann Wetlands Study
Center with its large hands-on exhibit room. Just outside, there is an
observation deck with panoramic views of the marsh and the Patuxent
River and a boardwalk that winds through the marsh and leads into
the forest. Children can learn about marsh ecology while exploring the
area by canoe, or by using dipnets and buckets to search a pond for
turtles, tadpoles, dragonflies and aquatic insects. For young natural-

ists, there are excellent volunteer opportunities as well as a summer science camp. Visitors may rent canoes or launch their own canoes from the park.

The Black Walnut Creek Nature Study Area is dedicated to nature study and environmental education. You can walk out on boardwalks through the marsh and swamp and on woodland trails for an up-close view of the wetlands. Nature hikes are available by reservation for groups of eight or more.

River Ecology Boat Tours offers you a chance to board a pontoon boat and learn about wetlands, wildlife and the history of the local area. These tours are available for school programs, adult groups and seniors, by reservation from April through October.

The Patuxent Rural Life Museums include seven buildings at the site: The Duvall Tool Museum, the Blacksmith Shop, the Farriar and Tack Shop, a Tobacco Farming Museum, and the 1880 Duckett Log Cabin with its privy, chicken coop and meat house, all of which depict life along the river. Tours are available for groups by reservation.

www.pgparks.com/places/parks/jugbay.html

301-627-6074

Park comprises several properties on the river along the eastern boundary of Prince George's County, Upper Marlboro, MD
Capital Beltway (I-495) to Pennsylvania Avenue, SE (exit 11A, Rt. 4). Go eight miles to Rt. 301 south. Go 1.7 miles to left on Croom Station Road; left on Croom Road, and then another left on Croom Airport Road. At park entrance, either go straight to group camp area or turn left and proceed 1.7 miles to park office.

Daily, 8 a.m.–dusk. Closed Thanksgiving, December 25 and January 1.

All parklands are considered "limited use natural areas" and require a permit or reservation. Call for more information on permits.

Hunting at Patuxent River State Park, Seneca Creek State Park and Monocacy NRMA.

Activities accommodate seniors and disabled visitors.

Historic sites.

Interpretive group boat tours on Jug Bay, April–October, by reservation.

Canoeing, cross-country skiing, camping, fishing, hiking.

Lake Artemesia Park

Lake Artemesia is a 38-acre, scenic man-made lake with over two miles of accessible trails, a beautiful aquatic garden and abundant fishing. The lake is stocked with several varieties of fish (bass, bluegill, sunfish, catfish and trout). The park was created during construction of the nearby Washington Metro rail line. Builders removed sand and gravel from the park area to use in the Metro rail project in exchange for building the lake and developing the natural area. Lake Artemesia is also part of the Anacostia Tributary branches of the Anacostia River.

www.pgparks.com/places/nature/artemesia.html

301-927-2163

600 Cleveland Avenue, College Park, MD
Capital Beltway (I-495) and exit at Kenilworth Avenue (Rt. 201) south (toward Bladensburg); turn right onto Greenbelt Road (Rt. 193), then right onto Branchville Road. The road will bear left and left again crossing under Greenbelt Road where it changes into Ballew Ave. Just after the stop sign at Berwyn Road, turn left into the parking lot for Lake Artemesia. Follow bike path to the lake.

Open year-round, sunrise to sunset.

Ample parking at Branchview/Ballew Avenue. No cars are permitted on park grounds.

For hiking/biking trails, enter the park at the 5200 block of Calvert Road in College Park or at Osage Street and Swarthmore Court in Berwyn Heights.

A stroller-accessible trail loops around the lake. Benches and resting areas are provided.

Wheelchair-accessible fishing pier.

Hiking, biking, fishing, aquatic garden.

Special activities include evening hikes and stream conservation programs.

Lake Frank Park

Lake Frank (or Lake Bernard Frank) is part of Rock Creek Regional Park and was created as a sister lake to Lake Needwood (see p. 131) to aid in flood control. Lake Frank and Lake Needwood are separated by Avery Road in Derwood, north of Rockville. Lake Frank is an idyllic spot which offers shoreline hiking, fishing and a peaceful place to "get away from it all." A long-time favorite of dog lovers, the parklands surrounding the 54-acre lake contain both paved and dirt trails. Leashes are required for dogs at all times, especially when near the water.

www.mc-mncpp.org/parks

301-495-2595

Bordered by Avery Road, Muncaster Mill Road and Norbeck Road in Derwood, MD
Parking available at Muncaster Mill and Avery roads. Capital Beltway (I-495) to I-270 north; exit at Shady Grove Road, then immediate right at fork to Redland Road; follow Redland and turn right on Needwood Road; continue on Needwood and turn right on Muncaster Mill Road. The entrance to the park is on the right side. The lake is a quarter-mile walk from the parking lot.

Daily, sunrise–sunset.

No swimming or boating.

Fishing, hiking. Detailed trail maps can be obtained from www.mc-mncppc.org/trails

Lake Needwood Park

Lake Needwood is a picturesque man-made lake nestled in wooded Rock Creek Regional Park. At the lake's edge you will find a boathouse, bait and tackle shop and picnic shelters.

The lake offers activities for a full day of outdoor fun. You can take a trip aboard the "Needwood Queen," a 20-passenger pontoon boat or rent a boat yourself. (Paddleboat, rowboats and canoes are available.) Private boats are allowed on the lake from March 1 through December 15. Stocked with fish, Lake Needwood is also a good place to go fishing. (Bait and fishing rods are available for purchase as well as the required fishing licenses for those over 16.) There are also easy hiking trails, play areas, picnic groves and a snack bar, as well as the Meadowside Nature Center (see p. 189).

www.derwood.net/Recreation/Lkneedwood.htm

301-495-2595

15700 Needwood Lake Circle, Derwood, MD
Capital Beltway (I-495) to Georgia Avenue north; turn left on Norbeck Road; turn right on Muncaster Mill Road; turn left on Avery Road; follow signs to Visitor's Center/Boat Rental.

Boat rentals available June–August, noon–6 Monday–Friday, 6:30–6 weekends. Open weekends only in the months of May and September. One person on each boat must be at least 16 years old or have a driver's license. Life jackets are required and provided for children.

Two golf courses, 18- and 9-hole. Schedule and fees, 301-948-1075.

Groups with advance boat reservations can ride the "Needwood Queen" during the week ($2/person with a ten-person minimum). The general public can ride on weekends ($2/person). For recorded boating information, call 301-762-9500.

Shelter rentals, 301-495-2525, 8:30–5.

Boating, fishing, hiking, playgrounds, wildlife watching.

Little Bennett Regional Park

A short ride north of Washington lies secluded camping and hiking in Little Bennett Regional Park. Sites include picnic tables and grills; sinks, showers and toilets; laundry rooms and water. Rental equipment fee and includes a four-person tent, two camp chairs, a propane stove and a lantern. This is also an excellent place for a day hike and lunch on one of the park's many trails. There are several open fields, horseshoe pits, volleyball courts and playgrounds. Located on the trails are remains of historic sites, including saw mills, a 19th-century schoolhouse and several houses. Nearby Little Seneca Lake offers fishing.

www.mc-mncppc.org/parks/enterprise/park_facilities/ little_bennett

301-495-2595

23701 Frederick Road, Clarksburg, MD
Capital Beltway (I-495) to I-270 north; exit at Boyds-Clarksburg (exit 18); turn right on Clarksburg Road and continue for one mile; turn left on Rt. 355; continue for 0.75 miles to park entrance on right.

Daily, dawn to dusk.

Check website for weekend activities at Hawk's Reach Activity Center.

Family camping (91 sites), April 1–October 31, maximum stay two weeks, weekend camping March–November; reservations accepted; fee. Primitive camping areas for groups; call campground registration, 301-972-9222. There is a camp store at the registration office.

Camping, hiking, biking, equestrian trails, playgrounds.

Old Rag Mountain (Shenandoah National Park)

A visit to the rocky top of Old Rag Mountain is a Green Acres Middle School tradition. The mountain stands alone in Virginia's Blue Ridge at 3,291 feet in a park filled with history and surprises. Old Rag's Ridge Trail is a tough climb over and through big boulders—but worth it for the spectacular views in every direction. (You can see Skyline Drive to the west and the Chesapeake Bay to the east.) This is a popular hiking spot; get to the trailhead early in peak seasons. Two shelters on the circuit have cooking fireplaces, though camping is not permitted above 2,500 feet.

www.nps.gov/shen

540-999-3500

Shenandoah National Park, near Luray, VA; about 2 hours from DC Capital Beltway I-495 to exit 49 to I-66 W toward Front Royal/Manassas. Exit 43A to Lee Hwy/US-29 S toward Gainesville/Warrenton. US-211 W exit toward Luray/Warrenton. US-211 W to left at Berryville Pike/US-522; then right at Fort Valley Rd/Rt. 231. Turn right at Sharp Rock Rd; right at Nethers Rd to parking.

Adults and teens over 16, $5–$8, depending on season; vehicle passes $10–$15, depending on season.

Patapsco Valley State Park

In 1608, Captain John Smith discovered the river that runs through this historic park. Battles of the Revolutionary War, War of 1812 and the Civil War were fought here. Look for the old stone viaduct, the country's first train depot and the dam that was the world's first underwater hydroelectric plant. Patapsco offers nature walks, campfire programs, picnicking, playgrounds, hiking, mountain bike and equestrian trails, canoeing and ball fields. Fishing is good in the river. Campers have access to fireplaces, picnic tables, water, showers and electricity.

www.dnr.state.md.us/publiclands/central/patapscovalley.html

410-461-5005

8020 Baltimore National Pike, Ellicott City, MD
Capital Beltway (I-495) to Rt. 29 north to Rt. 40 east. Entrance is a half-mile inside Howard County, on the Patapsco River between Elkridge and Sykesville, MD. From I-695 to exit 15B (I-40W), for three miles, right into park.

Year-round, 9–sunset. Closed Thanksgiving and December 25.

$2 admission. Seniors/disabled passes available by application.

Family camping (83 sites), April–October, $20 per night without electric and $25 with electric. Youth group camping (6 sites for up to 35–50 persons capacity) by reservation; 6 mini cabins, $50/night on Fridays and Saturdays.

Avalon Visitor Center: exhibits showing 300 years of history along Patapsco River.

Biking, boating, camping, fishing, hiking, playgrounds.

Piscataway National Park

Piscataway Park has many areas open to the public. Farmington Landing site, located on Piscataway Creek, is a nice place to launch small boats or to fish. Accokeek Creek has a boardwalk over a marsh area where you can see a variety of birds.

The Marshall Hall area was once a thriving plantation (only the walls remain) and in later years an amusement park visited by excursion boats from Washington, DC. Today visitors can launch boats, picnic or take a hike on a wetland trail. The Hard Bargain Farm Environmental Center offers educational programs for groups of school children. Students can study the wildlife found along the river, including beavers and great blue herons. The park's Visitor Center and a fishing dock are located in the National Colonial Farm area. The National Colonial Farm is an 18th-century farm and a modern day eco-farm (see p. 199).

www.nps.gov/pisc

301-763-4600

3400 Bryan Point Road, Accokeek, MD
Capital Beltway (I-495) or the Rt. 295 Bypass to Indian Head Highway south (Rt. 210). To reach the National Colonial Farm area, continue on Indian Head Highway for ten miles to a right turn on Bryan Point Road; follow to end of the road. To reach the Marshall Hall area, continue on Indian Head Highway for four more miles; then right turn on Marshall Hall Road (Rt. 227) and proceed for three miles to the park entrance.

Daily, dawn–dusk.

Limited wheelchair access.

Bikers and hikers can park either at the National Colonial Farm Visitor Center or at the parking areas off Bryan Point Road near the Accokeek Creek and travel along the shoreline for several miles.

Boating, hiking.

Seneca Creek State Park

This 6,300-acre stream valley park covers both sides of Great Seneca Creek for 14 miles from Route 355 north of Gaithersburg to the Potomac River. Approximately 1,000 acres are developed for public day-use including a self-guided tour which meanders through the area. Trail maps can be found at the Park Office. The maps cover five trails plus the self-guided Woodlands Trail of the old Clopper mansion ruins, and an historical mill. Also located within the park is the Schaeffer Farm area (off Schaeffer Road) with over ten miles of multi-use trails primarily suited for mountain biking. The Seneca Creek Greenway Trail offers over 16 miles of hiking following the Great Seneca creek from the Potomac River upstream to Route 355 and onward to the Maryland National Capital Park and Planning Commission park land.

www.dnr.state.md.us/publiclands/central/seneca.html

301-924-2127

11950 Clopper Road, Gaithersburg, MD
Capital Beltway (I-495) to Rt. 170 north; exit at 10, Clopper Road; continue two miles to park headquarters on the left.

Day-use area open year-round, 8 a.m.–sunset.

April–October: Weekends and holidays, $2 per person (seniors and children in car seats, free); November–March: no charge. (Out-of-state residents add $1 to all-day use charges).

Private picnic pavilions available for rent.

No pets, including horses, are permitted in the day-use area. For trail conditions, call 301-924-1998.

Park Office includes a 140-seat auditorium available for weekday meetings, $280/day.

Hunting.

Wheelchair access on pontoon boat tour, Park Office, Boat Center, picnic areas and restrooms.

Athletic fields, biking, boating, disk golf, fishing, hiking, kayaking and canoeing, playgrounds, 18-hole disk golf course, 90-acre lake, open fields.

Special activities include Gaithersburg's Winter Lights in December; the Shaker Forest Festival in September; and hay rides, bird walks, canoe tours, pontoon tours, moonlight walks, campfires, and Junior Ranger programs in the summer.

Sligo Creek Park

This peaceful park, which runs through Silver Spring and Takoma Park, is a pleasant place to bike, walk, or have an old-fashioned family picnic. A hiking/exercise course, playground equipment, basketball courts, and a flat bike trail paralleling the creek for ten miles, make for a delightful family outing. Follow the trail to Wheaton Regional Park.

www.mc-mncppc.org

301-495-2595

Parallels Sligo Creek Parkway from University Boulevard to New Hampshire Avenue, Silver Spring, MD
Begin at Piney Branch Road and Sligo Creek Parkway.

Daily, dawn–dusk.

Softball and other athletic fields, biking, golf course, hiking, playgrounds, tennis.

Sugarloaf Mountain

A visit to Sugarloaf is a pleasant way for the family to enjoy nature. This privately owned mountain is known for its lovely foliage and vistas. The auto road goes almost to the top, and there are plenty of good walking and climbing trails to match your family's hiking levels. Young children can climb to the top from the auto road. More experienced climbers may want to ascend via "Devils Kitchen." There's a great view at the top and picnic spots scattered on the mountain.

www.sugarloafmd.com

301-869-7846

7901 Comus Road, Dickerson, MD
Capital Beltway (I-495) to I-270 north to exit 22; turn right on Rt. 109 south toward Comus; go two and a half miles and turn right at Comus Road; sign at entrance. Park at the base of the mountain, or drive your car part of the way up the mountain and park at overlooks.

Visitors admitted daily, 8 a.m.–one hour prior to sunset. All visitors must leave by sunset.

No fires or cookouts allowed.

Underground Railroad Experience Trail

This two-mile long, wooded, scenic trail celebrates the history of the Sandy Spring Quaker community in helping to oppose slavery from the time that and commemorates the involvement of Montgomery County residents in the Underground Railroad, the system of safe houses and brave "conductors" who helped slaves travel north to freedom.

www.mc-mncppc.org/trails/trails_maps/Rural_legacy.shtm

301-563-3400

6501 Norwood Road Sandy Spring, MD (Woodlawn Manor)
Capital Beltway I-495, to Rt. 355 north (Rockville Pike/Frederick Road). Right onto First Street/MD 911E; continue onto Rt. 28 E/Norbeck Road. Left on Layhill Rd/ MD182; left onto Norwood Rd/MD182.

Free hikes, Saturdays, April–November, 10 a.m. Meet at the kiosk across from the stone barn at Woodlawn Manor.

HIKING, FISHING, BIKING AND BOATING IN VIRGINIA

♨ Bull Run Marina

This heavily wooded park on Lake Occoquan is an ideal spot for teaching children the art and lore of fishing (bait and tackle for fishing can be purchased in the park). Picnic tables and grills are scattered under the trees overlooking the water. The Marina has hiking trails and a playground, and offers outdoor education courses, as well as guided canoe trips.

www.nvrpa.org/bullrunmarina.html

703-250-9124

12619 Old Yates Ford Road, Clifton, VA
Capital Beltway (I-495) to I-66 west; exit at Fairfax, Rt. 123 south to Clifton Road; right on Clifton Road; turn left on Henderson then right onto Yates Ford Road.

Open March 17–November 11, Friday–Sunday and holidays, dawn to dark.

Rowboat, kayak and canoe rentals and boat launching.

Athletic fields, boating, canoe and kayak rentals, fishing, hiking, playgrounds.

Fountainhead Regional Park

Located at the widest point of Lake Occoquan, this scenic park is a conservation area that shelters a profusion of birds, geese, ducks, raccoons and deer. Picnic tables and grills overlook the water, and nature trails wind over hills and ravines to views of the lake and low marshlands. The park also offers miniature golf, and a five-mile mountain bike trail. It is an ideal spot to teach children to fish (licenses are sold at the park), and boats are available to rent.

www.nvrpa.org/fountainhead.html

703-250-9124

10875 Hampton Road, Fairfax Station, VA
Capital Beltway (I-495) to I-95 south to Rt. 123 north; go about five

miles and turn left on Hampton Road; go three miles to entrance on the left.

Open March 17–November 11, dawn–dark.

Mini golf open weekends in spring and fall and daily in the summer.

Mountain Bike Trail Conditions: 703-250-9124.

Picnic shelter rentals, 703-352-5900.

Access to the 17-mile Bull Run-Occoquan Trail.

Wheelchair access includes a fishing pier.

Mountain biking, boating, fishing, hiking, miniature golf, bridle trails.

Boat and electric motor rentals available.

Great Falls Park

Great Falls is an 800-acre park overlooking the magnificent Great Falls of the Potomac River. Families come here to explore the remains of the 18th-century Patowmack Canal, built to bypass the falls, or to fish in the river. There are many hiking and equestrian trails, and a snack bar (open seasonally).

www.nps.gov/grfa

703-285-2965

9200 Old Dominion Drive, McLean, VA
Capital Beltway (I-495) to Georgetown Pike (Rt. 193); go west four miles to right on Old Dominion Drive (Rt. 738); continue one mile to park entrance.

Daily, 7 a.m.–dark. Closed December 25.

Entrance fee, $3 per individual or $5 per vehicle; the parking lot may be full by the middle of the day on weekends, so plan accordingly. Annual Passes for Great Falls are available for $20.

WARNING: Do not wade in the water or climb on rocks in restricted areas. Stay away from the river's edge and watch children closely at all times. The current here is exceptionally powerful. Every year a number of people who disregard the warning signs drown.

Visitors Center is staffed by park rangers and volunteers. Special tours and walks are held all year. The Visitor Center is open from 10 a.m. until 4 p.m. daily, with extended hours during the spring and summer months.

Leashed pets are allowed.

Overlook 2, which provides a wonderful panoramic view of the falls, is a short walk from the Visitor Center and is wheelchair accessible.

ADA parking is near the Visitor Center. The Patowmack Canal Interpretive Trail is accessible by wheelchair as far as Lock 1.

Picnic area has picnic tables and small grills.

VA TimeTravelers site, fishing, hiking.

Huntley Meadows Park

This 1,424-acre park, tucked away in the midst of suburbia, will introduce your children to several diverse habitats: wetlands, forest and meadow. Dogue, Little Hunting, and Barnyard Run Creeks flow through the park on their way to the Potomac River. There are many species of plants and animals. A two-thirds-mile wetland boardwalk trail with observation platforms and a tower takes you into the marsh. Look for some of the park's residents, including raccoons, beavers, frogs, turtles, insects and abundant bird life. Be sure to bring your field guides, binoculars and curiosity.

The Visitor Center includes interactive exhibits depicting the cultural and natural history of the park and its natural habitats. Children especially enjoy the wetlands diorama and photomurals.

www.fairfaxcounty.gov/parks/Huntley

703-768-2525

3701 Lockheed Boulevard, Alexandria, VA
Capital Beltway (I-495) to Richmond Highway, Rt. 1; go south three and a half miles and turn right at Lockheed Boulevard. Proceed three blocks to the park entrance on the left at Harrison Lane.

Park open daily, dawn to dusk. Visitor Center open Monday, Wednesday, Thursday and Friday, 9–5. Additional summer hours: June weekends 9–5; July and August weekends 9–1. Closed Tuesday, Thanksgiving, December 25 and January 1.

Picnic at Stoneybrook or Lee District Park.

Trails and boardwalk are wheelchair and stroller accessible. Wheelchairs are available upon request.

Mason District Park

Mason District Park includes 121 acres in the heart of Fairfax County. The park features tennis and basketball courts, ball fields and jogging trails. Visitors can enjoy a wildlife pond, take a hike or follow self-guided nature trails. There are picnic and open play areas as well as a playground for young children. The Arts in the Parks series offers free family-friendly performances on Saturdays at 10 a.m. from May to September.

www.fairfaxcounty.gov/parks/omp.htm

703-941-1730

6621 Columbia Park, Annandale, VA
Capital Beltway (I-495) to Little River Turnpike east; continue for two miles to left at John Marr Drive; right on Columbia Pike to park entrance on the right, before Sleepy Hollow Road.

Daily, dawn–dusk.

Athletic fields, hiking, playgrounds, tennis.

Special activities include Mason Days with crafts and entertainment in September.

 Mount Vernon Trail

This 18.5-mile trail is a pleasure for joggers, bikers and walkers. There are numerous places to stop for a picnic lunch or to take a rest. At Roosevelt Island, you can walk the trails; LBJ Grove provides a clear view of the Washington skyline; Gravelly Point is a favorite place to watch planes take off and land; Daingerfield Island has water sports and a restaurant; Dyke Marsh is a 240-acre wetland where you might spot some rare species of birds; and Mount Vernon was George Washington's home.

www.nps.gov/gwmp/mvt.html

703-289-7500

George Washington Memorial Parkway
The trail parallels the Potomac River and the George Washington Memorial Parkway from Theodore Roosevelt Island to Mount Vernon.

Daily, dawn–dusk.

Parking available at Theodore Roosevelt Island, LBJ Memorial Grove, Gravelley Point, Daingerfield Island, Jones Point Lighthouse, Belle Haven, Fort Hunt Park, Riverside Park and Mount Vernon.

Restrooms at Theodore Roosevelt Island, LBJ Memorial Grove, Daingerfield Island, Belle Haven, Fort Hunt Park and Mount Vernon.

On the route is Mount Vernon District Park and Recreation Center with an indoor ice rink and swimming pool.

Connects to the Arlington County trail system and the Washington and Old Dominion bike trail at Theodore Roosevelt Island. Cross Memorial Bridge and connect to the C&O Canal bike trail.

Athletic fields, biking, boating, fishing, hiking, playgrounds.

 Potomac Overlook Regional Park

Here is a welcome open area in the heart of urban Arlington. Children will enjoy visiting the nature center and participating in its many natural and human history programs, concerts and community events. The park offers several hiking trails and picnic areas.

www.nvrpa.org/parks/potomacoverlook

703-528-5406

2845 Marcey Road, Arlington, VA
Capital Beltway (I-495) to George Washington Parkway East to Spout Run exit; go right on Lorcom Lane; right on Nellie Custis (becomes Military Road); right on Marcey Road to park entrance.

Daily, dawn–dusk.

Nature Center: Tuesday–Saturday, 10–5; Sunday, 1–5. Closed Monday.

Nature Center has wildlife and archaeological displays.

Vegetable, herb, butterfly and wildflower gardens.

Special activities include the Annual Open House and Heritage Festival on the first Sunday in May.

M Prince William Forest Park

Several campgrounds in this park offer a variety of camping experiences: Oak Ridge, with 80 sites for tents and trailers (no reservations); Chopawamsic, with primitive camping not accessible by cars (permits required); and Turkey Run Ridge, with group tent campsites for 25–40 people (reservations required). Camp Orenda, also knows as Cabin Camp 3, offers camping in historic cabins and is listed on the National Register of Historic Places. Ranger-guided programs are provided year-round. Groups may request special ranger-guided activities.

www.nps.gov/prwi

703-221-7181

Capital Beltway (I-495) to I-95 south for about 35 miles to Rt. 619 (near Quantico); follow signs.

Daily, dawn–dusk. Visitor Center open daily, 9–5. Closed Thanksgiving, December 25 and January 1.

Entrance fee, $5 per vehicle.

37 miles of hiking trails. 21 miles of bicycle-accessible roads and trails.

Swimming.

Red Rock Wilderness Overlook Regional Park

Discover a beautiful, out-of-the-way place. Hike over hills and through woods dotted with wildflowers to panoramic views of the Potomac River and the distant mountains.

www.nvrpa.org/parks/redrock

703-737-7800

43098 Edwards Ferry Road, Leesburg, VA
Capital Beltway (I-495) to Rt. 7 west toward Leesburg; Rt. 15 Bypass north; turn right on Edwards Ferry Road (Rt. 773). Drive 1.5 miles to park entrance on left. Parking on-site.

Open year-round, dawn to dusk.

Nature trails, scenic overlook, hiking.

No public restrooms.

Riverbend Park

Riverbend Park encompasses 409 acres of Potomac shoreline, meadows, forests and streams and has a visitor center with a wooden deck overlooking the Potomac River. The park features picnic areas with grills, a snack bar, walking trails and fishing.

www.fairfaxcounty.gov/parks/riverbend

703-759-9018

8700 Potomac Hills Street, Great Falls, VA
Capital Beltway (I-495) to Rt. 193 west; turn right on Riverbend Road; go 3 miles to right on Jeffery Road; continue 1.5 miles to the park.

Daily, 7 a.m.–dusk. Visitor center open Wednesday–Monday noon–5; closed Tuesday.

Hiking, nature and equestrian trails, boat launches and craft rooms.

The Riverbend Nature Center, 8814 Jeffery Road, is open only for scheduled programs, groups and appointments.

Wheelchair access includes a paved interpretive nature trail through upland forest.

Boating, fishing, hiking.

Scotts Run Nature Preserve

Fairfax County naturalists refer to Scotts Run as the "Hot Spot for Wild Flowers," plus hiking for all ages and abilities, bird watching, and spectacular foliage. It is said that many of the huge trees are more than 100 years old. The scenery includes an abundance of dogwood and papaw as well as wildflowers in the spring. A three-mile trail follows a "stepping-stone stream" to a small waterfall and an awe-inspiring view of the Potomac. The trail gets more challenging as it approaches the river.

www.fairfaxcounty.gov/dranesville/Parks.htm

703-324-8702

7400 Georgetown Pike, McLean, VA
Capital Beltway (I-495) to Rt. 193 west; proceed on Rt. 193 for less than a mile to parking lot on the right.

Daily, dawn–dusk.

No restrooms.

Hiking.

From the eastern edge of Scotts Run, there is access to the Potomac Heritage trail, which runs south along the Potomac River for 10 miles, to Theodore Roosevelt Island.

Theodore Roosevelt Island

From the parking lot, visitors cross over a footbridge to enter this 88-acre wildlife refuge, preserved in its natural state as a tribute to conservationist President Theodore Roosevelt. The deeply wooded island includes a clearing where a 23-foot bronze statue of Roosevelt rises from a plaza that incorporates small shallow pools. It is a pleasant place to rest or have a picnic lunch. The park boasts a vast variety of plants, beasts, birds and bugs in the swamps and forests, and is a good place to fish as well as canoe (bring your own). Sturdy low-heeled shoes are a must for exploring the two and a half miles of foot trails that meander through the varied habitats. Insect repellent is recommended, especially in the summer.

www.nps.gov/this/

703-289-2500

George Washington Memorial Parkway
Theodore Roosevelt Bridge to George Washington Memorial Parkway north, on the Virginia side of the Potomac River; follow signs to parking area for Roosevelt Island. Not accessible from the southbound lanes. From the south, Theodore Roosevelt Bridge to Constitution Avenue. Right on 23rd Street and cross Memorial Bridge. Bear right and return to the George Washington Memorial Parkway.

Daily, dawn–dusk.

Call for information on guided tours and lectures.

Wheelchair accessible with assistance.

Boating, fishing, hiking.

Special activities include nature walks by appointment; ranger-led activities; Theodore Roosevelt birthday celebration in October; and Mr. Lincoln's Soldiers, featuring Civil War reenactments, in May.

Washington and Old Dominion (W&OD) Railroad Regional Park

Called "the skinniest park in Virginia," this 45-mile strip of park follows the roadbed of the old W&OD Railroad. It is the most heavily used park in Northern Virginia. The 100-foot-wide paved path, which connects with numerous other trails and parks, serves bikers, hikers, joggers and skate boarders from Arlington to Purcellville. The trail begins in Arlington, and there are several access points near Metro stations. Restrooms are located at several community centers along the way.

www.nvrpa.org/parks/wod; www.wodfriends.org

703-352-5900

21293 Smiths Switch Road, Ashburn, VA
The railroad trail goes from Shirlington near I-395 to Purcellville in Loudon County. Additional places to access the W&OD are:

Shirlington: Capital Beltway (I-495) to I-395 north to the Shirlington exit, keep to the right and turn left onto South Four Mile Run Drive (second light). The W&OD Trail will be on the right alongside the road. You can park along the side of the road. Not recommended for leaving your car overnight.

Arlington: At Manchester and 4th Street, and at Wilson Boulevard, west of Bon Air Rose Gardens and tennis courts, on the south side of the road.

Dunn Loring: Capital Beltway (I-495) to Gallows Road north. Go past the trail and turn right on Idylwood Road and then right on Sandburg Street. There is a gravel lot on both sides of the road at the trail.
Vienna East: Capital Beltway (I-495) to Route 123 into Vienna. Turn left (coming from Tysons) onto Park Street and right into the Vienna Community Center parking lot. The trail runs between the parking lot and the Community Center.

Vienna West: Capital Beltway (I-495) to Route 123 into Vienna. Turn right (coming from Tysons) onto Park Street. Turn left at the four-way stop sign onto Church. Turn right onto Mill Street and then left onto Ayr Hill Road. There is parking in the gravel lot at the train station.
Reston: Capital Beltway (I-495) to Route 7 west, turn left onto Reston Parkway. Turn left onto Sunset Hills Road.

Sterling: Route 28 several miles north of the Dulles Airport. Watch for signs. This is a good lot for horse trailers. For additional locations in Ashburn, Herndon, Leesburg and Purcellville, see www.wodfriends. org/parking.html.

Daily, dawn to dusk.

Refreshment concession at Smith Switch in Ashburn (Loudon County), VA.

Call for information on bike rentals.

A 54-page, color Trail Guide is available for sale at all regional parks, NVRPA Headquarters and at www.wodfriends.org.

Dual equestrian trail west of Vienna to Purcellville.

Biking, hiking.

BATTLEFIELDS AND HISTORIC SITES

Antietam National Battlefield

The Visitor Center houses a small museum with period artifacts, and shows a 26-minute film every half hour that describes the Civil War battle of Antietam, the bloodiest one day battle in American history. A one-hour Antietam Documentary is shown daily at noon. For a more thorough understanding of the battle, take the self-guided driving tour around the battlefield. The eight and a half mile drive, with the audiotape or CD tour that can be purchased at the bookshop, takes about two hours and includes 11 stops.

www.nps.gov/anti

301-432-5124

5831 Dunker Church Road, Sharpsburg, MD
Capital Beltway (I-495) to I-270 north to I-70 west (in Frederick); exit at Rt. 65 south (Sharpsburg exit) outside Hagerstown; follow Rt. 65 for 11 miles to battlefield on left.

Memorial Day–Labor Day, 8–7; Labor Day–Memorial Day, 8:30–5. Closed Thanksgiving, December 25 and January 1.

$4 per person or $6 per family.

Ranger programs daily during the summer. A Junior Ranger program is available for children ages 6–12.

Shepherdstown, WV, five miles away, offers many fine restaurants.

Special activities include Living History Demonstrations (artillery, infantry, and encampment) by National Park Service volunteers, and an annual 4.5-mile Memorial Illumination in early December commemorates those lost, killed and wounded at the Battle of Antietam.

Ball's Bluff Regional Park

Interpretive signs with Civil War-era maps and photographs lead visitors along a one-mile trail into the days of the significant Battle of Ball's Bluff, the largest Civil War engagement to take place in Loudon County. The park encompasses much of the battlefield and surrounds the Ball's Bluff National Cemetery.

www.nvrpa.org/parks/ballsbluff

703-737-7800

Ball's Bluff Road, Leesburg, VA
Capital Beltway (I-495) to Rt. 7 west toward Leesburg. Exit on Rt. 15 Bypass north. Turn right on Battlefield Parkway and left on Ball's Bluff Road. The park is at the end of the street.

Daily, dawn–dusk.

Tours are offered the first Saturday in May through the last Sunday in October at 10 a.m. and noon. Sunday evening tours on holiday weekends at 6.

Fishing, hiking.

No public restrooms.

Special activities include living history lectures and walks on selected weekends.

Fort Ward Park

Fort Ward was the fifth largest of 68 Union forts built to defend Washington during the Civil War. Learn more about it at the park museum or enjoy the azalea and flower displays in the garden area of this 40-acre park, built on the highest point in the city. (See also Fort Ward Museum, p. 97.)

ci.alexandria.va.us/recreation/parks/fort_ward_park.html

703-838-4848

4301 West Braddock Road, Alexandria, VA
Capital Beltway (I-495) to I-395 north to Seminary Road east; after approximately one mile, turn left on north Howard Street; right on West Braddock Road to entrance. Parking on-site.

Daily April–October, 8–8; November–March, 8–dusk.

Park can be reserved for group picnics.

Hiking, playground.

Special activities include self-guided tours; free summer twilight concerts on Thursdays after 7; Scottish Fair the last weekend in September.

Fort Washington Park

The present Fort Washington Park is a 341-acre natural area along the Potomac River. A large masonry Civil War Fort, it was completed in 1824 as the only permanent fortification built to defend the Nation's Capital. It is an outstanding example of early 19th-century coastal defense with its 45-foot high stone and brick walls sitting on a hillside above the Potomac River, and offers an excellent upriver view of Washington, DC. After viewing the movie in the Visitor Center and touring the Fort, you can enjoy a picnic lunch on the grounds. Features include trails, playgrounds, picnic areas and recreational and educational opportunities.

www.nps.gov/fowa

301-763-4600

13551 Ft. Washington Road, Ft. Washington, MD
Capital Beltway (I-495) to Indian Head Highway south; continue for four miles and turn right onto Fort Washington Road, to park entrance. Parking on-site.

Park grounds open daily 8–sunset. Visitor Center and Historic Fort open early April through late October 9–5; late October through early April 9–4:30. Closed Thanksgiving, December 25 and January 1.

Three-day pass, $5 per vehicle; $3 per individual for walk-ins, bike riders.

Fee waiver for prearranged educational field trips.

Recommended for children age ten and older.

Fishing, hiking.

Fredericksburg and Spotsylvania National Military Park

This national military park represents three years of war during the height of the Confederacy as well as the beginning of the final campaign of the Civil War where commanders Robert E. Lee and Ulysses S. Grant first met on the field of battle. Two visitor centers include museum exhibits, paintings and audio-visual programs. There are four Civil War battlefields to tour, self-guided auto tours with numerous maps, and walking trails.

www.nps.gov/frsp/vc.htm

540-786-2880

120 Chatham Lane, Fredericksburg, VA
Capital Beltway (I-495) to I-95 south to Fredericksburg, (Rt. 3 east exit); proceed two miles to Business Rt. 1 (Lafayette Boulevard). Turn left and drive 0.5 miles to visitor center on the left.

Two visitor centers open daily, 8:30–6:30. Chatham Manor, which served as a Union headquarters and field hospital during the war, is open 9–4:30. The "Stonewall" Jackson Shrine, where Confederate General Thomas Jonathan Jackson died after his mortal wounding at Chancellorsville, is open daily 9–5. The shrine's hours change seasonally; contact the park for information on visiting the site, 540-786-2880.

$4 per person, children under age 17 free. Groups should call in advance. Visitor Center films cost $2, age 10–61; $1, over 61; under age 10 free.

Wheelchair accessibility in the Chancellorsville Visitor Center and Fredericksburg Visitor Center.

VA TimeTravelers site, hiking.

Manassas National Battlefield Park

This park commemorates one of the first battles of the Civil War in 1861. The Visitor Center features a museum with an electronic battle map, Civil War era uniforms and weapons and a park orientation film shown on the hour (additional fee required). The park offers several loop trails, and a junior ranger program for children. Ranger-guided tours are given during the summer, when the stone house is also open.

www.nps.gov/mana

703-361-1339

6511 Sudley Road, Manassas, VA
Capital Beltway (I-495) to I-66 west to Rt. 234 north (Sudley Road). The Visitors Center is on the right, past Northern Virginia Community College.

Park open daily from dawn–dusk. Visitor Center open daily 8:30–5. Closed Thanksgiving and December 25.

Adults, age 17 and older, $3; children, free. Pass is good for three days.

VA TimeTravelers site.

PICK YOUR OWN

Butler's Orchard

Families visiting the 300-acre Butler family farm will get an appealing and instructive view of fruits growing in the orchards and fields, and have an opportunity to pick their own produce. Kids of all ages will enjoy plucking the ripe fruit directly from the vine, tree, or bush. Bring your own baskets, which will be weighed before picking, or purchase them at Butler's for a small fee. Fresh seasonal produce is also for sale at the stand.

www.butlersorchard.com

301-972-3299, reservations 301-428-0444

22200 Davis Mill Road, Germantown, MD
Capital Beltway (I-495) to I-270 north; exit at Father Hurley Boulevard

(exit 16); bear right onto Rt. 27; after 1.3 miles turn right onto Brink Road and look for sign on the left.

Open May–Christmas; call to check exact days and hours. Closed Monday, except during strawberry season, Labor Day, and Columbus Day.

Call to hear a recorded message about the availability of specific crops.

Special activities include a hayride in Bunnyland in the spring, Strawberry Blossom tours in late April and early May, Pumpkin Festivals each weekend in October, Pumpkin Harvest Days from October–November, as well as group hayrides and Choose and Cut Christmas Trees in November and December. Fruit crops include strawberries, blueberries, tart cherries, blackberries, red raspberries, apples and pumpkins.

Cox Farms (Market and Pumpkin Patch)

Cox Farms is set on 116 acres overlooking a lake and the Blue Ridge Mountains. Offering a seasonal farm market and greenhouse items, the farm is a child-friendly place with climbing structures and wagons for children to use. It is open every day in October with extra activities on the weekends. The October theme is to experience harvest time at the farm. All activities center around outdoor physical activity in a rural environment such as pumpkin picking, hayrides, hay tunnels, mountain slide and swings that drop into hay pits. Weekend festivals include food, face painting, and four stages with live entertainment. Cowboy Jack entertains live every day.

www.coxfarms.com

703-830-4121

15621 Braddock Road, Centreville, VA
Capital Beltway (I-495) to Braddock Road; go five miles west on Rt. 28 in Fairfax County. Or Capital Beltway (I-495) to I-66 west; right onto exit 52 (Rt. 29 south); right at third light at Pleasant Valley Road; go four miles to four-way stop sign and turn left at first driveway.

Open April–December (call for hours). In October, open 10–6 daily; extra festival activities on the weekends.

Entrance fees for the Pumpkin Patch include all activities and a pumpkin. Weekends, $9, and weekdays, $7. Children under two are free.

Stroller and wheelchair accessible (although there is some farm terrain).

Special activities include a Spring Farm visit (with baby animals and greenhouse tour), Easter egg hunt, Summer Corn Roast and Watermelon Contest, December Christmas trees with Santa, Pumpkin Patch from the end of September till the first of November, with live entertainment, hay-rides, mountain slides, rope swings, cider, apples, farm animals, tunnels and mazes.

153

Homestead Farms

Homestead Farms opens in late May when the strawberries are ripe and ready to be picked. The summer season brings blackberries, peaches, and a variety of summer vegetables including vine ripened tomatoes and sweet corn picked fresh every day. At the farm market, you will find a large selection of jams and pickles as well as honey collected from beehives located on the farm. In mid-August, the red raspberry season begins, and later in the month, Gala apples are ready to be picked. These are the first of thirteen varieties of apples grown in the orchards. During the autumn harvest, Homestead's farm market is filled with apples, pumpkins, fall squash, Indian corn, gourds and fresh apple cider. Petting barnyard with pigs, chicken, sheep and goats. No pets please.

www.homestead-farm.net

301-977-3761, reservations 301-926-6299

15600 Sugarland Road, Poolesville, MD
Capital Beltway (I-495) to I-270 north; exit at Rt. 28 west through Darnestown to left on Rt. 107 toward Poolesville. Make first left on Sugarland Road; 1 mile on right.

Open mid-May–October 31, and weekends in December.

Hayrides to the pumpkin patch, weekends in October.

Educational tours for school groups are given on weekdays in September and October by reservation only. Call 301-926-6999.

Local personal checks and cash are accepted; no credit cards.

Larriland Farm

This 285-acre, pick-your-own produce farm is set in the rolling foothills of the Appalachian Mountains in Western Howard County. Sample fresh fruits and vegetables right in the field and take a hayride in October. With an eight-acre pond, woods, and a 125-year-old chestnut post and beam barn which houses a farm market, this is sure to be a delightful destination for the entire family. Please call ahead to verify specific hours and for listing of ripe fruits reading for picking. Pick-your-own fruits and vegetables. Containers are furnished. No pets please.

www.pickyourown.com

301-854-6110

2415 Woodbine Road, Woodbine, MD
Three miles south of I-70 (Exit 73) on Rt. 94, Woodbine Road. Capital Beltway (I-495) to Georgia Avenue; follow Georgia Avenue north, past Olney and Laytonsville; turn left on Jennings Chapel Road and right on Florence Road; turn right on Rt. 94; farm is on the right.

Open Tuesday–Sunday. Hours vary by season.

Cash or checks accepted; no credit cards. ATM available.

 ## Phillips Farm

All summer and fall, children will enjoy visiting Phillips Farm to pet and feed baby animals and to climb on haystacks. There is always fresh produce to buy. Each weekend in October, the Harvest Festival offers a corn maze, hayrides to the pumpkin patch and pick your own pumpkins. In the summer, head out to the farm to pick your own flowers. Farm animals to pet; Germantown history exhibits; Pumpkin Patch in October with hay rides (small fee); campfires in the evening, birthday parties, Scout campfires and activities.

www.phillipsfarmproduce.com

301-785-8621

13710 Schaeffer Road, Germantown, MD
Capital Beltway (I-495) to I-270 north to Exit 15 Germantown, Rt. 118 south. Continue on 118 for 1.5 miles to Clopper Road. Turn right on Clopper for 0.2 miles. Turn left onto Schaeffer. Entrance is 0.25 miles on the left.

Open June 28–October 31, 10–7. Closed Tuesdays.

Special activities include the Montgomery County Farm Tour the fourth Saturday and Sunday in July with free hay rides and pony rides.

 ## Potomac Vegetable Farms

This is a working, certified organic vegetable and berry farm with horses and chickens in a natural setting. The farm specializes in lettuce and greens, tomatoes, beans, squash, peppers, flowers and fresh eggs. Potomac Vegetable Farms also grows pumpkins and berries for pick-it-yourselfers. The proprietors encourage informal visits to their fields, animals, and ongoing operations. In addition to tours for young children, they also have tours for groups of older children who are interested in the connection between farming and the environment, health, and ecology issues. Bring your used egg cartons (in good condition) and plastic and paper bags to recycle.

www.potomacvegetablefarms.com

703-759-2119

9627 Leesburg Pike (Rt. 7), Vienna, VA
Capital Beltway (I-495) to Rt. 7 west; continue for four and a half miles to entrance on left.

Open July 1–October 31; call for hours.

$4 per person for guided farm tours.

School buses, vans and carpooling are advised.

Guided tours for groups of ten or more. Call to schedule school or community groups.

Wheelchair access limited, as there are no sidewalks.

GARDENS

 Brookside Gardens

This 50-acre public garden has outdoor plantings landscaped in formal and natural styles. In addition to the well-known azalea, rose, formal and fragrance gardens, there are aquatic and Japanese gardens with a Japanese teahouse. The lake is home to water snakes and fish. Geese and ducks can be found near the aquatic gardens, and butterflies are indeed attracted to the butterfly garden. Inside the two conservatories are colorful annuals and perennials and exotic plants. In the greenhouse, a stream with stepping stones is a delight for little ones. Two annual exhibits are not to be missed: Wings of Fancy live butterfly exhibit runs from May to September and the Garden of Lights runs from mid-November through early January.

The Visitors Center houses a horticultural library including a number of children's books (for use on site only). There are self-guided, recorded and staff-guided interpretations of the garden. A free audio self-tour is available. A class schedule lists all the scheduled lectures, workshops and programs.

www.mc-mncppc.org/parks/brookside

301-962-1400

1800 Glenallan Avenue, Wheaton, MD
Capital Beltway (I-495) to Georgia Avenue north to Randolph Road;
right on Randolph Road for two blocks; right on Glenallan Avenue; go
a half mile to entrance on right.

Gardens open sunrise to sunset.

Conservatory open 10–5. Closed Christmas.

Gift shop, visitors center, horticultural library.

Partial wheelchair access.

*Wedding, private receptions and corporate retreats are welcome, call
301-962-1404 for details.*

*Special activities include Saturday story times for ages 2–6, Groundhog
Day celebration on February 2.*

Green Spring Gardens Park

This park contains demonstration gardens for the home gardener, an
extensively renovated 18th-century house, and the Horticulture Center
with a greenhouse and a library. The grounds include formal rose, herb
and vegetable gardens, a fruit orchard and an iris bed. Smaller children
especially enjoy the woods and two ponds with ducks and geese. Horticulture classes are offered for children of all ages.

www.fairfaxcounty.gov/parks/gsgp

703-642-5173

4603 Green Spring Road, Alexandria, VA
Capital Beltway (I-495) to exit 54B (Braddock Road, East, Rt. 620). Trav-
el approximately 3 miles, crossing Little River Turnpike. Pass Pinecrest
Shopping Center. Stay in right lane and turn right onto Witch Hazel
Road. From I-395, exit 3B (Little River Turnpike, West, Rt. 236). Turn
right onto Braddock Road. Follow directions as shown above once on
Braddock Road.

Grounds open daily, dawn to dusk. Horticulture Center open Monday–Saturday, 9–4:30; Sunday, noon–4:30. Manor House (no strollers) open Wednesday–Sunday, noon–4:30. Park and buildings closed Thanksgiving, Christmas and New Year's Day; on other holidays, open noon–5.

Free admission and parking; progams/tours are fee-based.

Advance reservations for program/tours and for groups of 30 or more.

Kenilworth Park and Aquatic Gardens

Many varieties of flowering water plants thrive in the ponds of the Kenilworth Aquatic Gardens, a National Park Service site. Children love seeing the brightly colored flowers, watching frogs, turtles, birds and fish in the ponds, and exploring the River Trail that borders the Anacostia River. Wildflowers begin blooming in the marsh in early spring, and the water lilies begin blooming in early summer.

www.nps.gov/kepa

202-426-6905

1550 Anacostia Avenue, NE, Washington, DC
From Kenilworth Avenue, exit at Eastern Avenue and get on the southbound service road to Douglas Street; turn right on Anacostia Avenue; located across the Anacostia from the Arboretum. Parking lot on site.

Gardens open daily, 7–4. Visitor Center open 8–4, except Thanksgiving, Christmas and New Year's Day. Mid-morning is usually the best time to see summer flowers, earlier for wildlife.

Metrorail Orange line (Deanwood).

Reservations for ranger-led tour call 202-426-6905.

Special activities include the Waterlily Festival the third or fourth Saturday in July.

McCrillis Gardens and Gallery

Five acres of shaded gardens, a small art gallery, benches and a small pavilion make this a lovely place to visit. The gallery exhibits art in various styles and media by local artists.

www.mc-mncppc.org/parks/brookside/mccrilli.shtm

301-962-1657

6910 Greentree Road, Bethesda, MD
Capital Beltway (I-495) to Old Georgetown Road, heading south. Left onto Greentree Road. No parking on grounds. Limited parking is available on street. After 4:00 pm on weekdays and weekends, parking is available at the Woods Academy across the street.

Daily, 10 a.m.–sunset.

Meadowlark Botanical Gardens

This scenic public garden features 95 acres of natural and landscaped areas, a butterfly garden, herb garden, three wedding gazebos, three lakes and two miles of trails through woods, meadows and gardens. There are also three miles of paved trails, ideal for strollers and wheelchairs.

www.nvrpa.org/meadowlark.html

703-255-3651

9750 Meadowlark Gardens Court, Vienna, VA
Capital Beltway (I-495) to Rt. 7 west for five miles to Beulah Road south; go left on Beulah road for two miles and turn right into park. On-site parking.

Open year-round, except on Thanksgiving, December 24–25, New Year's Day and when snow or ice cover the trails. Hours vary.

Children (7–17 yrs) and senior citizens, $2.50; adults, $5.

Groups may schedule tours for a nominal fee.

About 80% of the garden is wheelchair and stroller accessible.

Hiking.

Special activities include gardening and biodiversity programs, tours of the gardens, plant sales and events throughout the year.

River Farm Garden Park

The elegant Main House at River Farm is set amidst 25 acres of lawns, gardens, meadows, and woods, and commands a sweeping view of the Potomac. Visitors can take self-guided tours of the Main House and the vast gardens; of particular interest are the Children's Gardens with their unique designs: Butterfly, Dinosaur, Bat Cave, Alphabet, Boat, and Zig-Zag.

www.ahs.org/river_farm

703-768-5700, 800-777-7931

The American Horticultural Society, 7931 East Boulevard Drive, Alexandria, VA
Located between Old Town and Mount Vernon. George Washington Parkway south through Old Town; turn left on East Boulevard Drive; follow the signs to River Farm Garden Park. On-site parking.

Grounds are open year-round, Monday–Friday, 9–5; Saturdays, April–September, 9–1. Closed on national holidays.

Limited wheelchair access to grounds and to house with assistance. Stroller accessible.

Special activities include Living Laboratory Tours for groups, by reservation only.

U.S. National Arboretum

Enjoy the varied shrubs and trees, gardens, overlooks, and ponds as you explore this 444-acre museum of living plants by road or footpath. It is most colorful in the spring when thousands of azaleas are in bloom, but is enjoyable year-round, as there is always something blooming and plenty of "stretching space" for children to expend a little excess energy. Favorite sections include the Dwarf Conifer Collection, about 1,500 specimens attractively planted and separated by grassy areas and walks; the Fern Valley Trail, a natural wooded area planted with ferns, wildflowers, and native trees and shrubs; and the Aquatic Garden, featuring tropical and local aquatic plants. The superb Bonsai Collection, a bicentennial gift from Japan, now includes a collection of Chinese and American bonsai. The National Herb Garden, approximately two acres, includes three sub-gardens: a formal "knot" garden with plants arranged in intricate patterns, resembling various kinds of knots; an historic rose garden; and a specialty garden which contains ten different "rooms" or plots, each featuring a different area of herb gardening.

Friendship Gardens feature perennials and ornamental grasses. The Asian Collections include a variety of exotic oriental plants.

Twenty-two of the original 24 National Capitol Columns that once formed the east central portico of the Capitol have been relocated here. The columns were in storage for many years before private funds were raised to finance their removal and reuse. The columns are placed in a nearly-square configuration, with a water stair, fountain and reflecting pool.

There are four beautiful areas that are easily accessible and situated adjacent to each other—the Aquatic Garden and Koi Pond surrounding the Administration Building, the Friendship Garden, the National Herb Garden, and the National Bonsai and Penjing Museum. Serious hikers will also find many intriguing trails throughout the Arboretum. A tram for touring the grounds was introduced in the fall of 1997. By car, bus or bicycle there are nine miles of roadways that wind through and connect the numerous gardens and collections on the 446-acre campus.

www.usna.usda.gov

202-245-2726

3501 New York Avenue, NE, Washington, DC
Capital Beltway (I-495) to Rt. 50 west (becomes New York Avenue); at first intersection, turn left onto Bladensburg Road; go three blocks; turn left on R Street, go 300 yards to the entrance. Plenty of free parking. Large lots are locate near the Grove of State Trees, near the R Street entrance, and near the New York Avenue entrance. Smaller lots are scattered throughout the grounds.

Daily, 8–5; Bonsai collection and Japanese garden open daily, 10–3:30. Closed Christmas.

Metro shuttle from Union Station on the weekends and holidays except December 25.

Gift shop open March 1–mid-December.

REGIONAL PARKS AND PLAYGROUNDS

Algonkian Regional Park

Located on the scenic Potomac shore, this 800-acre park is a day visit or overnight destination for families and groups. Downpour Water Park delivers waterslide fun and thrills throughout the summer months (see p. 265). In addition to a par-72 golf course, an a 18 hole miniature golf course and boating, there is a boat launch ramp that provides public access to the wide Seneca Lake section of the Potomac River. Picnic tables are scattered under trees along the shoreline and covered shelters may be reserved for group picnics. Twelve riverfront cottages with two to five bedrooms are available for rent as well as a meeting center and clubhouse.

www.nvrpa.org/algonkian

703-450-4655

47001 Fairway Drive, Sterling, VA
Capital Beltway (I-495) to Rt. 7 west; continue about 11 miles to Cascades Parkway north; drive three miles to park entrance, at the Loudoun-Fairfax county line.

Daily, dawn–dusk.

Downpour Water Park open daily, Memorial Day weekend–Labor Day.

Miniature golf open April–October. Hours vary.

Meeting center and clubhouse available for rent.

Golf course, athletic fields, fishing, hiking, swimming.

Riverfront vacation cottages available for rent.

Boat and RV storage, boat ramp.

Allen Pond Park

Allen Pond Park offers a wide variety of activities guaranteed to make for a fun-filled day. Take your pick of volleyball, softball, basketball and horseshoes, or play at the fully accessible Opportunity Park, go fishing or for a hike and end the day with a sunset concert in the amphitheater. Allen Park Pond Park is also home to the Bowie Ice Arena.

www.cityofbowie.org/comserv/parkFacilities.asp#allenpond

301-809-3011

3330 Northview Drive, Bowie, MD
Allen Pond is off Rt. 197, south of Rt. 50. Capital Beltway (I-495) to Rt. 50 eastbound to Exit 11 (Rt. 197 south); turn right at light at Northview Drive; go one mile to the park.

Boat rentals, 11–7; weekends, May and September; daily, Memorial Day–Labor Day. Opportunity Park open daily, 8:30–dusk.

Bowie Ice Arena, open for skating July 4–April 30, 301-809-3090.

Opportunity Park, a 100% fully accessible project including a tot lot, playground, fitness cluster, sensory trails, and stocked fishing pond.

Sunset Concerts, Sundays at 7 p.m., Memorial Day weekend–Labor Day weekend.

Biking, fishing, hiking, playgrounds.

Special activities include Bowiefest, first Saturday in June; British Car Day, fourth Sunday in June; a July 4 celebration; Antique Car Show, the third Saturday in August; and an Art Expo the first Saturday in October.

Audrey Moore RECenter/Wakefield Park

The Audrey Moore RECenter with its natatorium, gymnasium and fitness center is part of the 290 acre Wakefield Park. The RECenter has both indoor and outdoor recreational facilities. The outdoor facilities include 11 lighted tennis courts, a lighted practice court, shuffleboard and the newest addition, the Wakefield Skate Park. The indoor facility features a 50-meter pool with 3 and 1 meter diving boards and a super slide, sauna and showers, weight room, gymnasium, dance and exercise rooms, game room and courts for handball, squash and racquetball. The 2,600 square foot mural in the pool area depicts a marvelous underwater world, including submerged towers of Atlantis. Visitors enjoy the arts and crafts rooms as well as pottery and photography labs.

The surrounding Wakefield Park has nature and mountain biking trails. It is also connected by trail to Accotink Park which is located on the southern side of Braddock Road.

Wakefield Chapel, a historic nondenominational chapel built in 1899, is available for rental.

www.fairfaxcounty.gov/parks

703-329-7081

8100 Braddock Road, Annandale, VA
Capital Beltway (I-495) to Braddock Road west; continue to park entrance on right.

Pool is open Monday–Friday, 6:30 a.m.–9:30 p.m.; Saturdays, 7 a.m.–8 p.m.; lap lanes and classes, 9–noon; Sunday, 10–6.

Wakefield Skate Park.

Swimming, tennis, mountain biking,

Wakefield Farmers Market, May–October, Wednesdays, 2–6.

 Bluemont Park

Park facilities include basketball courts, baseball diamonds, athletic fields, lighted tennis courts, volleyball and a soccer and softball area. There are also picnic areas with grills, playground equipment, and bicycle trails. The park connects to Four Mile Run bike trail. Bluemont's two best features are the nine-hole disc golf course and its stream, which is stocked for trout fishing at the end of March.

www.arlingtonva.us

703-228-3323

601 North Manchester Street, Arlington, VA
From Rosslyn, Wilson Boulevard to left on North Manchester Street to park entrance.

Daily, dawn–dusk, sunrise to a half-hour after sunset, except for lighted facilities.

Tennis court reservations, 703-228-1805

Athletic fields, biking, fishing, hiking, playgrounds, tennis, disc golf.

Bull Run Regional Park

This park, deep in Civil War battlefield country, has 1,000 untouched acres of woods, fields and streams. It is a sanctuary for small animals and a wide variety of birds. A half-acre outdoor fantasy pool complex is one of its chief attractions. The park offers a colorful new playground, miniature and disc golf, open play fields, tent and tent-trailer camping sites, picnic areas with grills and some 18 miles of bridle paths. The "Blue Bell Walk" is a treat in spring when many wild flowers are in bloom. A sporting clays course, skeet and trap shooting gallery and indoor archery range help make this a park rich in activities to please virtually all interests.

Take Note

This is an ideal camping location when visiting Udvar-Hazy Center (see p. 110).

www.nvrpa.org

703-631-0550; 703-631-0552, pool

7700 Bull Run Drive, Centreville, VA
Capital Beltway (I-495) to I-66 west; exit on Rt. 29 west (Centreville); continue three miles to park signs.

Main park and sporting clays, skeet and trap shooting gallery, and archery range open daily all year.

Pool and water park open late June–Labor Day. Hours vary.

Access to the 18-mile Bull Run Occoquan Trail.

Park entrance fee for non-member jurisdictions: $7 per vehicle, per day; $14 per week; $11 per vehicle with more than 10 passengers; $4 per day with shelter rental.

Picnic shelter and rustic cabin fees, 703-352-5900.

Athletic fields, camping, disk golf, hiking, miniature golf, playgrounds, snack bar, swimming, wheelchair accessible.

Special activities include musical events, craft fairs, and a drive-through animated holiday lights show in December.

Burke Lake Park

Rent a rowboat, fish or follow the trails around this 888-acre park. The marina rents boats and sells bait for fishing (spring–fall) in the 218-acre lake. This park has a five-mile walking trail, over 150 wooded campsites and a camp store. For younger children, the park offers a miniature train, an old-fashioned carousel, a snack bar, ice cream parlor and playground. Picnic areas are plentiful in wooded spots. There are also 18-hole par-3 golf and 18-hole disc golf courses.

www.fairfaxcounty.gov/parks/burkelake

703-323-6601; 703-323-1641, golf course

7315 Ox Road, Fairfax Station, VA
Capital Beltway (I-495) to Braddock Road west; continue to left on Burke Lake Road (Rt. 645); proceed five miles to left on Ox Road (Rt. 123); park is on left.

Daily, dawn–dusk.

Admission fee per car for non-residents of county, $8 per passenger vehicle; $40 per bus.

Picnic areas with grills, playgrounds and fishing pier accessible to persons with disabilities. Boating, camping, fishing, hiking, playgrounds.

Cabin John Regional Park

Cabin John Park features 525 acres of climbing, sliding and swinging, including Adventure Playland, a large unit designed to encourage creative play on ropes, ladders and tube slides; wooded hiking trails; and a miniature train that offers a, pleasant trip through the woods (open daily in the summer, weekends and holidays in April and September).

Nearby, the park offers many recreational facilities, including indoor and outdoor tennis courts (301-469-7300); ice skating (301-365-2246); handball; volleyball court; Shirley Povich Field, a lighted baseball field; five softball fields (three lighted); a camping area with seven sites (301-299-0034); and picnic areas with tables, grills and shelters (301-495-2525). The park is also home to the Locust Grove Nature Center (see p. 188).

www.mncppc.org

301-299-0024

7400 Tuckerman Lane, Potomac, MD
Capital Beltway (I-495) to Old Georgetown Road; go north to left on
Tuckerman Lane; continue to the park's entrance just past Westlake
Drive on the left.

Daily, dawn–dusk. Closed Thanksgiving, December 25 and January 1.

*Train rides, April, May, September and October, weekends only, 10–4:30;
June–August,10:00–4:30, daily. $1.50 per person.*

Athletic fields, camping, hiking, playgrounds, skating, tennis.

Special activities include Summer Twilight Concerts,

*June–August; "Eye Spy" Halloween train ride for ages 8 and under, Thurs-
day–Saturday, evenings, late October.*

Cameron Run Regional Park and Great Waves Water Park

This water-oriented park is tremendous fun for both children and
adults. Cameron Run features a wave pool and a 3-flume, 40-foot high
water slide. The wave pool is most appropriate for strong swimmers.
Children under 13 must be accompanied by a person age 16 or older.
Younger children will enjoy the creative play pool featuring giant water creatures, rain jets and a shallow body flume. There is also a very
shallow wading pool for the youngest children. Cameron Run has a
sand volleyball court, batting cage, miniature golf course, pavilion for
rent (703-352-5900) and a fishing pond.

www.nvrpa.org

703-960-0767

4001 Eisenhower Avenue, Alexandria, VA
Capital Beltway (I-495 south) to the Eisenhower Connector (exit 174),
toward Alexandria; turn right at traffic light onto Eisenhower Avenue
and drive one-half mile to the park on the left.

The pool is open from Memorial Day–Labor Day; hours vary.

*Miniature golf and batting cages open end of March–November, weath-
er permitting. Call for hours.*

*Daily fees for the wave pool range from $10.25–$13.50 per person;
seniors, 55 and over, $6; under 2, free. Weekdays after 4, $6.25. Season
passes available.*

All facility passes for unlimited pool, miniature golf and one round batting cage, ranges $13–$15.

Pavilion rental mid-April–late October, 703-960-0767.

 ## Candy Cane City/Meadowbrook Community Park

With a variety of new equipment to crawl through, slide down, climb on and swing from, the Candy Cane City playground at Meadowbrook Park is a crowd pleaser for the very young. The name refers to the long ago time when the playground equipment was painted with red and white stripes. The elasticrete underneath helps cushion the feet and protect against injury. The adjacent recreation center, like other Montgomery County park centers, has ball fields, tennis courts, a well-equipped building, covered picnic area and a year-round activity program. Shaded play areas and water fountain.

7901 Meadowbrook Lane, Chevy Chase, MD
Capital Beltway (I-495) to Connecticut Avenue south; to East-West Highway; go left on East-West Highway to Beach Drive; right on Meadowbrook Lane, past stables to park entrance.

Daily, dawn–dusk.

Parking is available in a small lot on Beach Drive, off East-West Highway at Leland Street. Access to park is across a footbridge over Rock Creek.

Athletic fields, playgrounds, tennis.

 ## Chinquapin Center and Park

Chinquapin Park is a 44-acre park in the heart of Alexandria. It has a nature area and fitness trail, picnic tables, basketball and volleyball courts, lighted tennis courts, wheelchair accessible play module and large open fields.

The center is home to the Rixse Pool, a 25-meter indoor swimming pool with separate diving well, 3 racquetball courts, a fitness room, saunas, a snack bar and activity rooms.

www.alexandriava.gov/recreation

703-931-1127

3210 King Street, Alexandria, VA
Capital Beltway (I-495) I-395 to King Street (Rt. 7) east exit; turn right
onto Chinquapin Park Drive; entrance on left.

Center and Rixse Pool: Open weekdays, 6 a.m.–10 p.m.; weekends, 8–8.
Call for holiday hours.

Center and Rixse Pool: General admission fee covers use of pool, sauna,
and fitness rooms. Non-residents, $8; chaperones, $2; city residents,
adults age 16–59, $6, children 5–16 and seniors (60 plus), $6; chaper-
ones, $1. Discount passes and group rates available.

Tennis reservations can be made on-site, one hour prior to playing time,
Monday–Friday, 6 a.m.–10 p.m.; weekends and holidays 8–8.

Volleyball information: 703-931-6333.

Hiking, swimming, tennis,

Special activities include racquetball, fitness room, saunas for women
and men, nature trail and park, garden plots.

Clemyjontri Park

Clemyjontri Park is a two-acre playground with carousel
designed with the goal of creating accessible side by
side play for all children of all abilities. The design incorporates four outdoor "rooms" surrounding a centerpiece
carousel. The Rainbow Room archways and swings, the Schoolhouse
and Maze, the Movin' and Groovin' Transportation area and the Fitness
and Fun rooms are designed to include apparatus such as swings with
high backs, some easy access, lower monkey bars, ramps that make all
play areas wheelchair accessible, wide pathways between equipment
and non-slip, porous surfaces to ensure greater access for all children.
The carousel has chariots, a spinning teacup, prancing horses and is
recessed to ground level for wheelchair access.

www.fairfaxcounty.gov/parks/clemyjontri

703-388-2807

6317 Georgetown Pike (Rt. 193), McLean, VA
Capital Beltway (I-495) to Exit 44, Georgetown Pike (Rt. 193) toward
Langley. Travel approximately 2.2 miles. Park entrance on right.

Park open daily, 7 a.m.–dusk. Least crowded before 10 or after 3.

Carousel open seasonally, weather permitting. Check park website for current schedule. $1.50 per ride.

Limited parking includes a drop-off zone for passengers who need close access.

Overflow parking available at Langley Fork Park, 6250 Georgetown Pike (1/4 mile). For safety do not park on Georgetown Pike.

Picnic pavilion available for rent. Reservations requested for groups of 10 or more. Can submit form from park web site, via fax to 703-388-2821 with minimum of two weekss notice, or call 703-324-8732 for centralized park reservation system.

When not reserved the picnic pavilion is available first-come, first-served. The shelter includes six accessible tables and seats that will seat up to 48, including 16 wheelchairs. More picnic tables are available in the park.

Restrooms and water fountains.

No pets of any kind are permitted on the playground.

 ## East Potomac Park

East Potomac Park is run by the National Park Service and is a one and a half mile long finger of land between the Washington channel and the Potomac River. The path along the sea wall is fine for strolling, biking and fishing. A playground is nearby. Attractions include an outdoor pool, tennis, miniature golf, a driving range and two 18-hole golf courses. Hains Point, at the southern edge of the park, is a pleasant place to stay cool on a hot summer day. No matter how steamy the rest of the city is, there is always a breeze at Hains Point.

202-619-7222

1100 Ohio Drive, SW, Washington, DC
Turn off Maine Avenue, SW, near the 14th Street Bridge and follow signs; or follow Ohio Drive from the Lincoln Memorial.

Daily, dawn–dusk

Outdoor tennis courts, 202-554-5962.

Outdoor swimming pool, 202-863-1309.

Golf and miniature golf, 202-863-9007.

Biking, miniature golf, playgrounds, swimming, tennis.

Fairland Recreational Park/Fairland Regional Park

This bi-county park offers more than 150 acres of parkland in Prince George's County and 322 in Montgomery County. Trails for walking and biking run through wooded hills and streams throughout the park.

The Prince George's section of the park is home to the Sports and Aquatics Complex, including a heated 50-meter indoor pool with a moveable floor, a heated indoor 25-yard leisure pool with a fountain, a heated whirlpool with waterfall, a family changing room, locker rooms with coin-operated lockers and an outdoor deck area. The complex also includes a gymnastics center, racquetball courts, a weight-training center, indoor and outdoor tennis courts and sand volleyball courts. The Gardens Ice House year-round ice-skating rink is located on-site (see p. 255), as are the Fairland Batting Cages.

The Montgomery side of the park offers tennis courts, athletic fields, playgrounds, four picnic shelters available by permit and both hard and natural surface nature trails.

Take Note

There are separate entries from Prince George's and Montgomery Counties. See the item description for the activities in which you and your kids are most interested.

www.mc-mncppc.org/parks

301-495-2595

3928 Greencastle Road, Fairland, MD
Capital Beltway (I-495) to Rt. 29 North, right on Briggs Chaney Road, left on Robey Road. The park is at the end of the road. There are multiple entrances located behind the fields.

www.pgparks.com

301-699-2255

13950 Old Gunpowder Road, Laurel, MD
I-95 to exit 29 toward Beltsville. At first light, make a left onto Old Gunpowder Road. Follow Old Gunpowder Road for approximately 1.25 miles. Fairland Regional Park is on the left.

Aquatic Center and Athletic Complex: 301-362-6060; TTY, 301-362-6090.

Tennis Bubble: 301-953-0030

Gardens Ice House: 301-953-0100; 410-792-4947; 301-699-2544 (TTY).

Fairland offers nine state-of-the-art lighted batting cages for softball and baseball, April–October.

Hadley's Park

Hadley's Park is a one-acre, fully-accessible playground for children with disabilities. It was the model on which other Hadley's parks were designed. The one-acre park is designed so children of all abilities can have fun and challenge themselves on its creative play course, featuring a soft-play surface ideal for roller-skates, bikes and wheelchairs. The park is appropriate for preschool-age children.

www.hadleyspark.org

Falls Road Park on Falls Road at the intersection of Falls Chapel Way, Potomac, MD
Capital Beltway (I-495) to I-270 north; exit at Falls Road (Potomac); park is on the right after the second traffic light

Hadley's parks are located in Rockville, Damascus and Germantown, Maryland and Dulles Town Center, in Sterling Virginia.

Hemlock Overlook Center for Experiential Education

Hemlock Overlook is an outdoor center offering a variety of outdoor and team development programs for students, teachers, businesses, teams and churches. Activities are open to the public and special groups by reservation. Trails may be used without reservations.

www.nvrpa.org

703-993-2059

13220 Yates Ford Road, Clifton, VA
Capital Beltway (I-495) to I-66 west to Rt. 123 south. Turn right on Clifton Road; go 3.7 miles and left on Yates Ford Road.

Open year-round.

Camping, rope courses.

Special activities includes rope courses, outdoor challenge course with a zip wire. Access to the 17-mile Bull Run-Occoquan Trail (no bikes).

Jefferson District Park and Golf Course

This 60-acre park features a 9-hole executive golf course (par 35) and an 18-hole miniature golf course.

---

www.fairfaxcounty.gov/parks

703-573-0444

7900 Lee Highway, Falls Church, VA
Capital Beltway (I-495) to Rt. 50 west; right on Gallows Road; right on Lee Highway (Rt. 29/237) to park entrance on left at Hyson Lane.

Daily, dawn–dusk.

Lighted outdoor tennis courts, April–October. Courts can be reserved for a fee.

Miniature golf, tennis and basketball facilities are lighted until 11 p.m., April 1–October 31.

Special activities include a hayride in October and a junior golf tournament for 8–16 year olds in June.

Lake Accotink Park

Lake Accotink Park, in nearby Springfield, encompasses 493 acres offering year round enticement and unique views of waterfowl and marsh life with its 55 acre lake, wetlands and streams. Activities vary with the season. Waterfront possibilities include canoe, rowboat and pedal boat rentals, fishing, tour-boat rides, boat launch and bait and tackle sales. Small sailboats (under 15 feet) and kayaks are permitted, while windsurfing and gas powered motor boats are prohibited. Those who want to fish must have a Virginia State Fishing License. For those who want to focus on the natural habitat, there is a 3.75-mile hiking/biking trail.

---

www.fairfaxcounty.gov/parks

703-569-0285

7500 Accotink Park Road Springfield, VA
I-95 South to Old Keene Mill Road west; proceed on Old Keene Mill Road;. turn right on Hanover Ave; left on Highland Avenue; right on Accotink Park Road. Park Entrance will be on the left.

Daily, 7 a.m.–dusk. Includes playground, pavilions, trails and open play fields.

Boat rentals, tour boat, carousel, miniature golf.

May and June, weekends only, 11–8; end June–Labor Day, weekends, 11–8; weekdays noon–6; September–early October, weekends and Columbus Day only, 12–7. Call for off-season hours.

Boat Rentals, pedal boats, $6 per half hour, $10 per hour; row boats, $6 per half hour, $15 full day rental; canoes, $5 per hour; $2 launch fee for personal boats.

Antique carousel, $1.50 per person.

Lucky Duck miniature Ggolf, $4 for adults; $3 for juniors/seniors; $2 for second 9 holes. 2-for-1 coupons available for Mondays–Thursdays.

Special activities: boat rentals, cardboard boat regatta, children's fair, carousel, miniature golf, monthly events (listed on website).

 ## Lake Fairfax Park

This 476-acre park offers a 15-acre lake for boating (boat rentals and excursion pontoon boat rides available) and fishing, as well as a water park, the Water Mine Swimmin' Hole (see p. 271). Plan to spend an entire day at Lake Fairfax Park, starting with a few hours at the innovative pool with its numerous water slides and rambling river, followed by a ride on the miniature train and carousel. Rent a pedal boat and enjoy some quiet time on the lake, go for a hike on a nature trail, and enjoy a family picnic near the playgrounds.

www.fairfaxcounty.gov/parks

703-471-5415

1400 Lake Fairfax Drive, Reston, VA
Capital Beltway (I-495) to Rt. 7 west; continue about six miles and turn left on Rt. 606; turn left on Lake Fairfax Drive and follow it to park entrance.

Daily, 7–dusk, closed December 25.

Marina complex with redesigned boat dock and canoe launch.

Marina hours, 11–7, end May–Labor Day.

Bike, equestrian and hiking trails.

Amphitheater for rent.

Water Mine Swimmin' Hole (admission includes carousel and tour boat).

Family camping, March–November, reservations accepted.

Athletic fields, boating, camping, fishing, hiking, playgrounds, swimming.

🛉 Lee District Park and Robert E. Lee Recreation Center

The recreation center boasts a natatorium with a 50-meter indoor swimming pool and water slide, a fully equipped fitness center and a gymnasium with basketball and volleyball. In addition, there are racquetball, handball and wallyball courts. Saunas, exercise and meeting rooms are also avaialble. In addition to the train and carousel, the park features playing fields, tennis courts, a tot lot, softplay indoor playground, a sand volleyball court, an amphitheater, hiking trails and picnic areas.

www.fairfaxcounty.gov/parks

703-922-9841

6601 Telegraph Road, Alexandria, VA
Capital Beltway (I-495) to Telegraph Road south; go three miles to park entrance on left.

193-acre park open daily, dawn–dusk.

Amphitheater programs, June–August, Wednesdays, 7:30 p.m.

RECenter fees 19 and up, $8.70 (residents, $6.50); 5–18, $8.70 (residents, $5.25); under 4, free; chaperones, $1.50; Families (up to 4 in total), $25 (residents, $14).

Athletic fields, hiking, playgrounds, swimming, tennis.

Special activities include fireworks on July 4 and a Halloween train ride in October.

Montrose Park

Open space provides room for games at this popular Rock Creek Park location, featuring outdoor tennis courts (no reservations needed), a boxwood maze, a playground, and picnic tables. This is a nice place to visit after a trip to Dumbarton Oaks (see p. 43).

3001 R Street, NW at Avon Place, NW, in Georgetown, Washington, DC
Wisconsin Avenue north from Georgetown, turn right on R Street.
Park is on the left.

Daily, dawn–dusk.

Playgrounds, tennis.

 Norwood Local Park

This local park has been renovated to be a fully accessible playground for kids of all abilities. Among the recreation features of this park are a playground, softball field, lighted baseball field and five tennis courts. The park also has a picnic area and is home to the Norwood Recreation Building, which is available for rent.

www.mc-mncppc.org/parks

301-299-0024

4700 Norwood Park Bethesda, MD
Capital Beltway (I-495) to Wisconsin Avenue/Rt. 355 south through Bethesda past Bradley Blvd; turn right onto Norwood Drive.

Playground.

Recreation building available for rent.

Softball field, lighted baseball field,tennis courts.

  Occoquan Regional Park

This scenic park is located on the Occoquan River. The park offers 400 acres of recreational space, a touch of the past with its historic brick kilns and reminders of the women suffragists imprisoned here in the early 1900's. Features include batting cage, picnic tables, walking trails and water activities.

www.nvrpa.org

703-690-2121

9751 Ox Road, Lorton, VA
Across the water from the Town of Occoquan, VA, on the Fairfax County shore. Capital Beltway (I-495) to I-95 south to Rt. 123 north; follow for one and a half miles to the park's entrance on the right.

Open mid-March–November, 7 a.m.–dark; December, 7 a.m.–dusk; January–February, 8 a.m.–dusk. Gates closed December 24–25, January 1.

Fee for batting cage and boat launching ramps.

Picnic shelter and gazebo rentals: 703-352-5900.

Soccer, softball, and baseball fields.

Paved trails are stroller- and wheelchair-accessible.

Athletic fields, batting cages, biking, boating, fishing, hiking, snack bar.

 Pohick Bay Regional Park and Golf Course

"Pohick," the Algonquin word for "the water place," is an apt description of this 1000-acre waterside park. Visitors can swim, boat, canoe, kayak and fish. Other activities include family camping (hot showers available), flying kites, miniature and disc golf and picnicking. Golfers should find the 18-hole, par-72 course a challenge. The park also features a four-mile bridle path, hiking trails and an observation deck that overlooks the Potomac River. Most of the area around the park is maintained as a wildlife refuge and the recreation areas are planned to minimize the disturbance to the animals, especially the nesting area of the bald eagle.

www.nvrpa.org

703-339-6104

6501 Pohick Bay Drive, Lorton, VA
Capital Beltway (I-495) to I-95 south to Lorton exit; turn left on Lorton Road; right on Armistead; right on Rt. 1; left on Gunston Road. Continue 1 mile to golf course on left; Go three miles to main park entrance on the left.

Daily, dawn–dusk. Outdoor pool open Memorial Day weekend to Labor Day. Mini and disc golf are open late March–October. Hours vary.

$7 per vehicle per day; $14 per vehicle per week; $11 per vehicle with ten or more; annual pass, $25 for residents of member jurisdictions.

18-hole, par-72 golf course, 703-339-8585. Driving range, pro shop, lessons and tournament packages.

"Canoe the Marsh" day and evening trips available.

Boat launching, sailboat and pedal boat rentals.

Family campground reservations available April–October, 703-339-6104. Group campground reservations, 703-352-5900.

Nature trails and bridle paths.

Pool is wheelchair accessible, trails are not.

Special activities Easter Egg Carnival.

South Germantown Recreational Park

South Germantown Recreational Park's Central Park features two championship miniature golf courses and a splash playground with a tumbling buckets waterfall, rain tree, water tunnel and 36-foot water maze. The two unique 18-hole putting courses provide real challenges with water features, sand traps, rough turf and natural obstacles. (The miniature golf season may extend beyond October, weather permitting.) National Youth Soccer League championships games and some professional games are held here at the outdoor Maryland Soccer Plex. The park is home to the Germantown Golf Park Driving Range.

www.mc-mncppc.org/parks/facilities/south_germantown

301-601-4400

18401 Central Park Circle, Boyds, MD
I-270 north to exit 15B toward Germantown. Stay on MD Rt. 118 for 3 miles, passing Clopper Road (Rt. 117). Turn left at Germantown Park Drive; at traffic circle, second exit onto Central Park Circle.

Open late May–early September; hours vary by season.

Splash playground, $4; miniature golf, 18 holes, $4. Combination of one round of golf and splash playground, $6. Group rates available.

Lockers and cubbies, showers, dressing room, restrooms, vending area.

Huge wooden structure playground.

Swimming, soccer, ball fields.

Tuckahoe Park and Playfield

A unique playground features towers, tall slides and a maze that all appeal to 7–12 year olds. This wooded, well-loved park also has softball fields, a soccer area, lighted outdoor tennis courts, and picnic tables.

www.arlingtonva.us

2400 Sycamore Street, Arlington, VA
I-66 to Exit 69, Sycamore Street/Falls Church; make a left onto Sycamore Street; follow Sycamore Street north past Lee Highway; park is on the left.

Daily, dawn–dusk.

Metrorail Orange line (Falls Church).

Athletic fields, tennis.

Turtle Park (aka Friendship Park)

A visit to this shady neighborhood playground oasis, recreation center, tennis courts and ball field is always a treat. The park includes swings, slides, tunnels and climbing structures in addition to the large, turtle-shaped sandbox for which the park is named. This fenced-in retreat, with one of the few remaining public sand boxes in the DC area, is a welcome carefree escape for parents and children alike.

www.turtlepark.org

202-282-2198

45th and Van Ness Streets, NW, Washington, DC

Shady fenced playground with large sandbox is fenced.

Turtle Time and Story Time, winter activities for young children.

Restrooms available in the recreation center.

Friendship Recreation Center with two multi-purpose rooms can be reserved for private use.

Baseball fields, basketball courts, softball field, tennis courts.

Special activities: May fair, ice cream social, fall clean-up day, Halloween festival. Local baseball, Little League and soccer programs. Recreation Center hosts cooperative preschool and summer camp.

Upton Hill Regional Park

This park offers visitors a woodland oasis in the heart of the most populated area of Northern Virginia. Upton Hill has a large swimming pool complex with water park features and woodland nature trails. The popular miniature golf course in a garden setting features one of the longest miniature golf holes in the world. Other attractions feature a gazebo, picnic areas, batting cage, Bocce ball court, horseshoe pit and a playground.

www.nvrpa.org

703-534-3437

6060 Wilson Boulevard, Arlington, VA
Capital Beltway (I-495) to Rt. 50 east; at Seven Corners turn east on Wilson Boulevard to the park entrance at Patrick Henry Drive

Open daily, dawn–dusk; pool open daily, Memorial Day weekend–Labor Day. Call for schedule and fees.

Tennis, 703-228-1805.

Metrorail Orange line (East Falls Church), one mile.

Batting cages, hiking, miniature golf, swimming.

Watkins Regional Park

This 437-acre park offers a wide variety of activities from hiking and biking trails to a carousel and miniature golf to camping and athletic facilities—something to please every family member. The extensive playground has brightly colored equipment gentle enough for toddlers and challenging enough for 5–7 year olds. Additionally, Watkins Regional Park is home to Watkins Nature Center (see p. 194) and Old Maryland Farm.

Just behind the train station is Old Maryland Farm (301-218-6700), a great place for the whole family. The farm features animals (from hogs to hens), herb and vegetable gardens, antique farm equipment, educational exhibits and year-round volunteer opportunities.

www.pgparks.com/places/parks/watkins.html

301-218-6870

301 Watkins Park Drive, Upper Marlboro, MD
Capital Beltway (I-495) to exit 15A,Central Avenue east (Rt. 214); follow Rt. 214 through Largo; turn right on Watkins Park Drive (Rt. 193). Park is on the right.

Daily, 7:30 a.m.–dusk.

Indoor and outdoor tennis courts and hitting wall.

Free lighting for evening outdoor play. For fees and reservations, call 301-249-9325.

Grills, group areas and athletic fields.

Camping area with 34 campsites, and showers.

Miniature train ride, carousel and miniature golf open late May–Labor Day, Tuesday–Sunday, 10–7; September, weekends only.

Outdoor summer concerts, Thursdays, 7–8:30 p.m.

Athletic fields, biking, hiking, playgrounds.

Special activities include the Winter Festival of Lights from late November to January, dusk to 9:30 p.m.

Wheaton Regional Park

This 536-acre park abounds with child-pleasing features, including a two-mile miniature train ride, a carousel, a four-mile paved bicycle trail (also excellent for strollers, wheelchairs and skaters), two-mile hiking trails, fishing, ice skating, ball fields, horseback riding stables and picnic areas.

The Shorefield Area includes Pine Lake, a stocked five-acre lake with fishing and picnicking, the miniature train that will take you on a ten-minute tour of the park and the restored 1915 Hershel Spillman carousel.

Glenallan Area Among the attractions are the Brookside Nature Center (see p. 184) and Brookside Gardens (see p. 156), a 50-acre public display garden and riding stables where you can find riding lessons for novice through advanced levels at the indoor riding arena or the outdoor facilities.

The **F. Frank Rubin Athletic Complex** has four softball fields and two baseball fields for day and evening use. Permits must be obtained from the Park Permit Office to use softball and baseball fields. One outdoor basketball court and four handball courts are available on a first-come, first-served basis. For information, call 301-495-2525. Six outdoor tennis courts are lighted for day and evening use. There is also an indoor tennis facility with an additional six courts for year-round play. Indoor courts must be reserved. For information, call 301-649-4049.

The athletic complex also features the year-round **Wheaton Indoor Ice Arena,** which offers lessons, skating time and skate rentals. Sessions are available for youth and adults-only. Call 301-649-3640 for more information on fees and information about inline skating.

www.mc-mncppc.org/parks

301-680-3803

2000 Shorefield Road, Wheaton, MD
Capital Beltway (I-495) to Georgia Avenue north; right on Shorefield Road to park entrance.

Daily, sunrise–sunset.

The carousel and train ride operate weekends and school holidays only in April and September, daily May–August. Call 301-946-6396 (April–September, 301-942-6703) for schedules and fees.

Many of the facilities accommodate people with disabilities. The miniature train and Adventure Playground are designed with unique equipment to assist those with mobility challenges. Brookside Nature Center, Brookside Gardens, picnic areas, and restrooms are accessible.

Athletic fields, biking, fishing, hiking, playgrounds.

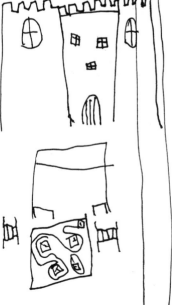

UNDERSTANDING THE NATURAL WORLD

 ## Agricultural Research Service National Visitors Center

This center is one of the largest and most diversified research farms in the world. Livestock experiments since 1910 here have led to the development of America's meaty Thanksgiving turkey and to the production of leaner pork. Visitors see first-hand the impact of agricultural science on daily life. After a brief orientation at the Visitors Center, visitors tour the facility by bus.

www.ars.usda.gov/is/nvc/welcome.htm

301-504-9403

Capital Beltway (I-495) to Exit 25A, Rt. 1, north to Beltsville. Drive about 2 miles and turn right on Rt. 212 (Power Mill Road). Go over bridge, cross thru light at Edmonston Road Into the Beltsville Agricultural Research Center (BARC)-East. The ARS National Visitor Center (Log Lodge, Building 302) is approximately 1.5 miles on right.

Weekdays, 8–4:30. Closed federal holidays.

Tours are given mostly to school and camp groups. Call ahead to make arrangements.

Wheelchair access at Visitors Center. Strollers allowed to point of bus departure.

Arlington Planetarium

Used primarily for school programs during the day, the planetarium also offers a variety of public programs on weekends throughout the year.

www.arlington.k12.va.us/instruct/science/planetarium

703-228-6070

1426 North Quincy Street, Arlington, VA
Capital Beltway (I-495) to I-66 east to the Glebe Road exit south. Planetarium is located on the right side before 14th street.

Open 7:30 p.m., Fridays–Saturdays, 1:30 and 3 p.m. Sundays; monthly sky lecture "Stars Tonight," 7:30 p.m. first Mondays (except holidays, when the planetarium is open the second Monday instead). Closed during the summer.

Admission: $3; Seniors or 12 and younger, $2.

Metrorail Orange line (Ballston).

Brookside Nature Center

The nature center is a focus for local natural history with live and mounted specimens from the Washington region, hands-on nature discovery areas, an observation beehive, habitat demonstration garden, self-guided nature trail, and wildlife viewing areas. Call for information about Brookside's nature programs for children and an Educator's Guide to Programs.

www.mc-mncppc.org/parks/nature_centers/ brookside/index.shtm

301-946-9071

Wheaton Regional Park, 1400 Glenallan Avenue, Wheaton, MD Capital Beltway (I-495) to Georgia Avenue north 3 miles toward Wheaton. Turn right on Randolph Road. At the second traffic light turn right onto Glenallan Avenue. Continue on Glenallan Avenue to a 4-way stop sign. Right into the second entrance on the right.

Tuesday–Saturday, 9–5; Sunday, 1–5. Closed Monday and federal holidays.

Clearwater Nature Center

Located in the Cosca Regional Park, this Nature Center features the "Natural Treasures of Prince George's County," exhibit which shows a view of life underground. Other highlights include a variety of live reptiles, birds of prey, a fish and indoor turtle pond, and other surprises. Herb and butterfly gardens allow you to explore the fully equipped lapidary laboratory. Five miles of hiking trails criss-cross the park where you can observe local wildlife at the lake and streams.

301-297-4575

Cosca Regional Park, 11000 Thrift Road, Clinton, MD
Capital Beltway (I-495) to Rt. 5 south; turn right onto Surrats Road;
turn left on Brandywine Road (Rt. 381); right onto Thrift Road to the
entrance.

Monday–Saturday, 8:30–5 and Sundays 11–4. Closed some holidays.

Hiking.

*Special activities include Birds of Prey Day, Prehistoric Party, theme hikes,
scout badge programs.*

Croydon Creek Nature Center

Take a walk and explore the field, forest and stream surrounding this
nature center. An Exhibit Room and Discovery Room provide interactive fun and educational environmental exhibits for all ages.

The Discovery Room is geared for children in preschool through elementary school. Children learn about animals that live in and around
Rockville, conduct research experiments, and make a picture from
granite rubbing tiles. Puzzles abound.

The Exhibit Room has more for the middle school and older set. Here
visitors can bird-watch through the binoculars, relax on the oak and
hickory bent-wood benches, discover how to live with urban wildlife,
learn about national, state and city symbols, and use a computer to
learn more about bird songs and birds of prey.

ww.ci.rockville.md.us

301-294-2752

Rockville Civic Center Park, 852 Avery Road, Rockville, MD
Capital Beltway (I-495) to I-270 north to Rt. 28 east (Montgomery
Avenue). Montgomery Avenue turns into Viers Mill Road after you
cross Rt. 355 (Rockville Pike) for about 1 block. Follow Rt. 28 (left turn
from Viers Mill Road). Right onto Baltimore Road. Go past the main
entrance to Glenview Mansion and F. Scott Fitzgerald Theatre Civic
Center. Turn left on Avery Road. Follow Avery Road to the nature
center.

*Monday–Saturday, 9–5:30; Sundays, 1–5:30. Closed New Year's Day,
Memorial Day, July 4, Labor Day, Thanksgiving, and Christmas.*

Hiking.

Gulf Branch Nature Center

Located in a 38-acre wooded stream valley, this nature center features interpretive displays on Arlington and Virginia plants, animals, and natural history. Attractions include a Native-American display with a dugout canoe, a moderately strenuous 0.75-mile trail to the Potomac River, and an observation beehive. Educational programs are offered year round to organized groups and the general public. Points of interest include a stream, pond, and access to the Potomac River.

703-228-3403

3608 North Military Road, Arlington, VA
Capital Beltway (I-495) exit north to the George Washington Memorial Parkway. Exit onto Spout Run, turn right onto Lorcom Lane, right onto Nelly Custis and then merge with Military Road. Parking available on-site.

Tuesday–Saturday, 10–5; Sunday, 1–5. Closed Mondays and federal holidays.

Not stroller or wheelchair accessible.

VA TimeTravelers site, hiking.

Hidden Oaks Nature Center

The Nature Center focuses on the discovery of evidence of landscape changes caused by the forces of nature and man. There are seasonal displays and small live animals such as turtles and snakes. Many of the exhibits provide hands-on options. The surroundings, including an oak forest, woodland stream, and traces of a Civil War railroad, as well as timbering and farming lands, make for an interesting visit.

www.fairfaxcounty.gov/parks/nature

703-941-1065

Annandale Community Park, 7701 Royce Street, Annandale, VA
Capital Beltway (I-495) to Little River Turnpike east (Rt. 236); turn left at first traffic light onto Hummer Road; proceed one half mile; turn left into Annandale Community Park; follow signs to Nature Center.

Weekdays except Tuesday, 9–5; Saturday–Sunday, noon–5. January–February, open daily, 12–5. Closed Thanksgiving, December 25, and January 1.

Reservations required for discovery programs and special events.

Group tours for schools or other youth organizations.

Special activities include "Forest Fledgling," a program for children ages 3–5 years and their parents offering stories, crafts, nature activities, and outdoor exploration.

Hidden Pond Nature Center

Acres of undisturbed woodland, quiet trails, splashing streams and a tranquil pond are just a few reasons to visit Hidden Pond Park and Nature Center. Situated along the Pohick Stream Valley, the park offers solitude and opportunities for exploration and discovery.

The Nature Center prepares the visitor for investigating and experiencing the ecology of ponds, streams and wetlands. Exhibits include a live display of many of the inhabitants of the pond, a touch-table, a parent and child corner and displays of "feature creatures" and current events in the natural world. The building also offers a lab/all-purpose meeting room for visiting school groups or special programs, and a small retail sales area with items for the nature lover.

Outside, there are self-guided trails which lead to the stream valley and surrounding woodlands. If treasure hunting is more your thing, the naturalists will gladly loan you nets, so you can go on your own to search in and around Hidden Pond. (Treasures must be returned to the pond before leaving.)

www.co.fairfax.va.us/parks/hiddenpond

703-451-9588

Hidden Pond Park, 8511 Greeley Boulevard, Springfield, VA Capital Beltway (I-495) to I-95 south to Old Keen Mill Road (Rt. 644) west for 3.3 miles. Left onto Greeley Boulevard (second left after Rolling Road) to park entrance at the end of the street. From Fairfax County Parkway, Old Keene Mill Road east 2.9 miles to a right onto Greeley Boulevard

Weekdays, 9–5; Saturday and Sunday, noon–5; closed Tuesdays. January and February, open daily, noon–5, closed on Tuesdays.

Wide variety of programs for all ages. Group tours by reservation.

Hiking, playgrounds, tennis.

Howard B. Owens Science Center and Planetarium

This modern science center emphasizes participatory exhibits and interactive programs. The Summer Science Enrichment Program is open to preschool through high school students on a first-come, first-served basis. The center primarily serves students of the Prince George's County Public Schools.

Public Planetarium programs are held on the 2nd Friday of each month at 7:30 p.m. Other showings on request for scout groups, civic or fraternal organizations and non-public school groups.

www.pgcps.org/~hbowens

301-918-8750

9601 Greenbelt Road, Lanham-Seabrook, MD
Capital Beltway (I-495) to Greenbelt Road; continue for three miles to entrance on right.

Adults, $4; senior citizens and students, kindergarten through college, $2.

Open house in November.

 Locust Grove Nature Center, Cabin John Regional Park

This Nature Center has a small collection of nature books, games, puzzles, a tree exhibit and some native snakes and frogs on display. There are several wooded trails for moderate hikes. A one-quarter-mile trail leads to a naturalist garden and wildlife meadow. Another one-quarter-mile trail leaves the nature center and follows numerous steps downhill to a meadow that borders the Cabin John Creek.

www.mc-mncppc.org

301-299-1990

7777 Democracy Boulevard, Bethesda, MD
Capital Beltway (I-495) to Old Georgetown Road/Rt. 187 exit north; turn left on Democracy Boulevard; the Center is beyond Westlake Drive, next to the tennis courts.

Tuesday–Saturday, 9–5. Closed Sunday, Monday, and holidays. Trails open sunrise to sunset.

Specially designed group programs for schools, camps and families by reservation.

Special activities include full moon hikes, campfires, story times, toddler programs and bird walks. The Nutshell News lists schedule.

Long Branch Nature Center

This Nature Center is in a hardwood forest with hiking and biking trails, swamp, meadow and streams. The Washington and Old Dominion Bike Path (see p. 146) passes through the area. The Nature Center offers many things for children and adults to explore, including displays of live reptiles and amphibians, an indoor turtle/fish pond, seasonal displays and a discovery corner for young naturalists. Although most programs are free, reservations are required and can be made by calling the Nature Center.

www.arlington.va.us

703-228-6535

625 South Carlin Springs Road, Arlington, VA
Capital Beltway (I-495) to Rt. 50 west to South Carlin Springs Road; turn left on South Carlin Springs Road; look for the Long Branch Nature Center sign on the left side of the road. Park at the Nature Center or in adjoining Glencarlyn Park.

Tuesday–Saturday, 10–5; Sunday, 1–5. Closed Monday and holidays.

Picnic in nearby Glencarlyn Park.

Playgrounds.

Meadowside Nature Center

This Nature Center is surrounded by 350 acres, including 7.5 miles of trails, a lake, marsh, pond, herb garden, raptor cage (with live owl, hawk, and turkey vulture), two butterfly gardens and a mid-1800s farmstead. Inside the Center is a Curiosity Corner Room with a microscope table and other interactive activities. There are live animal exhibits and a wildlife observation window as well. Legacy of the Land is a diorama of Maryland habitats. Kids love crawling into and sliding out of the cave and enjoy looking at an underground cross-section of the earth, which shows tree roots and a view into the bottom of a pond.

Summer Conservation Clubs, adult volunteer program and Junior Naturalist program are available.

www.mncpp.org

301-924-5965

Rock Creek Regional Park, 5100 Meadowside Lane, Rockville, MD Capital Beltway (I-495) to Georgia Avenue north; continue to left turn on Norbeck Road; turn right on Muncaster Mill Road; left on Meadowside Lane.

Tuesday–Saturday, 9–5; closed Sundays, Mondays and federal holidays.

Hiking.

Special activities include programs for individuals and families throughout the year and are listed in the Nutshell News website calendar.

National Wildlife Visitor Center, Patuxent Research Refuge

The $18 million National Wildlife Visitor Center is one of the largest science and environmental education centers in the Department of the Interior. Interactive exhibits focus on global environmental issues, migratory bird studies, habitats, endangered species, creature life cycles and the research tools and techniques used by scientists. The Visitor Center offers wildlife management demonstration areas and outdoor education sites for school classes. There are also hiking trails, interpretive programs, tram tours, wildlife observations and films.

Take an interpretative tour around the refuge's Lake Reddington where you can see wildlife and evidence of wildlife activity. Learn about the habitats the refuge manages for the success of migratory birds, mammals, reptiles and amphibians.

www.fws.gov/northeast/patuxent

301-497-5760

US Department of the Interior, 10901 Scarlet Tanager Loop, Laurel, MD Capital Beltway (I-495) to the Baltimore-Washington Parkway (Rt. 295) north to the Beltsville / Powder Mill Road exit; turn right onto Powder Mill Road; go 1.9 miles; turn right into Visitor Center entrance. Parking on site.

Daily, 10–5:30. Closed January 1, Thanksgiving, and December 25.

Tram tickets $3 adult, $2 senior, and $1 child.

Workshops for teachers.

Facility and parts of trails are wheelchair and stroller accessible.

Fishing, hiking.

Special activities include children's education games throughout the year, crafts and refuge trail walks. Wildlife Tram tours mid-March through mid-November.

Peace Park/Kunzang Palyul Chöling

Kunzang Palyul Chöling is one of largest communities of monks ordained in the Tibetan Buddhist tradition in North America. The beautiful temple complex is on 72 acres in rural Montgomery County, Maryland. It provides monastic living quarters for monks and nuns, a large wildlife refuge, peaceful walking trails and 28 consecrated stupas. The 65-acre Peace Park has six gardens in which the traditional peaceful meditation is a clockwise 30-minute walk. The Prayer Room, with its 24-hour-a-day prayer vigil, is also open to the public for meditation and prayer.

301-349-0440

18400 River Road, Poolesville, MD
Capital Beltway (I-495) to River Road exit toward Potomac.

 ## Rock Creek Nature Center and Planetarium

One of the best in the area, this Nature Center offers many exhibits of the flora and fauna of its surrounding woodland. Children find the live reptiles and beehive especially interesting. There are also two self-guided nature trails.

The Nature Discovery Room contains hands-on activities, puppets and books to help children learn about their environment.

An exciting part of the Nature Center is the planetarium show. The room darkens, stars appear and the audience is transported outdoors on a clear night. The show for younger children concentrates on the identification of major constellations and the movement of the heavenly bodies through the night sky. The later show, for older children, is divided into a study of the sky as it will appear that night and an in-depth astronomy presentation. Evening stargazing sessions, run in conjunction with the National Capital Astronomers, are held approximately once a month, May through October. Also see Rock Creek Park (on p. 118).

www.nps/gov/rocr

202-426-6829

5200 Glover Road, NW, Washington, DC
Connecticut Avenue north, turn right on Military Road, turn right at Glover Road to the Nature Center.

Daily, 9–5 Wednesday–Sunday. December 25, January 1 and Thanksgiving. Planetarium shows on Saturday and Sunday at 1 p.m. for children age four and older (children must be accompanied by adults), and on Wednesday at 4 p.m. for children age seven and older.

Special programs available by reservation for groups of ten or more, Wednesday–Friday only. Call at least two weeks in advance.

No food or drink in the Nature Center.

Strollers are permitted in the Nature Center, but not in the Planetarium.

Rust Sanctuary (Audubon Naturalist Society)

The Rust Sanctuary property in Loudoun County, Virginia, includes a manor house, formally called Yoecomico, and 62 acres of land. Rust Sanctuary is committed to protecting the integrity of the natural area while providing opportunities and resources that encourage the discovery and appreciation of the natural world. The sanctuary protects six different kinds of habitats including: wildlife habitat gardens, meadows, hedge rows, mixed hardwood forest, pine plantation and a pond. The manor house is equipped with offices, classrooms, meeting rooms and a small nature center.

www.audubonnaturalist.org

703-669-0008

802 Children's Center Road, Leesburg, VA
Capital Beltway (I-495) to Leesburg Pike west (Rt. 7) to Leesburg. Left on Catoctin Circle, right on Children's Center Road to Sanctuary Drive, ignore the no outlet sign. Parking available on-site.

Grounds open daily, dawn–dusk. Building open weekdays, 9–5; building closed weekends.

Hiking.

Special activities include regular bird walks, nature programs and seasonal events for children. The Sanctuary's trails and meadows are open daily for exploration and discovery.

U.S. Naval Observatory

The work of the U.S. Naval Observatory consists primarily of determining the precise time and the measurements of star positions. Tours include a short movie on the Observatory, a look at the highly accurate electronic clocks and other exhibits and an explanation of the workings of the 12-inch Alvan Clark refractor telescope. On clear nights, the tours include a look through the telescope.

www.usno.navy.mil/tour_info.shtml

Massachusetts Avenue at 34th Street, NW, Washington, DC
Parking is available just outside the South Gate on Observatory Circle across from the New Zealand Embassy.

Half-hour public tours are offered on a limited basis on Monday evenings at 8:30 p.m. Reservations must be submitted online 4–6 weeks in advance and all adult visitors must present a photo ID. No one is admitted without a reservation.

University of Maryland Observatory

Looking through telescopes at stars, planets, nebulae, and galaxies makes for a fascinating visit at the University of Maryland Observatory. The Observatory is open to the public on the 5th and 20th of each month November–April, at 8 pm, and May–October, at 9pm, for a short presentation by a guest speaker, tour of the observatory and observation if weather permits.

www.astro.umd.edu/openhouse

301-405-0355

Metzerott Road, College Park, MD
Capital Beltway (I-495) to the Rt. 1/College Park exit; go south on Rt. 1 to Rt. 193 (University Boulevard) west. Turn right at the first light

(Metzerott Road). The observatory is past the stop light on the left. Free parking at the observatory or across the street at the University System Administration.

The lecture hall and observatory are wheelchair-accessible, but to look through the telescopes requires ascending a ladder.

Watkins Nature Center

Watkins Nature Center, located within Watkins Regional Park, offers indoor and outdoor ponds, native wildlife displays, a children's discovery corner, butterfly and herb gardens, six miles of marked trails and a puppet theater. The Nature Center is only a five-minute walk from the picnic areas and the playground. Call for a schedule of children's nature programs and family special events.

www.pgparks.com/places/parks/watkins.html

301-218-6870

301 Watkins Park Drive, Upper Marlboro, MD
Capital Beltway (I-495) to exit 15A,Central Avenue east (Rt. 214); follow Rt. 124 through Largo; turn right on Watkins Park Drive (Rt. 193). Park is on the right.

Monday–Saturday, 8:30–5; Sundays and holidays, 11–4.

Webb Sanctuary (Audubon Naturalist Society)

This 20-acre nature sanctuary has hiking and nature trails through woods and meadows on rolling terrain outside the quiet village of Clifton. Enjoy free programs or enjoy a walk with nature. Look for resident and migrating birds, search for salamanders, discover frogs and toads or watch for butterflies and wildflowers.

www.audubonnaturalist.org

703-737-0021

12829 Chestnut Street, Clifton, VA
Capital Beltway (I-495) to I-66 west to the Fairfax County Parkway (Rt. 7100) south. Follow Rt. 7100 to the next exit, Lee Highway (Rt. 29) south. At the second stoplight, turn left on Clifton Road. Follow Clifton Road until it ends and turn right into the town of Clifton. Right

on Chestnut Street; first right after the stop sign to the sanctuary. Parking on site.

Daily, dawn–dusk.

Hiking.

 Woodend Nature Sanctuary (Audubon Naturalist Society)

Woodend is a tranquil 40-acre wildlife sanctuary. The pond, meadows and woods are fun to explore; a self-guided nature trail is available. Inside the main house is the Wilbur Fisk Banks Bird Collection, consisting of 594 specimens, mostly from eastern North America.

www.audubonnaturalist.org

301-652-9188

8940 Jones Mill Road, Chevy Chase, MD
Capital Beltway (I-495) to the Connecticut Avenue exit South for one half mile. Turn left onto Manor Road, right on Jones Bridge Road, and left on Jones Mill Road. Entrance to Sanctuary is one third mile on the left. Parking on-site.

Daily, dawn–dusk.

Special activities include after-school and summer programs for children; also offered are family and adult activities, including day and weekend trips, a Holiday Fair in December and a Nature Fair in May.

HISTORICAL FARMS

Carroll County Farm Museum

Visitors get a look back in history in this 1800s farmhouse surrounded by 140 rolling acres of countryside. Offerings include guided tours of the farmhouse and self-guided tours of the Living History Center and exhibit buildings—including a Spring House, Blacksmith Shop, Tinsmith Shop, Transportation Exhibit and gardens. Farm animals are stabled in the pasture area, a play area for children and nature trails are also available. Demonstrations scheduled throughout the season may include quilting, weaving, broom making, tinsmithing and blacksmithing. The General Store sells candy, souvenirs and handcrafted items made by resident artisans.

ccgov.carr.org/farm

800-654-4645, 410-876-2667

500 South Center Street, Westminster, MD
Capital Beltway (I-495) to Georgia Avenue (route 97) north; continue about 35 miles to left turn on Rt. 132; follow to left on Center Street; continue a half mile to entrance on right. Parking on site.

Group tours in April, Tuesday–Friday, 10–4; in May, facility open to general public, weekends, noon–5. Additional hours: July and August, Tuesday–Friday, 10–4. Open for tours during Christmas season. Closed Mondays and some holidays.

Adults, $3; children 7–18 and adults over 60, $2; 6 and under, free. Groups of 20 or more (by reservation), $2.50 per person.

Strollers permitted outside, but not in Farmhouse.

Hiking.

Special activities include Blacksmith Days and Civil War Living History Encampment in May; Spring Muster of Antique Fire Equipment and Fiddlers' Convention in June; an Old-Fashioned July 4th Celebration in July; Steamshow Days in September; Fall Harvest Days in October, and a Holiday Theme Tour in December.

Cedarvale Farm

This farm features a herd of 20 bison, raised primarily to preserve the species and to educate school children about our American heritage. Bring your apples and stale bread to feed the bison.

cedarvalefarm.com

410-734-7467

2915 Coale Lane, Churchville, MD
Capital Beltway (I-495) to I-95 north past Baltimore to exit 80; turn left on Rt. 543; go to traffic light and then turn right on Rt. 136 and follow for 3 miles; turn right on Coale Lane (look for bison on Cedarvale Farm sign).

Sundays, 1–5.

Recreation facilities available.

Claude Moore Colonial Farm at Turkey Run

The Claude Moore Farm at Turkey Run is a living history museum that portrays family life on a small, modest farm just before the Revolutionary War. The farm uses hands on, interactive programs to further understanding of agriculture and everyday life in 18th-century Virginia.

703-442-7557

www.1771.org

6310 Georgetown Pike, McLean, VA
Capital Beltway (I-495) to Georgetown Pike (Rt. 193) east two and a half miles; go left onto access road; farm is a half-mile on the left. Or George Washington Memorial Parkway to Rt. 123 south; after one mile, turn left on Rt. 193; right onto access road; farm is a half-mile on the left. Public parking available.

Open April–December, Wednesday–Sunday, 10–4:30. Closed January–March, holidays and rainy days.

Adults, $2; children 3–12 and seniors, $1.

Group visits must be scheduled in advance.

Gravel paths with moderate inclines.

VA TimeTravelers site.

Special activities include an 18th-century Market Fair in May, July, and October, with merchants, crafts and a colonial orchestra. Participate in the wheat and tobacco harvest days and many food preservation events.

 Frying Pan Farm Park

Frying Pan Farm Park is home to Kidwell Farm, a working dairy demonstration farm that portrays family farm life in the 1930's. Greet the friendly farm animals, take a wagon ride or watch the farm hands at work. Sit on the front porch or take a tour of the farm. Kids can visit with farm animals including draft horses, lambs, goats and calves. See the aspects of a working farm in action, including hay storage, milking parlor, stalls and a blacksmith's shop. A variety of classes for children, adults and preschoolers are available.

Frying Farm Park is also the home of Fairfax County's only public equestrian facility. There are two outdoor riding rings and an indoor center. The Equestrian Center has a riding arena (110 feet x 235 feet) with spectator seating for 800.

www.fairfaxcounty.gov/parks/fryingpanpark.htm

703-437-9101

2709 West Ox Road,, Herndon, VA
Capital Beltway (I-495) to Exit 49 (Rt. I-66 West); I-66 to Fairfax County Parkway (Rt. 7100); north on Fairfax County Parkway approximately 6 miles; turn left on West Ox Road; proceed 1.4 miles to park entrance on the right.

Frying Pan Farm Park, daily dawn–dusk.

Kidwell Farm, daily 9–5; check website for animal birthing schedule.

Hayrides March–November, 10–4:30. Call to confirm availability.

Equestrian facilities for show and practice. Park does not rent horses or provide riding lessons.

Country store, March–December, 10–4:30.

Farmer's Market, Wednesday mornings, May–October.

Visitors' center with auditorium and classroom available for rental; birthday party facility rental.

Special activities: Acoustic Jam, country store, Easter egg hunt, farm show, 4H Fair, horse shows, Fall Fun Festival.

National Colonial Farm

At this beautiful site on the Potomac opposite Mount Vernon the Accokeek Foundation, in cooperation with the National Park Service, has recreated a working farm. It features demonstration gardens and animals of a middle-class tobacco plantation in the mid-18th century. Seasonal farm work goes on every day, as well as daily domestic activities. On the interpretive tours, children of all ages have the chance to observe the farming methods and family life characteristic of the period. Bird enthusiasts will be pleased to know that the farm is home to three pairs of bald eagles. See Piscataway Park (see p. 134).

www.accokeek.org/ncf.htm

301-283-2113

Piscataway National Park, 3400 Bryan Point Road, Accokeek, MD Capital Beltway (I-495) to Indian Head Highway (Rt. 210) south; proceed south on Indian Head Highway for ten miles; turn right at Bryan Point Road; follow for four miles to farm parking lot on right.

Tuesday–Sunday, 10–4. Closed Thanksgiving, Veterans Day, December 25, and January 1.

A vehicle for people with special needs is available. Call during the week to make arrangements.

Special activities include the Potomac River Heritage Festival in late September, featuring demonstrations of a variety of colonial crafts; Children's Day in the spring and fall.

 Oxon Hill Farm

Oxon Hill is a working farm with daily demonstrations of farm chores, animals, crops and equipment typical of those on farms in the early 1900s. Children can pet the animals, and learn about animal care and farming methods. There are craft demonstrations, a natural spring, and a self-guided nature walk that explains how farms utilized the surrounding woods. An additional bonus: the spectacular view of the Potomac River, Washington and Virginia.

www.nps.gov/oxhi

301-839-1176

6411 Oxon Hill Road, Oxon Hill, MD
Capital Beltway (I-495) to Indian Head Highway, exit 3A south; go right at end of ramp to Oxon Hill Road; make immediate right into farm.

Daily, 8:30–4:30. Closed Thanksgiving, December 25 and January 1.

Cow milking weekdays at 10, 11:30, and 3:30 by reservation; on weekends, first-come, first-served basis at 10 and 3:30. Chicken feeding and egg gathering at 11 weekdays, by reservation.

Appropriate for preschool age children.

Athletic fields, fishing, hiking.

Special activities include sheep-shearing, gardening, threshing, cider pressing, butter churning, ice cream making, corn harvesting and sorghum syrup cooking.

Temple Hall Farm Regional Park

This self-sustaining 286-acre working farm raises farm animals (cows, goats, hogs, peacocks, chicken, ducks and sheep) and produces Orchard grass and Alfalfa hay. Interpretive programs designed as outdoor classrooms are offered to educate children about the diverse aspects of farm life, animals and crops. A farm interpreter leads tours and guides children as they participate in farm-related activities such as feeding the animals or working in the garden. All animals are in fenced pens; this is not a petting farm.

www.nvrpa.org/templehall.html

703-779-9372

15789 Temple Hall Lane, Leesburg, VA
Capital Beltway (I-495) to Rt. 15 north through Leesburg. Turn right onto Limestone School Road (Rt. 661). Go approximately one mile; the farm entrance is on the left.

Sundays, April–October, 11–4.

Interpretive tours last 1–2 hours, depending on the age level of the group.

Special activities include a corn maize event held the last week in August through October. The farm also has pick-your-own-pumpkins and hayrides, and an open house by appointment twice a year during the spring and fall.

Walney Visitor Center/Ellanor C. Lawrence Park

A large preserve of open space, the park's 660 acres are home to many features including: the Walney Pond, historic ruins, Walney Visitor Center, Cabell's Mill/Middlegate complex, picnic facilities, athletic fields and hiking trails.

The Walney Visitor Center is a converted 1780 farmhouse with live animal exhibits, historical exhibits, greenhouse and classrooms. The Walney house was a home to families who farmed the Walney farm during the 18th, 19th and early 20th centuries. Outbuildings include a smokehouse, ruins of an icehouse and diary complex and demonstration gardens.

www.fairfaxcounty.gov/parks/ecl

703-631-0013

5040 Walney Road, Chantilly, VA
Capital Beltway (I-495) to Rt. 66 west for eleven miles to Sully Road/Rt. 28 north (exit 49) north. Make an immediate right turn onto Walney Road; the entrance is one mile on the left.

Daily, dawn–dusk.

Mostly accessible with assistance.

Tours, self-guided studies, and summer camps offered.

VA TimeTravelers site, athletic fields, hiking.

6

ARTS AND ENTERTAINMENT

Whether you live around Washington or you're a visitor, be sure to take advantage of the city's many opportunities to introduce your children to the performing arts. The entertainment sections and Web sites of local newspapers list up-to-date information on performances. There are many options for finding lower-cost tickets. Here are a few ideas:

TICKETplace offers half-price tickets that can be purchased on the day of the performance. TICKETplace is located at 407 7th St. NW, close to the Archives/Navy Memorial Metro station (Yellow or Green line) and Gallery Place station (Red, Yellow or Green line). TICKETplace is open Tuesday–Friday, 11–6, and Saturday, 10–5. Call 202-TICKETS for information on what is available on a particular day. Some shows are also available online, Tuesday–Friday, noon–4 at www.ticketplace.org. TICKETplace accepts credit and debit cards only.

Sign up on the Goldstar Events Web site (www.goldstarevents. com) for regular emails regarding half-price offerings at local theaters, concerts and sporting events. If you travel outside of Washington, you can use this site to find half price tickets at Goldstar Events' locations in Los Angeles, San Francisco, San Diego, Orange County, and San Jose, Calif., as well as in Chicago, New York, Boston and Las Vegas.

"Stages for All Ages" is a program of the League of Washington Theaters designed to introduce people 17 and under to live, professional theater. More than 25 area theaters offer a free ticket to a child age 17 or under with each adult ticket purchased, for select performances. The schedule varies, but tickets generally are available for performances in the spring. Check the Web site www.lowt.org/stages/stages.html for a list of performances, or call 202-638-4270 to request a brochure. Contact theaters directly for tickets.

Some organizations offer "pay as you can" performances or student discounts; ask at the box office. Some additional discounts specific to particular venues are listed below.

Adventure Theatre at Glen Echo Park

The Washington area's longest-running children's theater boasts a year-round schedule of performances and classes at historic Glen Echo Park. Major productions provide good professional entertainment; an on-site education program offers classes after school and on weekends, and summer workshops for ages 6–15. After the matinees, children can collect autographs from the performers and then run off for a ride on the carousel (open May–September, see Glen Echo Park on p. 80).

www.adventuretheatre.org

301-320-5331

Glen Echo Park, 7300 MacArthur Boulevard, Glen Echo, MD
Near Goldsboro Road

Performances on Saturday and Sunday, 11 and 1:30; separate weekday productions on Tuesday at 11 and Thursday at 10.

Tickets are $12 per person. Group rates available.

Sign language available; call to make arrangements.

African Heritage Center for African Dance and Music

The Center is a dance studio where classes and performances in African dance and music are held. The African Heritage Dancers and Drummers, one of the first African-American dance companies in the Washington area, specializes in the traditional dance of West Africa. Harvest dances, mask dances and stick dances, many performed in colorful robes, are all fascinating to watch. The Center also offers workshops in West African dance, drumming and instrument making.

www.ahdd.org

202-399-5252

4018 Minnesota Avenue, NE, Washington, DC
Located near RFK Stadium at Minnesota and Benning Road.

Weekend performances. During the first week in August, daily performances around noon.

Admission varies.

Metrorail Orange line (Minnesota Avenue, south).

American Film Institute/Silver Theatre and Cultural Center

This three-screen complex offers a year-round program of the best in American and international cinema, featuring an eclectic mix of festivals, premieres, retrospectives, special events, tributes, on-stage guest appearances and educational programs.

301-495-6720

8633 Colesville Road, Silver Spring, MD

Special activities include Silver Spring Outdoor Movie Series, "Silver Screen Under the Stars," family fun and entertainment in July.

Arena Stage

The Arena Stage complex houses three theaters: an in-the-round (Fichandler) stage, a standard proscenium (Kreeger) stage, and a cabaret-style (Old Vat) room. Although most performances are intended for adult audiences, some shows are geared for the whole family. Arena offers several savings programs for children and adults: Students with ID may receive 35% off regular ticket prices for every performance except Saturday evenings. A limited number of $10 tickets is available to patrons ages 5–25 on the day of the performance. These tickets are available until 30 minutes before curtain and one day in advance on the weekend, and can be ordered by phone; call 202-488-3300. In addition, half-price HOTTIX are available to all patrons for most performances from 90 minutes before curtain to 30 minutes before curtain and must be purchased in person.

Arena also offers summer camp and education programs, including an annual student playwriting contest in which the winners' plays are staged at the theater. Also available are student group sales packages with a curriculum guide, copy of the play script and in-class visit from an Arena artist.

www.arenastage.org

202-554-9066

1101 6th Street, SW, Washington, DC
Capital Beltway (I-495) to I-395 North / US-1 North toward Washington via 14th Street. Exit at I-395 north, and then the Maine Avenue exit. Keep left at the fork in the ramp and merge onto 9th Street, SW. In less than 0.5 miles turn left onto Maine Avenue, and then left onto 6th Street, SW.

Metered parking on the street and several pay lots within easy walking distance.

Metrorail Green line (Waterfront-SEU).

Arlington Cinema 'n' Drafthouse

This historic 1930s Art Deco theater has been converted into a restaurant/theater with comfortable chairs and table-side service. The Drafthouse offers many family-friendly events, including movies, improvisational children's theater, magic shows, live music and more. Family-friendly events are smoke-free and require that children under 21 be accompanied by parent or guardian.

www.arlingtondrafthouse.com

703-486-2345

2903 Columbia Pike, Arlington, VA
Capital Beltway (I-495), to I-66 east to Fairfax Drive/Glebe Road. Go south on Glebe Road to the intersection of Columbia Pike. Turn left. The Drafthouse is about two blocks down on the left side of the street.

Family-friendly events are scheduled Saturdays and Sundays.

Metrorail Blue or Yellow line (Pentagon City). Take Route 16 bus or a cab.

Blackrock Center for the Arts

This center provides venues for performances in dance and theater along with film presentations, lectures and arts education. Classes in the performing, literary and visual arts are offered seven days a week for children, teens and adults, including classes specifically for children with special needs. Summer camps also are featured. Some performances include "enrichment activities" such as a musical instrument "petting zoo" or post-show lectures and master classes.

www.blackrockcenter.org

301-528-2260

12901 Town Commons Drive, Germantown, MD
I-270 north to Middlebrook Road West. Cross MD Rt. 118. Right into the Town Center Shopping area. Go two short blocks and turn left. Blackrock is on the right. The parking lot is behind the building.

Classika Theater

A relative newcomer to the region's arts scene, this children's theater offers wonderful productions geared to children ages 4–12+. The company comprises professional actors trained in movement and Eastern European–style acting. Plays often include puppets as well as actors. In addition to performances at their intimate 75-seat theater in Shirlington, the company also has brought plays to the National Theater in Washington and to the Arts Barn Theatre in Gaithersburg. The Theater offers classes and summer camps in performing and visual arts.

www.classika.org

703-824-6200

Village at Shirlington, 4041 S. 28th Street, Arlington, VA
George Washington Parkway past Memorial Bridge exit. Exit at I-395
South/Boundary Channel Drive. Go right at the fork, following signs
to enter I-395 south. Exit 7 to Glebe Road/Shirlington. Follow signs for
Shirlington. Go through one traffic light. Turn left at the first street, S.
Quincy Street. Turn right at the first street, S. 28th Street The theater is
at the end of the street on the right.

$12 in advance, $15 at the door.

Arts Barn: 311 Kent Square Road, Gaithersburg, MD.
www.gaithersburgmd.gov

Comedy Sportz Arena

Bring the whole family to experience this entertaining comedy sporting event. Two teams of performers compete in a battle of wits by
playing a series of improvisational games, all based on suggestions
from the audience. A referee governs the action on the playing field,
keeping time and calling fouls when comments make the audience
groan or a player says anything in poor taste. Audience participation
encouraged. Suitable for all ages.

www.cszdc.com

703-486-5233

Ballston Commons Mall, 4238 Wilson Blvd, Arlington, VA.
Capital Beltway (I-495) to I-66 East, exit 71. Stay right onto Glebe
Road. Ballston Commons Mall is on the left at Wilson Lane.

Performances Thursday, Friday, Sunday, 8 p.m.; Saturday, 7:30 p.m.

Kidz show, 3 p.m., first Saturday of every month.

Ticket prices $10–$14.

Metrorail Orange line (Ballston)

Encore Stage and Studio/The Children's Theater

The Children's Theater offers fully staged and beautifully costumed musicals and dramas for children by children. Some are original, some are traditional, but all are professional and performed by talented young actors. Open auditions for ages 9–14 are held for each production. Call or visit the website for a schedule of performances as well as year-round classes and workshops.

www.encorestage.org

703-548-1154

2515 North Randolph Street, Arlington, VA
Performances are at the Thomas Jefferson Community Theatre, 125 South Old Glebe Road, Arlington, VA.

Five weekend productions per year.

Act III Young Adult Program for high school and college students and young adults

Adults, $10; Students and seniors, $8; Groups (10 or more), $7 each.

Fairfax Symphony Orchestra

This concert series features a mix of folk, contemporary and classical music. Each summer, the Fairfax Symphony performs 40 free concerts in area parks and historic sites. You can pack a picnic and have a relaxing meal while you listen to the music in a beautiful outdoor setting. About 15 concerts, called "Overture to Orchestra," are designed to introduce children to the different instrument sections in an orchestra: percussion, string, brass and woodwind. Other concerts feature instrumental soloists or a particular style of music, such as a Dixieland or German band. Call or visit the website for a calendar of the summer offerings and information about school programs.

www.fairfaxsymphony.org

703-642-7200

Packard Center, 2nd Floor, 4024 Hummer Road, Annandale, VA

"Sounds of Summer" performances from June–September in the late morning, early afternoon and early evening at Fairfax County parks and historic sites.

Folger Shakespeare Theatre

This 250-seat theater is constructed to suggest an open-air 17th-century theater, and is home to three Shakespeare and contemporary theater productions each year.

www.folger.edu

202-544-7077

201 E. Capitol Street, SE, Washington, DC

See Folger Shakespeare Library, p. 34.

Friday Night in the Park Concerts

This concert series features a mix of folk, bluegrass, contemporary and classical music. Call or visit the website for a summer schedule. (See p. 142 for more information about Potomac Overlook Regional Park.)

www.nvrpa.org/potomacoverlook.html

703-528-5406

Potomac Overlook Regional Park, 2845 Marcey Road, Arlington, VA

Performances summer through early fall, every other Saturday, 7 p.m.

No alcohol permitted at picnics.

Harman Center for the Arts/Shakespeare Theatre Company

The Harman Center for the Arts opened in 2007 to combine the Lansburgh Theatre and Sidney Harman Hall, home of the Shakespeare Theatre Company. The Center provides a Washington venue for local, national and international performing arts companies.

www.shakespearetheatre.org/harman

202-547-1122

Lansburgh Theatre: 450 7th Street NW, Washington, DC

Sidney Harman Hall: 610 F Street NW, Washington, DC

Students, $10 with student ID.

Metrorail Yellow or Green line (Archives/Navy Memorial/Penn Quarter); Red, Yellow or Green line (Gallery Place/Chinatown), Red line (Judiciary Square)

Imagination Stage

The Bethesda Academy for the Performing Arts was founded in 1979. Today BAPA's Imagination Stage is the largest and most respected multi-disciplinary theater arts organization for young people in the region. The Imagination Stage season offers professional shows for families as well as year-round classes, performance opportunities and school outreach programs for young people. Imagination Stage is committed to making the arts inclusive and accessible to all children regardless of physical, cognitive or financial abilities.

Imagination Stage's facility includes a 450-seat professional theater and a 200-seat theater for student productions. Studios for drama, dance, music, and digital media, production rooms, birthday party rooms, a café and a toy shop are located in this theater arts center.

www.imaginationstage.org

301-881-5106

4908 Auburn Avenue, Bethesda, MD
Capital Beltway (I-495) to Wisconsin Avenue/Rt. 355 south toward Bethesda. Turn right on Woodmont Avenue, past the National Library of Medicine. Turn right onto Rugby Avenue; left onto Auburn Avenue. Public parking garage.

Daily, 9:30–6. Performances weekends, holidays and summer days.

$14–$18 per ticket; $5–6 for school tickets; group rates available.

Metrorail Red line (Bethesda).

Programs for the hearing impaired.

Special activities include productions and performances for preschool through young adult. Summer camps.

John F. Kennedy Center for the Performing Arts

The Kennedy Center is America's living memorial to President Kennedy and home to six theaters that host great artists and performances of music, dance and theater from around the world. Offerings include National Symphony Orchestra concerts, plays and musicals, opera, ballet and modern dance, jazz and chamber music, performances for young people and more.

The **National Symphony Orchestra** has continued to reach both young people and adults with educational performances, lectures/demonstrations and artistic training for aspiring musicians. Written performance guides for all productions are available prior to the events for teachers and families.

Kennedy Center Youth and Family Programs include classics as well as commissioned works performed in the Theater Lab and Terrace Theater by groups from all over the United States. Programs include performances in theater, dance, music, puppetry and opera for families and school groups. Tickets are sometimes available the day of the performance, though it is best to order in advance.

The Kennedy Center's 324-seat **Family Theater** is home to world-class performances for the nation's youth. Located on the site formerly occupied by the AFI Film Theater, it incorporates the most modern theatrical innovations available, including premium audio technologies and a digital video projection system.

National Symphony Orchestra Family Concerts are scheduled in fall and spring on Saturday and Sunday. The December concerts usually have a holiday theme. Prior to each concert there is a hands-on activity in the grand foyer. One of the most popular of these activities is the instrument "petting zoo," where children may try out all the instruments that will be played professionally on the stage.

The Center also offers free performances every day at 6 p.m. on its Millennium Stage. The Stage was created as part of the Kennedy Center's Performing Arts for Everyone initiative. These free, hour-long performances include presentations of music, dance and theater for all ages.

www.kennedy-center.org

For a list of forthcoming programs, click on "Calendar," then "Discover Our Programs," and finally "Performances for Young Audiences."

202-467-4600, 800-444-1324 (ticket information)

2700 F Street, NW, Washington, DC
Capital Beltway (I-495) to I-66 east across the Roosevelt Bridge. Bear right to exit to Independence Avenue. Go under Roosevelt Bridge and Kennedy Center is the second entrance on the right. Parking garage on site.

Commercial parking at the Kennedy Center and nearby Watergate and Columbia Plaza garages.

Metrorail Orange or Blue line (Foggy Bottom). A free shuttle is provided from the Foggy Bottom metro station to and from the Kennedy Center.

Tickets to all performances may be purchased at the box office.

A limited number of Specially Priced Tickets (SPTs) are available to students in advance of the first performance for some Kennedy Center attractions, excluding Saturday evenings. Advance SPTs are available until curtain time of the first performance of the run of the show. After the first performance, SPTs can only be purchased in person by the student on the day of the performance, subject to availability, for designated performances. Specially Priced Tickets are NOT available for preschool age children or infants.

Sixty minutes of free parking is available for patrons making ticket purchases and exchanges with validation from the Box Office. Free parking is NOT available from the Columbia Plaza garage.

Call the Education Office at 202-416-8830 and ask to be put on the mailing list for children's programs and for brochures on specific events.

Special activities include an Arts Festival in the fall with free music, dance and other entertainment for children; a multicultural children's book and author festival in November; and Holiday Festivals with sing-a-longs, free performances and concerts in December.

 ## Marine Barracks Evening Parade

The U.S. Marine Band concerts are followed by a 90-minute parade featuring the U.S. Marine Drum and Bugle Corps, the U.S. Marine Corps Silent Drill Platoon, the U.S. Marine Corps Color Guard, and two companies of marching Marines. Marines, in full dress, escort each group to their sets. It is an impressive spectacle and a wonderful way to spend a summer evening.

www.mbw.usmc.mil

202-433-6060

Marine Barracks, 8th and I Streets, SE, Washington, DC
Park at Arlington National Cemetery Visitors' Center and take the free shuttle bus to and from the barracks.

Parades on Friday evenings at 8:45, May–August (arrive no later than 8). For reservations (required), write at least three weeks in advance. For group reservations, write at least two months in advance or fill out teh online reservation form at the website.

Call for information on wheelchair accessibility.

Security: All guests pass through security checkpoints.

Maryland Hall for the Creative Arts

Visit this home to the arts in Anne Arundel County featuring live theater, hands-on art activities, gallery exhibitions, performances and a wide variety of classes. Resident companies include the Annapolis Symphony Orchestra, Annapolis Opera and Ballet Theatre of Maryland.

www.marylandhall.org

410-263-5544

801 Chase Street, Annapolis, MD
Capital Beltway (I-495) to Rt. 50 east to Annapolis; exit at Rowe Boulevard, turning right; turn right at second light (Taylor Avenue); turn right on Spa Road; first left on Greenfield.

Monday–Friday, 8–11; Saturday, 8–5. Some classes and performances are held Sundays.

Montgomery College
Robert E. Parilla Performing Arts Center

The Saturday Morning Children's Series held at this Montgomery College performing arts center features four to five musical theater events each year, based on books for young audiences. Designed for short attention spans, these performances are 50–60 minutes long.

www.montgomerycollege.edu/pac

301-279-5301

51 Mannakee Street, Rockville, MD
Capital Beltway to I-270 North, to exit 6A, Rt. 28 (W. Montgomery Avenue.). At end of exit ramp, go straight across Rt. 28; it will become Nelson Street. Go to first light at Mannakee Street, turn left. The campus is 1.5 blocks on the left.

Adults,$7; children, students and seniors, $6.

Metrorail Red line (Rockville or Shady Grove). Take MetroBus Q2 or Ride-On Bus 46 or 55.

 ## Mount Vernon Community Children's Theater

Mount Vernon Community Children's Theater (MVCCT) has presented scores of theatrical productions featuring young actors from the Washington metropolitan community since its incorporation in 1980. Performed by children for children, MVCCT has consistently won awards for its productions and programs. Workshops, classes, summer camp and full-scale productions of musicals and dramas fulfill the theater's mission to provide opportunities for children and their families to participate in the creative process of live theater. Actors, musicians, set designers, make-up artists, costume designers and technical production staff are provided opportunities to learn the crafts and skills required for the presentation of live theater.

www.mvcct.org

703-360-0686

1900 Elkin Street, Alexandria, VA

Adults, $10; students and seniors, $8.

National Gallery of Art Children's Film Program

The Children's Film Program offers innovative programming, enhances enjoyment of the Gallery's collections and exhibitions and fosters an understanding of film as an art form. The program represents a broad range of recent foreign and domestic films, including a variety of animation styles, live-action and classics. A listing of scheduled films, descriptions, appropriate age ranges, dates and times can be found on the gallery's website by clicking on NGAKids, or by calling 202-789-3030.

All programs are shown in the East Building Auditorium, unless otherwise noted. Programs are free and eating is offered on a first-come, first-seated basis. Groups are welcome.

www.nga.gov

202-737-4215

Located on the National Mall between 3rd and 7th Streets at Constitution Avenue NW

Monday–Saturday, 10–5; Sunday, 11–6. Closed December 25, January 1.

National Theatre: Saturday Morning at the National and Monday Night at the National

These dynamic one-hour shows invite audience participation and are irresistible to kids age 4 and older. Magicians, dancers, mimes and puppets are among the performers of local and national renown. Adult programs are also offered on Mondays at 6 and 7:30 p.m.; some may be appropriate for adolescents.

www.nationaltheatre.org

800-447-7400 (tickets)**; 202-628-6161** (info)

1321 Pennsylvania Avenue, NW, Washington, DC

Performances throughout the school year, Saturday at 9:30 and 11. Monday nights at 6 and 7:30 for teens and adults.

Tickets distributed 30 minutes before show, first-come, first-served.

Metrorail Red, Orange or Blue line (Metro Center). Parking in nearby commercial lots.

Netherlands Carillon Concerts

Come sit on the grass to hear the free carillon concerts of popular, classical and religious music. A gift from the people of the Netherlands, the 50-bell carillon, housed in its open steel structure, is an impressive auditory and visual experience. Visitors may go up into the tower to watch the carillonneur perform and to view the city of Washington.

www.nps.gov/gwmp/carillon.htm

703-289-2500

Located off Marshall Drive in Rosslyn, VA
Near Iwo Jima Memorial and Arlington National Cemetery. From Rosslyn, VA: follow Ft. Myer Drive, which turns into Meade Street, to Marshall Drive; left on Marshall Drive; then first left into park.

Performances are held Saturdays and national holidays, May–September. In May and September, 2–4; in June–August, 6–8.

This is a good place to view the July 4 fireworks.

Now This! Kids!

Now This! Kids! presents a delightfully innovative and totally improvisational musical children's theater show appropriate for children ages 5-12. Every skit is an original, based on suggestions from the audience with funny and amazing results. Group rates are available.

www.nowthisimprov.com

202-364-8292

Blair Mansion, 7711 Eastern Avenue, Silver Spring, MD, and Arlington Cinema 'n' Drafthouse, Arlington, VA (See p. 207.)

Select Saturdays at Blair Mansion, and one Sunday each month at Arlington Cinema 'n' Drafthouse.

Metrorail Red line (Silver Spring).

Olney Theatre Center

The Olney Theatre Center is a professional theater with four performing venues, including seating for up to 500 on the west lawn for the Theatre's Summer Shakespeare Festival. The season includes a family entertainment series, as well as staging of classic and contemporary plays.

www.olneytheatre.org

301-924-3400

2001 Rt. 108, Olney, MD
Georgia Avenue north to Olney; turn right on Rt. 108 in the center of town. Theatre is a half-mile on the left.

Metrorail Red line (Glenmont) and transfer to the 22 bus, which stops directly in front of the theater.

Tickets, $15 for all family series events; $6 lap seats for children under 3.

Publick Playhouse for the Performing Arts

The Playhouse, originally the 1947 art deco Cheverly Theatre, was renovated and reopened in 1975 as a theater committed to cultural diversity in the arts. Known throughout the metropolitan area for the quality and affordability of its programs, this 462-seat theater features nationally recognized touring companies in dance, music and theater, and is home to many community arts groups.

www.pgparks.com/places/artsfac/publick.html

301-277-1710

5445 Landover Road, Cheverly, MD
One-half mile off the Baltimore-Washington Parkway (Rt. 295) at the Cheverly exit, at the intersection of Landover and Annapolis roads. Free parking.

Midweek performances are offered at 10:15, 11, and noon.

Children, $6–$15 for children; adults, up to $20.

Special activities include a monthly Saturday Morning at the Movies, Vaudeville Style, which starts with a half-hour of live entertainment that includes lots of audience involvement, followed by a family-friendly movie.

Puppet Company Playhouse

The Puppet Company performs delightful productions with clever interpretations of many children's classics in a new 200-seat theater at historic Glen Echo Park. Audience members sit on the carpeted floor while master puppeteers spellbind audience members.

www.thepuppetco.org

301-320-6668

Glen Echo Park, 7300 MacArthur Boulevard, Glen Echo, MD
Located at the intersection of MacArthur Boulevard and Goldsboro Road. Capital Beltway (I-495) to exit 30, River Road. Go up the ramp and stay right, going east toward Washington DC At the fifth light turn right onto Goldsboro Road. Follow Goldsboro until it dead-ends at MacArthur Boulevard Turn right onto MacArthur, then first left onto Oxford Road. The parking lot is on the left.

Age 2 and older, $8. "No obligation" reservations (see "Take Note") are strongly recommended. Group rates available with advance reservations. Coupon books of 10 tickets for $70 are good for one year. "Tiny Tot Tuesday" tickets are $5 each.

Take Note

Puppet Co. theater staff have high expectations for the behavior of their young patrons. Children who need to walk around or speak in loud voices will be asked to do so in the lobby, where there are TVs monitoring the show. "No obligation" reservations allow you to stay home if a child is sick or if plans change at the last minute.

Performances Wednesday–Friday, 10 and 11:30; Saturday–Sunday, 11:30 and 1. "Tiny Tot Tuesdays," at 10:30 and 11:30, feature 35 minute shows set on the theater floor, rather than the stage, to give a more intimate feeling. Baby bottles, water bottles and sippy cups are permitted during "Tiny Tot" performances, but all other food and drink must stay outside.

Productions change approximately every six weeks.

Appropriate for preschool age children through early elementary school.

Special activities include the carousel, open May–October, an annual exhibit showcasing puppets from recent productions, classes and workshops for children and adults and puppet-making demonstrations.

Round House Theatre

Round House offers a variety of stage productions each season, exploring different forms of theater and the performing arts. Limited engagements, contemporary adaptations of the classics, world premieres and works-in-progress can all be found on the stages at Bethesda (capacity 400) and Silver Spring (capacity 100–150). While most productions are for adults, some are suitable for the whole family.

Round House also provides theater education through special student matinees, a year-round theater school and an arts-centered summer day camp program.

> **Take Note**
>
> Round House offers free on-site childcare for one weekend matinee of each production. Children must be at least 3 and toilet-trained. Reservations must be made in advance; call the box office.

www.roundhousetheatre.org

240-644-1100 (box office); **240-644-1099** (main office)

4545 East-West Highway at Waverly Street, Bethesda, MD
Capital Beltway (I-495) to Rt. 355/Wisconsin Avenue south. One block past East-West Highway/Rt. 410 East, turn left on Montgomery Avenue. Turn left on Waverly at the first light to the county parking garage on Waverly; or cross East-West Highway and park in the Round House paid attended garage on the left.

8641 Colesville Road, Silver Spring, MD

Education Center, 925 Wayne Avenue, Silver Spring
Capital Beltway (I-495) to Colesville Road south to left on Spring Street. Right on Ellsworth or continue to right on Wayne Avenue. Public parking decks at Colesville Road and Fenton Street and at Ellsworth Avenue.

Metrorail Red line (Bethesda or Silver Spring, depending on which theater you are attending)

Smithsonian Discovery Theater

Thousands of children in the Washington area have had their introduction to theater at these performances. Discovery Theater offers new and diverse programming by artists of local and national renown, including many live performances and outstanding puppet shows, in a newly constructed performance space near the Smithsonian Castle.

www.discoverytheater.org

202-357-3030

The Ripley Center, 1100 Jefferson Drive, SW, Washington, DC
On the National Mall, just east of 12th Street.

Shows Monday–Friday 10 and 11:30 a.m.

Performances and workshops throughout the year; call for information on shows, dates, and times.

Adults, $6–$10; children, $5–$9.

Metrorail Blue or Orange line (Smithsonian, Mall exit) or Yellow or Green line (L'Enfant Plaza).

Appropriate for preschool age children through age 14.

Strathmore

Located one-half mile outside the Capital Beltway in North Bethesda, MD, Strathmore provides accessible, multi-disciplinary arts programming in the Mansion at Strathmore, the Music Center at Strathmore, and on its scenic 11-acre site. Artistic offerings presented by Strathmore in the Music Center include world-class performances by major national artists of folk, blues, pop, jazz, show tunes and classical music. The Music Center is home to five resident artistic partner organizations that present performances in the Concert Hall and classes in the Education Center. These include the Baltimore Symphony Orchestra (BSO at Strathmore), the National Philharmonic, the Washington Performing Arts Society, the Levine School of Music, CityDance Ensemble, the Maryland Classic Youth Orchestras and interPLAY. Each of the resident partners offers its own programs.

The Mansion at Strathmore is home to more intimate artistic programs presented by Strathmore in the warm and acoustically superb 100-seat Dorothy M. and Maurice C. Shapiro Music Room, the Gudelsky Gallery

Suite exhibition spaces, the outdoor Gudelsky Concert Pavilion, and outdoor Sculpture Gardens.

Every Thursday in July, two performances per day are presented on Strathmore's Backyard Theatre Stage. One-hour performances begin at 9:30 and 11:30 a.m. Free family-friendly outdoor concerts are held every Wednesday night from June through August. The Comcast Outdoor Film Festival, held the second week in August, offers 10 nights of free movies beginning at dark, about 8:30. The series usually includes 2–3 family friendly movies.

www.strathmore.org

301-581-5100 (ticket office)**; 301-581-5108** (tea reservations)

The Music Center at Strathmore: 5301 Tuckerman Lane
The Mansion at Strathmore: 10701 Rockville Pike
Both in North Bethesda, MD

Located at the intersection of Rockville Pike (Route 355) and Tuckerman Lane, north of the Capital Beltway (I-495). Entrance to (Grosvenor) Metro parking garage is on Tuckerman. Take the stairs or elevators to level 4 of the garage, and walk across the sky bridge into the Music Center's main entrance. Parking for the Mansion at Strathmore is at 10701 Rockville Pike.

Admission for Backyard Theatre Stage is $6 for adults and children over 3; under 3 is free. The summer concert series and movie series are free.

There is a handicapped entrance on the side of the Mansion building with an elevator.

Metrorail Red line (Grosvenor).

Parking is free for ticketed events at the Music Center. Park at the Grosvenor-Strathmore Metro garage on Tuckerman Lane; you must show your ticket stub to the attendant to exit.

The National Philharmonic orchestra performs about 18 concerts a year; children ages 7–17 are free with the purchase of an adult ticket.

Two resident companies offer classes for children ages 3 and up: CityDance Ensemble and the Levine School of Music.

Special activities include the Youth Art Exhibition, a display of artwork by elementary school children and a family-friendly Presidents Day Open House with free performances and classes. There is also a summer camp program as well as special arts classes and workshops throughout the year.

Children's Talks and Tours at The Mansion at Strathmore are available for children to learn about the artists, content and creation of the pieces in the current art exhibitions. Each talk and tour includes an art-related story and hands-on art project. Children must be accompanied by an adult, and must be at least 5 years old. Reservations are required; call 301-581-5109.

Sunset Serenades at the National Zoo

This summertime six-concert series features a diverse mix of ethnic and contemporary music. Past performances have included a mariachi band, classic rock and roll from the 50s and 60s, progressive reggae, and traditional Andean folk songs. Bring a picnic dinner or purchase snacks at the Mane Restaurant. Children love to dance in this relaxed outdoor environment. (See the National Zoo, p. 58.)

www.nationalzoo.si.edu

202-673-4717

National Zoological Park, Washington, DC
Rock Creek Park entrances at Adams Mill Road and Beach Drive, main entrance at 3000 block of Connecticut Avenue, NW.

Summer performances on Thursday evenings, late June to early August, 6:30–8, at the Lion/Tiger Hill Stage.

Metrorail Red line (Woodley Park-Zoo, a seven-minute, uphill walk; or Cleveland Park, a six-minute, level walk.)

Summer Concerts on the National Mall and Capitol Concerts: Armed Forces Bands and National Symphony

Spend a pleasant summer evening on the steps of the Capitol listening to patriotic and pops concerts presented by the Armed Forces bands. Enjoy the full majesty of the National Symphony Orchestra as it performs its holiday concerts al fresco.

Musicals, military concerts and July 4 celebrations under the stars are some of the attractions offered at Washington's outdoor downtown theater, the Sylvan Theater, and on the National Mall from Memorial Day through Labor Day. Bring picnics, blankets and insect repellent.

An impressive Torchlight Tattoo is presented by the U.S. Army Band and The Old Guard during mid-week at 7 p.m., mid-July to mid-August on the Ellipse near the White House. See www.usarmyband.com or www.mdw.army.mil/tlt/tlt.htm for schedule.

The U.S. Navy Band performs free concerts on Monday evenings at 8 from June through August on the West side of the U.S. Capitol grounds. Call 202-433-2525 for information, or see www.navyband.navy.mil/summerconcerts.shtml.

www.usarmyband.com

202-224-2985

119 D Street, NE, Washington, DC (National Symphony)
Located at the west front plaza steps and lawn of the Capitol.

Summer performances Mondays, Tuesdays, Wednesdays, and Fridays at 8 p.m. by the Armed Forces Band, weather permitting.

The National Symphony performs on July 4 and the Sundays prior to Memorial Day and Labor Day, rain or shine. Grounds open about 2 p.m.

Security: Bags and backpacks will be searched; no glass containers.

Performances at the outdoor Sylvan Theater on the grounds of the Washington Monument, weather permitting. Summer concert schedule at www.nps.gov/ncro/PublicAffairs/SummerintheCity.htm. Handicapped parking available off Independence Avenue at the rear of the theater.

Metrorail Red line (Union Station) or Blue or Orange line (Capitol South and Smithsonian, Mall exit)

Toby's Dinner Theatre

Since 1979, Toby's Dinner Theatre of Columbia has brought "the best of Broadway" musicals to a modern theater-in-the-round. The only regional dinner theater with a live orchestra, Toby's offers four family-friendly musicals each year.

Toby's Youth Theatre presents various productions throughout the year. Contact the theater for information and group reservations.

www.tobysdinnertheatre.com

301-596-6161

5900 Columbia Woods Road, Columbia, MD
Capital Beltway (I-495) to I-95 North to route 32 West. Rt. 32 west to
Rt. 29. Rt. 29 North to Exit 18B (Broken Land Parkway). Turn right at
Little Patuxent Parkway; turn right at South Entrance Road.

M The Washington Ballet

While many of the Washington Ballet's performances at
the Warner Theater and Kennedy Center are meant for
adults, the troupe offers a "family series" that includes intimate performances in its studios that appeal to boys and
girls of all ages. Past family series events have included invitations to
working rehearsals; performances based on children's literature staged
in the rehearsal studios at ballet headquarters; and the chance for children to come up on stage and perform a dance choreographed on
the spot by the troupe's artistic director. Kids are wowed by the close
proximity to the dancers, who may be no more than 10 feet away, and
enjoy the behind-the-scenes atmosphere that allows them to watch
muscular men and graceful women warm up at the barre. Ballets are
performed to music that ranges from Bach to the Beatles to the blues.

The Washington School of Ballet offers a wide range of classes from
pre-ballet for 6-year-olds to pre-professional for teens serious about
a ballet career. The school also offers special classes for boys as well
as for adults.

www.washingtonballet.org

202-362-3606

3515 Wisconsin Avenue, NW, Washington, DC
Located a few blocks north of the National Cathedral at the intersection of Wisconsin Avenue and Porter Road.

Metrorail Red line (Cleveland Park or Tenleytown)

Wolf Trap National Park for the Performing Arts

America's first national park for the performing arts offers world-class performances and classes for people of all ages. The Filene Center, surrounded by 100 acres of rolling hills, woods and streams, combines under-the-roof and under-the-stars seating. Resident professional companies, as well as world-renowned artists, perform during the summer. During the fall and winter, performances for adults are scheduled in the Barns at Wolf Trap. A wide variety of programs is offered, from folk singing to jazz. Children's Theatre-in-the-Woods presents music, puppetry, theater, dance and storytelling shows for children between kindergarten and sixth grade. Park Rangers lead programs about nature, theater and performing arts after most Theatre-in-the-Woods performances. The Center for Education features master classes, performances, distance learning, performings arts classes and workshops taught by internationally acclaimed Wolf Trap Teaching Artists for participants of all ages.

www.wolftrap.org

703-255-1900 (general information)**; 877-WolfTrap** (tickets)

1645 Trap Road, Vienna, VA
Capital Beltway (I-495) to the Dulles Toll Road / Rt. 267 West; go to Wolf Trap exit (open for performances only).

Filene Center is open May–September. The Barns is open October–May.

Children's Theatre-in-the-Woods is open from late June through early August at 10 and 11:15 a.m. on Tuesday through Saturday.

$5 shuttle at West Falls Church Metro (Orange line) for Filene Center performances.

Special activities include the International Children's Festival, featuring songs, dances, costumes, and crafts from around the world, held in early September; participatory theater, puppet, and dance programs for children in the summer; an Irish Festival with traditional music, dance, crafts and more on Memorial Day weekend; and a Christmas Carol Sing-a-Long featuring a military band, local choral groups and a candlelight procession (bring your own candle), the first Sunday in December.

Aladdin's Lamp Children's Books and Other Treasures

The store stocks a wide selection of books for infants and toddlers to young adults, plus parenting books and teacher resources, along with children's media, puppets, educational toys and games, greeting cards, posters, stickers, rubber stamps, and wooden puzzles. Special activities include programs for children ages 2½–6 on Wednesdays and Saturdays at 11, and for children 18 months to 3 years at 11 a.m. on Friday (call ahead for current information). Author visits and special events are held throughout the year. Summer programs include weekly book discussion groups for grades K–2 and 3–6, an end-of-summer reading celebration, and summer reading programs for children ages 6–12.

703-241-8281

2499 Harrison Street, Suite 10, Arlington, VA
Lee-Harrison Shopping Center, Lower Level (Near Harris Teeter Supermarket). Free parking behind the store.

Monday, Wednesday, Friday, Saturday 10–6; Tuesday and Thursday, 10–8; Sunday 11–4.

Metrorail Orange line (East Falls Church and West Falls Church).

Audubon Sanctuary Shop

Located at Woodend Sanctuary (see p. 195), the home of the Audubon Naturalist Society, this shop stocks an extensive selection of books on animals and plants, nature books for children, unusual puppets and puzzles, nature games and bird feeders.

www.audubonnaturalist.org

301-652-3606

8940 Jones Mill Road, Chevy Chase, MD
Capital Beltway (I-495) to the Connecticut Avenue exit south toward
Chevy Chase; turn left onto Manor Road and then right on Jones
Bridge Road; turn left onto Jones Mill Road to 8940 on the left.

Monday–Friday 10–5; Saturday 9–5; Sunday noon–5.

 Barnes and Noble

A selection of books for babies through young adult readers, along
with regularly scheduled children's events such as children's author
visits, story times and children's activities.

www.barnesandnoble.com

301-881-0237

12089 Rockville Pike, Rockville, MD
Montrose Crossing Shopping Center, 2.3 miles from Green Acres
School. Other locations throughout the area.

Barston's Child's Play

This popular toy store, well known for its extremely knowledgeable and helpful staff and fine selection of toys, includes a small but well-selected children's book section. The store features an extensive section of board and pop-up books for young children, along with many puzzle, game, sticker and joke books, especially good for traveling families. There is also a large selection of early readers, math and English workbooks, science and animal books, and "how to" books, such as children's cookbooks. This is a great source for book-related toys and media. The selection of toys, craft and art supplies, costumes and games is excellent, and spans a range of interests and ages.

www.barstonschildsplay.com

202-244-3602 (DC store)**; 301-230-9040** (Rockville store)

5536 Connecticut Avenue, NW, Washington, DC
Free parking behind store.

1661 Rockville Pike, Rockville, MD
In the Congressional Plaza shopping center.

DC store: Monday–Friday, 9:30–7 (Thursdays until 8); Saturday, 9:30–6; Sunday, noon–5.

Rockville: store Monday–Friday, 10–9; Saturday, 9:30–6; Sunday, 11–6.

Borders Books

Books for children, young adult and adult readers; story times, author visits.

www.borders.com

301-816-1067

White Flint Mall, 11301 Rockville Pike, Kensington, MD
Other locations throughout the area.

Color Book Gallery

This multicultural, multilingual children's bookstore in historic Occoquan celebrates the diversity of the Washington Metropolitan area with children's books (many bilingual) and musical instruments and fair trade crafts from around the world, along with weekly story and craft activities.

www.colorbookgallery.com

703-494-1994

308D Poplar Alley, Occoquan, VA
Capital Beltway (I-495) to I-95 S toward Richmond. Exit 160 to VA123/ Gordon Blvd toward Occoquan/Lake Ridge. Left at Commerce Street; right at Washington Street; left at Poplar Alley.

M Fairy Godmother

This small store on Capitol Hill carries a wide range of fiction and non-fiction for infants through teens, as well as foreign language children's books and media. Fairy Godmother also has a large selection of creative toys and art materials, music and book-related media, and stuffed animals and is a good place to look for hard to find titles.

202-547-5474

319 7th Street, SE, Washington, DC

Open Monday–Friday, 11–6; Saturday, 10–5; call for Sunday and holiday hours.

Metrorail Orange or Blue line (Eastern Market).

Karibu Books

This independent chain of bookstores specializes in books by and about African and African-American people, including children and teens—and parents.

www.karibubooks.com

301-559-1140 Hyattsville store, 301-352-4110 Bowie store

3500 East-West Highway Hyattsville MD
Capital Beltway (I-495) to exit 25 (Rt. 1 South) to right on East-West
Highway/410 to The Mall at Prince George's on the right.

15624 Emerald Way Bowie MD
Capital Beltway (I-495) to exit 19 to U.S. 50 East to exit 11/MD 197
(Collington Road). Turn right on 197 South to Bowie Town Center on
the right.

Monday–Saturday, 10–9:30, Sunday, 12–6 (11–6 at Bowie location).

*KaribuKIDS Time is 11–1 on the third Saturday of the month at the Bowie
Town Center location.*

 ## Kinder Haus Toys

This independently owned store features a well-considered selection
of fine children's toys, including a great selection of wood toys and
Folkmanis puppets, as well as books and crafts, and children's clothing
and shoes. Story times Mondays and Fridays at 10:30.

www.kinderhaus.com

703-527-5929

1220 N. FillmoreStreet Arlington, VA
South of Clarendon Boulevard, two blocks from the Clarendon Metro
stop, with parking across the street.

Open Monday–Friday, 10–7; Saturday, 10–6; Sunday, 10–4.

A Likely Story Children's Bookstore

This child-friendly store offers an impressive selection of books for
children, as well as parenting titles and professional books for teachers, children's media, puppets, puzzles, games, foreign language books
and best of all, a knowledgeable staff to assist in book selection.

www.alikelystorybooks.com

703-836-2498

1555 King Street, Alexandria, VA
Capital Beltway (I-495) to Rt. 193 exit (exit 43/44), toward George

Washington Memorial Parkway/Georgetown Pike; merge into GW Parkway south, which becomes George Washington Memorial Parkway south. Turn slight right onto North Washington Street. Go about one-half mile; turn right onto King Street (Rt. 7). On-street parking.

Open Monday–Saturday, 10–6 p.m.; Sunday, 1–5 p.m.

Metrorail Blue or Yellow line (King Street).

Special summer programs and book clubs are offered for all ages. Weekly storytimes for under-2s and for over-2s, as well as lap-sit programs for babies, bilingual storytimes and special events.

Noyes Library for Young Children

This charming one-room library, built as a library in 1863 is the Washington area's oldest library building and an historic landmark. It sits on its own triangular island surrounded by old trees and turreted Victorian homes. Once inside, children immediately sense the intimacy of this library meant just for them. There are programs and special events for babies and toddlers, two- and three-year-olds and preschoolers. Adults can borrow special Grandparents Kits with books, toys, and media centered on a particular theme to have on hand for visiting youngsters.

www.montgomerycountymd.gov/library

240-773-9570

10237 Carroll Place, Kensington, MD
Capital Beltway (I-495) to Connecticut Avenue north exit, toward Kensington. Turn right onto Howard Avenue. Go three blocks past all the antique shops to the stop sign. The road bears right and becomes Montgomery Avenue, immediately after Kensington Parkway forks off to the left. Continue one more block to Carroll Place. Noyes Library is straight ahead, a small beige house at the intersection of Carroll Place and Montgomery Avenue. Limited on-street parking.

Tuesday, Thursday, and Saturday, 9–5.

Note: the library is not accessible to strollers or wheelchairs.

Appropriate for preschool-age children.

Take Note

Story Times and Summer Readings

Libraries offer far more than books—there are story times for babies and toddlers, preschoolers and older children, as well as movies, science programs, crafts and puppet shows. Most bookstores and some toy stores also offer excellent story times. We love that these rousing renditions of favorite books are generally free.

Many museums offer great story times too. One of our favorites is the monthly program at the Kreeger Museum in northwest Washington, where you and your child ages 3 to 5 can listen to a story while gazing at paintings by Monet, Miro or Renoir, then head downstairs for an art project, for $5.

Summer reading programs at your public library provide reading encouragement to young children through teens (and sometimes adults) along with literature and arts programs during the summer months.

National Book Festival

The National Book Festival, held on the National Mall each September, is a free event offering readings and book signings by well-known writers for children, teens and adults. (See www.loc.gov/bookfest.)

Olsson's Books and Records

Olsson's is the oldest independent book and music store in the Washington area. The Alexandria store has a good selection of children's books, as well as adult reading and music.

www.olssons.com

703-684-0077

106 S. Union Street, Alexandria, VA
One block from King Street. Other locations throughout the area.

Politics and Prose

The superb children's department of this nationally known, independent, community-centered bookstore sprouted from the Cheshire Cat Children's Bookstore, which was founded by former librarians and teachers. The staff is wonderfully friendly and helpful; their knowledge of children's books and literature is formidable. The store is home to an extensive selection of paperback and hardback books for and about children and teens, along with book-related toys and media and some foreign language children's books. Politics and Prose features frequent author talks and story hours.

www.politics-prose.com

202-364-1919

5015 Connecticut Avenue, NW, Washington, DC
At the intersection with Nebraska Avenue, N.W.

Open 9 a.m.–10 p.m., Monday–Saturday; 10 a.m.–8 p.m., Sunday.

Metrorail Red line (Van Ness). Walk 1 mile north on Connecticut Avenue.

Events are announced on the store's website, and in email and print newsletters. Staff experts write reviews of new children's books for the newsletter; members enjoy discounts on featured titles (and others).

Sullivan's Toy Store

This store has packed a lot of toys in a small space and offers personal service to find appropriate items. There is a selection of books and art supplies, along with dress-up clothes, party items, games and classic toys. The book section features boardbooks, picturebooks, activity and travel books and math and reading workbooks, and appeals primarily to very young children. The same family has owned Sullivan's since it was founded. It was also the first store to carry *Going Places With Children in Washington, DC,* in 1958.

202-362-1343

3412 Wisconsin Avenue, NW, Washington, DC
A few blocks north of the National Cathedral.

Monday, Tuesday and Saturday, 10–6, Wednesday, Thursday and Friday, 10–7; Sunday, 12–5.

Strollers are permitted, but the aisles are quite narrow

Toy Kingdom

Just the right size for a toy store: large enough to have an excellent and well-chosen selection of toys, cards, books and games, and small enough to feel welcoming and friendly. The staff is approachable and helpful.

301-251-0220

36 Maryland Avenue, Rockville MD
Capital Beltway (I-495) to I-270 North to Falls Road exit. Bear right onto Maryland Avenue and continue on to the Rockville Town Plaza. On-street and garage parking.

Metrorail Red line (Rockville).

Monday–Saturday, 10–8; Sunday, 12–5.

Treetop Kids

These stores around the Washington area offer high-quality toys and good selections of favorite books and media. Knowledgeable sales personnel are able and willing to make appropriate suggestions for any age child.

www.treetopkids.com

301-299-8300 (Cabin John)**; 301-897-4940** (Bethesda)

11325 Seven Locks Road, Potomac, MD
Capital Beltway (I-495) to I-270 north to Montrose Road west. Left on Seven Locks to Cabin John Mall.

102019 Old Georgetown Road, Bethesda, MD
Capital Beltway (I-495) to the Old Georgetown Road exit toward Rockville; one mile on the right to the Wildwood Shopping center.

Special activities include guest appearances by storybook favorites and children's book authors.

SPECTATORS

Baltimore Orioles

Glorious structure, good food, spectacular views and, of course, America's pastime—Oriole Park at Camden Yards is nothing like the stadiums of yesteryear. A fun family outing, sure to inspire enthusiasm from the first-time or veteran fan. While you're there, visit the Babe Ruth Museum (see p. 299).

www.theorioles.com

888-848-BIRD(2473) or 410-547-6113 (tour office)

Oriole Park at Camden Yards, 333 West Camden Street, Baltimore, MD
I-95 north to Baltimore; follow the signs to Camden Yards.

*Games generally Saturday and weekdays, 7:05 p.m.;
Sunday, 1:35 p.m.*

*Ticket prices range from $8 for standing room to $65
for field or club boxes. Most tickets cost $15–$30.*

*MARC trains run from Union Station to Camden Yards,
800-325-RAIL.*

*Daily tours available during baseball season. Tours
last approximately 90 minutes and cover all areas of
the ballpark, including the Orioles dugout. Call for
times, 410-547-6234.*

*Security: No large bags or backpacks; park is monitored by security
guards and cameras.*

Take Note

*Kids 14 and under can join the
Orioles Dugout Club. For $17
per season, they get one ticket
to each of 10 Orioles games,
a club hat and lunch box.
Members' families can buy
tickets to club games for $6.*

Bowie Baysox

This Class AA affiliate of the Baltimore Orioles plays approximately 70 games per year. Seeing the Baysox play is a chance to watch professional baseball inexpensively and comfortably. The fireworks on special occasions are said to be "better than the Fourth of July." Mascot "Louie" is always on hand. There is a kids' play area for additional fun, as well as group picnic areas.

www.baysox.com

301-805-6000

4101 N.E. Crain Highway, Bowie, MD
Capital Beltway (I-495) to Rt. 50 east toward Annapolis; follow Rt. 301 south to left at second traffic light; follow the signs to Prince George's Stadium.

Game times vary, but generally: April–September, Monday–Saturday, 7:05 p.m.; Sunday, 2:05 p.m. or 6:05 p.m.

General admission: adults, $9; senior citizens, active military and children 6–12, $6; children 5 and under, free; reserved seats, $9–$14.

Security: Local park police check bags at main gate.

Cal Ripken, Sr. Collegiate Baseball League and Clark Griffith Collegiate Baseball League

Enjoy a wooden bat baseball game at one of the area's best fields for a family summer night at the ball game. Both the Cal Ripken, Sr. League teams and the Clark Griffith League teams present promising college players, many from our area. The ballparks feature concessions, raffles, trivia contests, special activities for children, and best of all, that great hometown feeling on game nights.

www.ripkensrcollegebaseball.org; www.clarkgriffithbaseball.org

410-588-9900; 703-BSEBALL/703-273-2255

Games in June and July, 5–7 nights each week.

Adults, $5–10; children under 5 or in baseball uniforms, free.

Bethesda Big Train

www.bigtrain.org

301-983-1006

Shirley Povich Field, 10600 Westlake Drive, Bethesda, MD

Fairfax Nationals

www.fairfaxnationals.com

Nellis Stadium at Panther Field, 10675 Fairfax Blvd, Fairfax, VA

Herndon Braves

www.herndonbraves.com

Herndon High School Stadium, 700 Bennett Street, Herndon, VA

Rockville Express

www.rockvilleexpress.org

301-340-1697

Knights Field, Montgomery College, 51 MannakeeStreet, Rockville, MD

Silver Spring–Takoma Thunderbolts

www.tbolts.org

301-270-0598

Montgomery Blair High School Stadium, 51 East University Blvd, Silver Spring, MD

M DC United

DC United has thrilled soccer fans in the nation's capital since the birth of Major League Soccer in 1996, earning domestic and international honors. The team plays at the 56,000 seat RFK Stadium.

www.dcunited.com

202-587-5000

RFK Memorial Stadium, 2400 East CapitolStreet, SE, Washington, DC Capital Beltway (I-495) to Baltimore-Washington Parkway (Rt. 295). Exit onto East Capitol Street.

Metrorail Blue or Orange line (Stadium-Armory)

Frederick Keys

The Frederick Keys baseball team is the Carolina League Class A affiliate of the Baltimore Orioles. It is considered a high-quality farm team in the Carolina League. The Keys play 70 home games a season, so you have a good chance of finding a game scheduled when you are planning to visit Frederick.

www.frederickkeys.com

301-662-0013

Harry Grove Stadium, 21 Stadium Drive, Frederick, MD
Capital Beltway (I-495) to I-270 north to I-70 Baltimore/Hagerstown. I-70 east toward Baltimore to Exit 54, then a right on Market Street, left onto Stadium Drive.

Open spring and summer.

General admission: adults, $8; children age 3–12, $5; children age 2 and under, free. Box seats, $11. Little Leaguers in uniform, free on weekdays. Call for information on group rates.

Fireworks shows, Junior Keys Club, and the team mascot, Keyote.

Potomac Nationals

A Minor League baseball club, the Potomac Nationals are the Carolina League Class A affiliate of the Washington Nationals.

www.potomacnationals.com

703-590-2311

G. Richard Pfitzner Stadium, 7 County Complex Court, Woodbridge, VA

Tickets, $6–$12.

 ## Washington Capitals

Known to fans as "The Caps," this NHL hockey team thrills fans at the Verizon Center in the heart of downtown DC.

www.washingtoncaps.com

202-266-2200 (executive offices); **202-397-SEAT** (tickets)

Verizon Center, 601 F Street, NW, Washington, DC.

Metrorail Red/Yellow/Green lines (Gallery Place/Chinatown)

Washington Freedom

Professional women's soccer returns to the DC area with the re-launch of the pro league in 2008. The Washington Freedom is considered one of the world's premiere soccer clubs and offers camps and clinics throughout the region, in addition to their own games played at the Maryland SoccerPlex.

www.washingtonfreedom.com/

443-259-0020

Maryland SoccerPlex, Germantown, MD
Capital Beltway (I-495) to I-270 north to exit 15B (Rt. 118 south) toward Germantown. Continue on Rt. 118 south for 2.8 miles; right on Richter Farm Road. Go 1 mile to Schaeffer Road (4-way stop) and turn left. Park entrance, 18031 Central Park Circle, is 0.3 miles on the right.

M Washington Nationals

Major league baseball returned to Washington when the former Montreal Expos relocated and took on the Nationals moniker. The Nationals actually took their name from *two* former Washington Senators baseball teams known affectionately as the "Nats." The team's 2005 relocation to Washington was the first in Major League Baseball since 1972, when the second Washington Senators moved to Texas, becoming the Rangers.

The Nationals played their first three seasons in a temporary home at RFK Stadium. The 2008 season inaugurates a state-of-the-art ballpark in Southeast Washington, along the Anacostia River, with great views of the Capitol and the Washington Monument.

Take Note

Tickets for the Washington Redskins are sold on a seasonal basis only; no individual game tickets are available through the team itself. For more information, see www.redskins.com.

www.nationals.mlb.com

202-675-NATS

Nationals Park, South Capitol Street and Potomac Avenue, SE, Washington, DC

Games generally weekdays and Saturdays, 7:05 p.m.; Sundays, 1:35 p.m.

Tickets prices for single tickets range from $5 to $55.

Metrorail Green line (Navy Yard).

Plan on a short wait to get back on the Metro after the game.

M Washington Wizards

Once the Baltimore Bullets, then the Washington Bullets, this NBA team settled into its current name and home in downtown Washington in 1997. The team's roster has included three players named to the list of the 50 Greatest in NBA History—Earl Monroe, Wes Unseld and Elvin Hayes.

www.nba.com/wizards

202-661-5000

Verizon Center, 601 F Street, NW, Washington, DC

Metrorail Red, Yellow, or Green line (Gallery Place/Chinatown)

CANOEING, KAYAKING AND SAILING

Belle Haven Marina

Belle Haven Marina is owned by the National Park Service; the Mariner Sailing School there is owned and operated by sailors. The rental fleet includes 19-foot Flying Scots, 14-foot Sunfish, kayaks, rowboats and canoes, as well as a 34-foot sloop with a captain. The sailing school offers classes for adults and children ages 8 and up. Classes are offered April through October, weather permitting.

www.saildc.com

703-768-0018

1201 Belle Haven Road, Alexandria, VA
Capital Beltway (I-495) to George Washington Parkway south past Reagan National Airport and through Old Town Alexandria. (The parkway becomes Washington Street, and then again becomes GW Parkway). About one mile past Old Town, turn left into Belle Haven Marina.

Weekdays, 8:30–8 or until sunset, whichever comes first. Weekends, 8:30–6.

The marina sells only water, soda and juices in vending machines; pack your own lunch to enjoy at the picnic tables in the surrounding park.

Fletcher's Boathouse

Fletcher's Boathouse has been in operation since the mid-1800s. Situated close to Georgetown, this landmark offers the perfect embarkation point from which to rent boats, canoes and bicycles to use on the Potomac, the canal, and the tow path. You also can purchase fishing licenses, bait, tackle and cane poles to fish from the shoreline or from the boats. Even though summer is the best time for many of the water activities, a walk in the woods in the wintertime from this point in the C&O National Park is memorable.

www.fletcherscove.com

202-244-0461

4940 Canal Road, NW, Washington, DC
Capital Beltway (I-495) to Glen Echo exit (Clara Barton Parkway)
toward Washington; the Clara Barton Parkway becomes Canal Road
at Chain Bridge in Washington. Fletcher's is near the intersection of
Canal and Reservoir Roads.

*Canoes and kayaks $15/hour, $35/day; rowboats $14/hour, $28/day;
bicycles $6/hour, $25/day; fishing license $10 for DC residents and $13
for non-residents.*

*Hours vary with the seasons and conditions; usually open March–
November, dawn–dusk.*

Limited wheelchair access.

Biking, boating, canoe and kayak rentals.

Thompson Boat Center

Enjoy a day on or along the Potomac River. Bicycle rentals include
all-terrains and cruisers. Boat rentals include: kayaks (both single and
doubles); canoes (can hold up to two people); rowing shells (single
recreational, single racing, and double racing); and sailboats (Sunfish).

www.thompsonboatcenter.com

202-333-9543

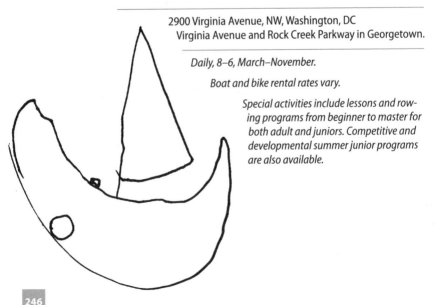

2900 Virginia Avenue, NW, Washington, DC
Virginia Avenue and Rock Creek Parkway in Georgetown.

Daily, 8–6, March–November.

Boat and bike rental rates vary.

*Special activities include lessons and row-
ing programs from beginner to master for
both adult and juniors. Competitive and
developmental summer junior programs
are also available.*

✕ Washington Sailing Marina

This National Park Service concession is the place to rent a Sunfish or Flying Scot for a few hours for a sail around the lagoon or to see Old Town Alexandria or Haines Point from the water. The Marina is home to several sailing clubs, and offers lessons and camps for all levels.

www.washingtonsailingmarina.com

703-548-9027

1 Marina Drive at Dangerfield Island, George Washington Memorial Parkway, Alexandria, VA
On the George Washington Memorial Parkway, one mile south of Reagan National Airport.

Sailboat rentals, spring through mid-October, 11–5. Last boats out at 4. Boat rentals by reservation only and require certification from a recognized sailing school or a written test at the marina.

Bike rentals year-round. Mount Vernon is 12 miles south along the Mount Vernon Trail. A 6-mile ride north will take you to the Washington Monument.

EQUESTRIAN

Meadowbrook Stables

The horseback riding facility at Meadowbrook Stables offers trail rides as well as a full lesson program for ages six and older, and is home to many "A"-rated horse shows.

www.meadowbrookstables.com

301-589-9026

8200 Meadowbrook Lane, Chevy Chase, MD
Capital Beltway (I-495) to Connecticut Avenue south to East-West Highway; turn left on Meadowbrook Lane; entrance to the stables is on the right.

Closed Monday. Office hours Tuesday–Friday, 10–7; Saturday–Sunday 8:30–3. Call for schedule and fees.

Potomac Horse Center

This nationally known riding school has three indoor arenas, two outdoor rings, and extensive trails, and offers lessons and a therapeutic riding program for children and adults of all levels. The center also offers horse boarding.

www.potomachorse.com

301-208-0200

14211 Quince Orchard Road, Gaithersburg, MD
Capital Beltway (I-495) to I-270 north; Exit 6B (Rt. 28, west); follow it for about two and a half miles; turn left on Muddy Branch Road; proceed two miles and turn right on Quince Orchard Road.

Monday–Friday, 9–9; Saturday–Sunday, 9–5.

Hiking.

Special activities include a ten-week summer camp program, horse shows and clinics.

Woodland Horse Center

Woodland Horse Center is has a lighted outdoor ring, dressage ring and an indoor ring as well as riding fields. Woodland offers a complete program of equestrian activities, including grooming and working student programs, boarding, horse sales and a fully equipped Tack Shop. While lessons are mainly English balance seat, Western lessons are available on a limited basis for adults only.

www.woodlandhorse.com

301-421-9156

16301 New Hampshire Avenue, Silver Spring, MD
Capital Beltway (I-495) to New Hampshire Avenue exit north. Continue 8 miles; the stables are just north of Spencerville Road (Rt. 198).

Classes for students 5 and up, including adults.

Woodland offers a free introductory lesson every Sunday at 1 (except on holidays), for about 90 minutes.

Rock Creek Park Horse Center

See beautiful Rock Creek Park by horseback. This horse center is DC's only full-service equestrian facility. Weekend and midweek trail rides must be reserved in advance. All riders must be at least 12 years old and must wear a helmet, which will be provided. Riding lessons for all levels, from beginner through basic dressage, as well as summer day camp, are offered for children eight years and older.

www.rockcreekhorsecenter.com

202-362-0118

5100 Glover Road, NW, Washington, DC
Located off Military Road between Connecticut Avenue and 16th Street (follow brown Park Service signs).

Tuesday–Friday, noon–6; Saturday–Sunday, 9–5. Closed Mondays and Thanksgiving, December 25 and January 1.

Call ahead for availability and reservations.

GOLF AND MINIATURE GOLF

Miniature golf courses that share facilities with pools are listed in the Swimming and Splashing section of this chapter (see p. 264). See Bohrer Park and South Germantown Recreational Park.

Brambleton Regional Park

Brambleton Regional Park is a championship 18-hole par-72 golf course, with a variety of challenging holes in the scenic woods and water holes, large bunkers, and plush putting greens. Discounted play after 2 p.m.

www.nvrpa.org

703-327-3403

Brambleton Regional Park Golf Course, 42180 Ryan Road, Ashburn VA Capital Beltway (I-495) to Rt. 7 west toward Leesburg; turn right on Belmont Ridge Road (Rt. 659); drive seven miles and turn right on Ryan Road (Rt. 772); continue for 1 mile to the entrance on the right.

Open, weather-permitting, all year long.

Fees vary by season, call for specifics.

Discounted play after 2 p.m.

Advance tee reservations: non-subscribers, two days; associate subscribers, 7 days; full subscribers, 14 days.

Tee reservations online (www.teetimes.com).

Tournaments or groups can be scheduled with a minimum of 24 players Monday through Wednesday.

Driving range, professional instruction and pro shop.

Mid Atlantic Golf Center

This lovely miniature golf center features waterfalls, bridges, trees and rocks, loop-the-loops, and even hollow logs through which players drive their golf balls. There is also a driving range and a pro shop.

301-924-8444

3701 Norbeck Road, Silver Spring, MD
Capital Beltway (I-495) to the Connecticut Avenue exit. Follow Connecticut Avenue north several miles, until it intersects with Georgia Avenue. (Rt. 97). Turn left (north) on Georgia. Right (east) on Norbeck Road (Rt. 28). Golf center is on the left.

Open Sunday–Thursday 10–10; Friday and Saturday 9 a.m.–10 p.m.

Miniature golf: adults, $6; children under 12, $4.

Driving range: $10 large bucket of balls, $7 regular bucket.

Rocky Gorge 4 Seasons Golf Fairway

The batting range boasts a 300-foot Home-Run Fence and sheltered cages for baseball or slow pitch softball. The 19-hole miniature golf range includes one of the world's longest miniature golf holes. The golf driving range features sheltered tees and a lighted putting green.

> **Take Note**
>
> The Rocky Gorge website offers printable coupons for the batting range and miniature golf.

www.rockygorgegolf.com

301-725-0888-golf; 301-725-8947-batting cages

Rt. 29 and Old Columbia Road Laurel, MD
Capital Beltway (I-495) to US 29 north 2.5 miles past Burtonsville, to entrance on the right before Rt. 216.

Open in all weather, seven days a week, year round.

Driving range; miniature golf; batting cages; arcade.

Batting cages 10–10. 18 pitches for $1.

Miniature golf 10–10. Play all you want for $4 Monday–Saturday, 10–6, and for $6 Sundays, holidays and after 6 p.m.

TopGolf

With nearly 80 covered and heated golfing bays, parents and children can experience a "near real" golf experience all year round in a fun game center equipped with the latest technology. Using real clubs and special golf balls embedded with computer chips to tee off from a driving bay onto a landscaped outfield with targets, players receive instant feedback from a computer screen in their bay.

www.topgolfusa.com

703-924-2600

6625 South Van Dorn Street, Alexandria, VA
TopGolf is less than 5 minutes outside of the Capital Beltway (I-495) and is across from the shops at Kingstowne Center.

Daily 8 a.m.–11p.m.

Two outdoor miniature golf courses.

Special children's programs.

SKATING, BOARDING AND BLADING

Bowie Skate Park

The park provides 8,000 square feet for skateboard and rollerblade use and offers skating equipment for all skill levels. Equipment includes a 5-foot kicker wedge, Special safety equipment is required.

www.cityofbowie.org/leisure/skatepark.htm

301-262-6200, 301-809-3001 (after 5 p.m. and on weekends)

Gallant Fox Lane at Rt. 197, Bowie, MD

Open Wednesday–Sunday, April–October. Weekends, noon–dusk; week-day hours vary.

Admission to the Skatepark is free, but all skaters are required to obtain a City of Bowie Skatepark User Identification Card to use the facility. This identification card must be obtained at the City Gymnasium, 4300 Northview Drive.

The Skate Park may be closed in the event of rain or extreme heat.

Features: 5' kicker wedge; 2.5' fun box with grind rail; 1.5' low wedge; 3' medium wedge; kinked grind rail; straight grind rail

Helmet, elbow pads and kneepads required at all times.

 ## Cabin John Ice Rink

Cabin John Ice Rink has two large rinks for free-style skating and ice hockey games, and a smaller rink for lessons. This state-of-the-art rink is open year-round and offers a variety of open-skating sessions, as well as private and group lessons.

www.mc-mncppc.org/parks/enterprise/ice/cabin_john

301-365-2246, 301-365-0585 (recording)

10610 Westlake Drive, Rockville, MD
Capital Beltway (I-495) to I-270 north, to the Old Georgetown Road exit. Head north on Old Georgetown, to a left on Tuckerman Lane; left on Westlake Drive. Rink is on the right.

$3.50–$6. Skate rental is $3. Discount books are available.

Family sessions, which are restricted to children under 12 accompanied by an adult, are offered on Sundays.

Party room.

 ## Fairfax Ice Arena

Fairfax Ice Arena offers year-round public skating and lessons for children age 4 and older and adults. The rink also offers adult hockey leagues, summer camp programs and arcade games.

www.fairfaxicearena.com

703-323-1131, 703-323-1132

3779 Pickett Road, Fairfax, VA
Capital Beltway (I-495) to Little River Turnpike exit, Rt. 236 west); at the eighth traffic light at Pickett Road, turn right; ice rink is on the right after passing three traffic lights.

Hours for public sessions vary season to season.

Weekday admission: Adults, $6.75; children 12 and under, $6.25; children 5 and under, $5.25; skate rental, $2.50 (hockey skates, $3.50). Weekend and holiday sessions are slightly higher. Discount cards available.

Wheelchair ramp on the side of the building.

 ## Franconia Roller Rink

Visit this family-oriented rink for roller skating fun. Special sessions are reserved for children and families, as well as adults and teens.

703-971-3334

5508 Franconia Road, Alexandria, VA
Capital Beltway (I-495) to Franconia/Van Dorn Street exit; at light, bear right; go to fourth light (half a mile) and turn left on Franconia Road; go one-quarter mile; at Crown station, turn left to rink.

Open Friday, 7–11 p.m.; Saturday, 10–12 and 1–4; Sunday, 1–7; all other evenings, 7–10.

Admission, $3.50–$6; skate rental, $1.65.

Toe-stops must be light colored.

Gardens Ice House

The Gardens is an impressive year-round skating facility for hockey, figure skating, speed skating, in-line skating, ice dancing, and even indoor soccer and curling. The facilities include an Olympic size rink and two National Hockey League size rinks with spectator seating.

www.thegardensicehouse.com

301-953-0100

13800 Old Gunpowder Road, Laurel, MD
Capital Beltway (I-495) to I-95 North toward Baltimore. First exit to Powder Mill Road East (Rt. 212). Turn left on Old Gunpowder Road. (first left). The rink is about 2 miles down the road on the left side.

Public skating Monday–Friday, 11:30–1:20; Friday 8 p.m.–10 p.m.; Saturday–Sunday, 1–3.

$5 Weekdays; $6 weekends; $3.50 skate rental.

Game room, fitness club, locker rooms.

 Herbert W. Wells Ice Rink

Open for ice skating from October through March, this rink is used for roller skating and/or street hockey during the summer. Rental skates are available. Call for information about general skating sessions, lessons, hockey, and fees.

www.pgparks.com/places/sportsfac/icerinks.html

301-277-3717 (general inquiries)**; TTY 301-454-1493**

5211 Paint Branch Parkway (formerly Calvert Road), College Park, MD
Capital Beltway (I-495), toward College Park, to exit 23 south, Kenilworth Avenue (Rt. 201). Proceed for 1.5 miles and turn right onto Paint Branch Parkway. Turn left into the parking lot (across from the 94th Aero squadron).

Metrorail Green line (College Park)

Mount Vernon Ice Arena

Fairfax County's only publicly-owned indoor ice arena is designed for year-round use. It offers skating and hockey lessons for all ages and abilities in an NHL-sized rink, as well as pick-up hockey sessions. Home rink of the Northern Virginia Ice Dogs Youth Hockey Club.

www.fairfaxcounty.gov/parks/rec/mvrec.htm

703-768-3224

2017 Belle View Boulevard, Alexandria, VA

Olney Manor Skate Park

The 90- by 160-foot Skate Park accommodates skaters of all skill levels. Skateboarders can test their skills on the Hubba Ledge, the Steps with Handrail, the Fun Box with Flat Rail, the Pyramid Ledge and in the large Bowl.

www.montgomerycountymd.gov/content/rec/sports/skatepark/olneyskate.asp

240-777-4979

16605 Georgia Avenue, Olney, MD
The Skate Park is located at Olney Manor Regional Park, adjacent to the Olney Indoor Swim Center.

Open March–November (weather permitting). The Skate Park will be closed if the temperature and/or windchill is below 35 degrees.

Spring hours: Monday–Friday, 3 p.m.–dusk; Saturday, noon–dusk; Sunday, 11 a.m.–noon (6–10 year olds), noon–dusk (all ages).

Yearly membership: residents, $35; non-residents, $45; guest pass, $5.

Daily equipment rental fees: knee pads, $1; elbow pads, $1; helmet, $2.

Skaters must be at least 6 years old. All skaters are required to wear a helmet. Check the website for additional Skate Park rules, the user waiver form and seasonal schedule.

Reston Ice Skating Pavilion

This beautiful outdoor rink in the middle of Reston Town Center is surrounded by restaurants, shops and a movie theater. Rentals include children's double-bladed skates and helmets.

www.restontowncenter.com

703-709-6300

1818 Discovery Lane, Reston, VA
Capital Beltway (I-495) to the Dulles Toll Road to Reston Parkway exit; go two blocks and turn left on Bluemont Way.

Daily, mid-November–mid-March: Monday and Thursday, 11–7; Tuesday and Wednesday, 11–9; Friday and Saturday, 11–11.

Adults, $5.75; children age 12 and under, $4.75; skate rental, $2.50.

Rockville Ice Arena

Formerly ARC IceSports, this state-of-the-art indoor facility is centrally located in Montgomery County. In addition to two NHL-sized rinks, there is a skate shop, Spike's Diner, an electronic game arcade and several party rooms for celebrations. Skating, of course, is the heart of it all, and there are lessons for every age and skill level in figure skating and hockey. Group skating lessons are offered beginning at age 3.

For the more advanced, there is a comprehensive figure skating training program featuring training sessions, workshops and clinics with National and Olympic coaches. There is plenty of hockey here too, with hockey initiation programs and Montgomery Youth Hockey Association, as well as Adult and Junior leagues.

www.rockvilleicearena.com

301-294-8101, 301-315-5650

50 Southlawn Court, Rockville, MD
Rt. 355 north; turn right on 1st Street, which becomes Rt. 28 (Norbeck Road); turn left on E. Gude Drive; turn right on Southlawn Lane and then right on Southlawn Court. Parking available.

Hours vary daily.

$6 weekdays; $7.50 weekends; $2.50 skate rental. Group rates available.

Rockville Roller Skating Center

Whether you're an in-line or traditional quad skater, you'll appreciate the real maple wood skate floor of this large family-oriented rink which has been operating for some 30 years.

301-340-7767

1632 E. Gude Drive, Rockville, MD
Located two blocks off Norbeck Road (Rt. 28 east). Capital Beltway (I-495) to I-270 north to Montrose Road east, forking left toward Tower Oaks Boulevard Turn left at the light onto Tower Oaks Blvd; turn right onto Wooton Parkway, which becomes 1st Street, which becomes MD 28 east. MD 28 east becomes Norbeck Road after approximately 0.25 miles. Turn left onto East Gude Drive.

Open Saturday and Sunday, as well as Montgomery County school holidays, 1–4; evening skating on Friday–Sunday nights; Tuesday evening session for adults only, 7–10; and Saturday mornings sessions for young children, 10–noon. Private sessions available for groups or fundraisers, Monday–Wednesday.

Afternoons, $7.50; evenings, $8.25; Saturday mornings, $6.05. Skate rental, $1.65.

Rockville Skate Park at Welsh Park

This 10,300–square-foot skating arena is a great place for in-line skaters, skateboarders and free style bikers.

www.rockvillemd.gov/parks-facilities/skatepark.htm

240-876-2655 (office)**; 240-314-8765 (**Information/conditions)

355 Martins Lane (at Mannakee Street), Rockville, MD
Capital Beltway (I-495) to I-270 north to Rt. 28 (West Montgomery Avenue) toward Rockville. Left onto Mannakee Road. Continue around the traffic circle on Mannakee Road. Right onto Martins Lane. Park is on the right.

Sculpture Garden Ice-Skating Rink

View fascinating art sculptures as you ice skate outdoors in the garden across from the National Gallery of Art. The skating rink is open mid-November through mid-March, weather permitting; in warmer weather, it becomes a fountain.

www.nga.gov/ginfo/skating/shtm

Located at the National Gallery of Art Sculpture Garden, 7th Street and Constitution Avenue, NW, Washington, DC

Monday–Thursday 10–9; Friday and Saturday 10 a.m. to 11 p.m.; Sunday 11–9.

Adults $7; children and seniors $6; skate rentals $3.

Metrorail Red line (Gallery Place-Chinatown) or Yellow or Green line (Archives-Navy Memorial)

Skate-N-Fun Zone

Skate-N-Fun offers in-line and roller-skating, as well as "Laser Storm," a laser tag game, a soft-play area, rock climbing wall and a video arcade. Skating lessons and private parties also are available.

www.skatenfunzone.com

703-361-7465, 800-203-4605

7878 Sudley Road, Manassas, VA
Capital Beltway (I-495) to I-66 west to Exit 47A (Rt. 234 south); go straight through four traffic lights to Skate-N-Fun on the right on Sudley Road.

Hours and admission prices vary.

Playground.

Tucker Road Ice Rink

The Tucker Road Ice Rink is open year round for ice skating. The facility includes the rink, a warming room, party room and spectator viewing room. Rental skates are available for all general skating sessions. Ice skating lessons, hockey clinics, day camps and facility rental are available.

www.pgparks.com/places/sportsfac/icerinks.html

301-265-1525

1770 Tucker Road, Fort Washington, MD
Between Palmer and St. Barnabas Roads

 ### Wheaton Ice Arena

This year-round NHL-sized rink offers sessions for all skating abilities, as well as lessons.

www.wheatonicearena.com

301-649-2250 recording; 301-649-3640

11717 Orebaugh Avenue, Wheaton, MD
Capital Beltway (I-495) to Georgia Avenue north. Turn right on Arcola Avenue, then left on Orebaugh Avenue.

Admission ranges from $3.50–$6 depending on age and time of day. Skate rental, $3. Discount books available.

Teen skate nights monthly during the school year.

SNOWBOARDING AND SKIING

Liberty Mountain Resort

Take a day trip to the slopes at Ski Liberty, which offers many instructional choices for children and adults, from all-day children's ski camps and childcare, to skiing, to snowboarding and snow tubing. The resort offers 16 trails, 9 lifts, and a 620-foot vertical drop, as well as night skiing seven days a week.

www.skiliberty.com

717-642-8282

78 Country Club Drive, Carroll Valley, PA
Capital Beltway (I-495) to I-270 north to Frederick. Rt. 15 north to Emmitsburg; exit left onto South Seton Avenue (blinking light near Getty station). At light, left onto Rt. 140 west; follow it to Pennsylvania Rt. 116 east. Right onto Rt. 116 east; Liberty Mountain is three miles on right. Liberty is about 60–90 minutes from the Beltway.

Open non-holiday weekdays, 9 a.m.–10 p.m.; weekends and holidays, 8 a.m.–10 p.m.

Rates for rentals and lift tickets vary.

> **Take Note**
>
> For a less expensive option, try snow tubing at the resort's separate "Boulder Ridge" area (with separate parking). Kids five and over can ride the comfortable carpet lift to the top of the main tubing runs; patrons can hook two or more tubes together, meaning smaller kids can be connected to a grown-up's tube. There's a separate "kiddie tubing area" for ages four and under. Bring a Thermos of hot chocolate so you can avoid the lines in the lodge.

Roundtop

Roundtop is primarily a ski and snowboard resort with 16 trails, 10 lifts, and a 600-foot vertical drop. Snow tubing also is popular. In the summer, Roundtop offers three paintball fields and ropes courses. Rental equipment is available for all activities.

www.skiroundtop.com

717-432-9631

925 Roundtop Road, Lewisberry, PA
Capital Beltway (I-495) to I-270 north to Frederick. Rt. 15 north to Dillsburg, PA. Turn right at the first light (Harrisburg Street). At top of hill, turn right. At next light, turn left onto Rt. 177. Turn left onto Pineforest Road to left on Roundtop Road.

Open in winter for skiing and snowboarding, 9 a.m.–10 p.m.; for tubing, 10–10. In the summer, paintball is open 9–9.

Admission varies; group rates available.

Whitetail Resort

The Whitetail Resort features skiing, snowboarding and snow tubing on 108 acres of terrain with 17 trails, 6 lifts and a 935-foot vertical drop. Whitetail offers a variety of ski school programs for children as well as childcare and ski camp packages. In spring, summer and fall, Whitetail offers more than 30 miles of hiking trails, scenic chairlift rides, fly-fishing and outdoor skills programs. There is also a summer Junior Adventure Camp program for children ages 12–16.

www.skiwhitetail.com

717-328-9400

13805 Blair Valley Road, Mercersburg, PA
Capital Beltway (I-495) to I-270 north to I-70 west to Exit 18, Clear Spring. Turn right at the end of the exit; go through the traffic light; at the island, turn right onto Broadfording Road. Go one-half mile to left on Blairs Valley Road. Whitetail is about 1.5 hours from Washington.

Daily in the winter for skiing, 8:30 a.m.–10 p.m. (Opens at noon December 25.)

Snow tubing, 4–10, Monday–Thursday, and 10–10 Friday–Sunday and holidays. There is a shuttle that will take you to the tubing area. Wear warm boots; ski boots are not allowed on the tubes.

Ski rental, lift ticket, and lesson prices vary.

Be sure to arrive early to reserve a snowboard.

Free ski and snowboard checking available.

Camping, fishing, hiking.

Wisp at Deep Creek Mountain Resort

Wisp is near Deep Creek Lake, and offers 22 ski trails covering 100 acres of terrain. Children's programs for ages 3–14 are available for half- and full-days, by advance reservations.

The year-round resort includes an 18-hole championship golf course, driving range, and Outdoor Adventures with a 20,000 square foot paved and wood skate park, paintball, scenic chairlift rides, mountain boarding, mountain biking, kayaking and a spa. An artificial "ski slide" lets patrons "ski" even in the summer.

A new "Mountain Coaster," a hybrid of an alpine slide and a roller coaster, lets visitors zip down, in, out and through the forest. It operates year-round. A new 1,700-foot manmade white-water course is open to participants age seven and up.

Club Wisp Kids' Night Out lets kids enjoy dinner and games while parents have a night out. Advance reservations required.

---

www.skiwisp.com

301-387-4911

---

296 Marsh Hill Road, McHenry, MD
I-270 to Frederick, MD; then I-70 West to Handcock, MD to I-68 West to Cumberland. Exit 14A to U.S. Rt. 219 South to McHenry. Follow signs one mile to Wisp. Wisp is about 180 miles from Washington.

SWIMMING AND SPLASHING

Washingtonians love their pools, and the region is home to numerous private community pools. Most public pools in the region now boast water slides, splash buckets, or other interactive features, blurring the line between "pool" and "water park." A sampling is listed below.

Bohrer Park Water Park at Summit Hall Farm

This park features an outdoor pool with a double water slide that is 250 feet long, a raindrop water umbrella, and a zero-depth entry. For children under five, the splash pool features a frog slide and a crab spray. The miniature golf course in a natural park setting has a large waterfall and garden pond, which empty into streams that flow through the course. The park also has three putting greens, a children's playground, and a skate park. The Activity Center at the park features two gymnasiums, three multi-purpose rooms and a fitness center.

www.gaithersburgmd.gov

301-258-6350, 301-258-6445 (pool)**; 301-258-6350** (activity center)

506 South Frederick Avenue, Gaithersburg, MD
Capital Beltway (I-495) to I-270 north; exit at Shady Grove Road; turn right on Shady Grove Road to left turn on Frederick Avenue (Rt. 355) for approximately 1.5 miles. The Farm Park is on the left on Education Boulevard.

Park offices open Monday–Friday, 8–5. Pool open daily in summer, 11–8.

Non-resident daily admission to the water park: Adults $6.75, children $5, seniors $5.50. Putt-n-pool pass $8.50.

Miniature golf open daily in the summer, 11–11. $5 per game for non-Gaithersburg residents, $4 for seniors, $7 for unlimited play.

Take Note
Kids love the small playground behind the concessions area at the water park, where they can run and climb during adult swim. The pool does not have a deep end or diving area.

Claude Moore Recreation Center

Loudon County's newest Recreation Center features a 50-meter indoor competition pool with diving boards, a leisure pool with water slide, a state-of-the-art rock climbing wall and indoor track aerobics studio.

www.co.loudoun.va.us/prcs/claudemoorerec/index.htm

571-258-3600

46105 Loudoun Park Lane, Sterling, VA

Monday–Friday, 5:30 a.m.–10 p.m., Saturday–Sunday, 8–8. (Call ahead for availability of the leisure pool and rock wall, as hours vary.) Closed Memorial Day, Labor Day, Thanksgiving, December 25 and January 1.

Admission: residents, $5.50; non-residents, $8.25; youth and seniors, $3.75($5.50 for non-residents). 25-coupon books and annual passes are available.

Downpour at Algonkian Regional Park

Downpour, the water playground at Algonkian Regional Park, is brimming with buckets of summertime water fun. A huge water bucket pours 800 gallons into the play pool every three minutes, drenching everyone in range. The bucket tops an intricate interactive tower in the play pool that invites children to climb, shoot water cannons, slide down one of two slides and activate a variety of water jets. In the main pool, a 20-foot slide tower leads to two slides. Floating polyethylene-foam alligators and snakes, and a shipwreck slide add to the water fun in this free-form pool.

Algonkian Regional Park offers a popular 18-hole champion-ship golf course, a meeting and reception complex, 12 vacation cottages, group and family picnicking, boat launching, fishing, miniature golf and a nature trail. (See Algonkian Regional Park, p. 162, for additional information.)

www.nvrpa.org/downpour.html

703-430-7683, 703-359-4603

47001 Fairway Drive, Sterling, VA
Capital Beltway (I-495) to Rt. 7 west for 15 miles to the Cascades Park-

way north exit. Continue on Cascades Parkway for three miles to the park entrance.

Daily, 11–7, from the last weekend in May through the middle of August, when weekday hours may be limited.

Daily admission: Individuals 48" or taller, $7.50; Individuals 48" or shorter, $6.50; Seniors (60+), $4.50; Children age two or younger, free. Fees are reduced after 3:30 on weekdays. Discount tickets available.

Montgomery County Public Pools

Montgomery County boasts four indoor swimming pools (Germantown, Silver Spring, Rockville and Olney) and seven outdoor pools (Bethesda, Germantown, Silver Spring, Gaithersburg, Poolesville, Wheaton), all of which offer classes for a full range of ages and abilities; swim teams; and recreational swim hours. The pools include one or more of the following features: water slides, mushroom fountains, beach-style entry, and/or tumble buckets.

The indoor pools also feature weight and exercise rooms, saunas, and hydrotherapy pools, all for adults.

General information for county pools is available at www.montgom-erycountymd.gov/rec. For locations, directions, hours of operation, or other information, click on Locations and then click on Montgomery County Aquatic Centers. Locations include:

Germantown Indoor Swim Center

In South Germantown Recreation Park (see p. 269, park entry, for direc-tions). Spectacular indoor facility that includes a competition pool, a recreation pool and a leisure pool with ramp areas.

240-777-6830

18000 Central Park Circle, Boyds, MD

Martin Luther King, Jr. Swim Center

Olympic-sized indoor swimming pool and separate kiddie pool; out-door water park open Memorial Day to Labor Day includes a "lazy river" complete with inner tubes.

301-989-1206

1201 Jackson Road, Silver Spring, MD
Capital Beltway (I-495) to New Hampshire Avenue north; turn right on Jackson Road.

Montgomery Aquatic Center

Indoor pool that features one- and three-meter springboards for div-ers, and an 18-foot diving well, as well as a 233-foot water slide. Call ahead to make sure the water slide is open; due to staffing shortages, it is not always open during published hours.

301-468-4211

5900 Executive Boulevard, Rockville, MD
Rockville Pike (Rt. 355) north to left on Nicholson Lane; turn right on Executive Boulevard. Turn left into the pool complex at traffic light.

Metrorail Red line (White Flint), 10-minute walk.

Olney Indoor Swim Center

301-570-1210

Olney Manor Park, 16601 Georgia Avenue, Olney, MD
Capital Beltway (I-495) to George Avenue north to Olney; swim center is on the right.

Wheaton/Glenmont Outdoor Pool

This outdoor water park features an activity pool with floating alligators to walk over, flume slides, and a leisure pool with fountains, sprays and kiddie slides.

301-929-5460

12601 Dalewood Drive, Wheaton, MD
Wheaton High School, off Randolph Road between Connecticut and Georgia Avenues.

Rockville Municipal Swim Center

The Rockville Swim Center has two indoor and two outdoor pools (one with a water slide and "beach"), a tot pool with fountains, a new "sprayground" and exercise rooms.

www.rockvillemd.gov/swimcenter/index.htm

301-309-3040, schedule and fees, 301-309-3045

355 Martins Lane, Rockville, MD
Capital Beltway (I-495) to I-270 north to Rt. 28 (West Montgomery Avenue) toward Rockville. Left onto Mannakee Road. Continue around the traffic circle on Mannakee Road. Right onto Martins Lane. The swim center is on the right.

Daily; hours vary.

Rockville residents: adults, $5; age 17 and younger, $4. Nonresidents pay $1 more.

Athletic fields are at adjacent park.

Playground; tennis.

Rollingcrest-Chillum Splash Pool

Open year-round, Rollingcrest-Chillum Splash Pool offers aquatics opportunities for people of all ages and swimming abilities. The indoor pool facility includes: a heated, 20-yard lap pool with a drop slide and lily pad walk; a heated family pool with beach grade entry, a tube slide, otter slide, and water play features; a heated whirlpool; a heated children's pool with beach grade entry, water play features and fun slides; a lobby observation area; locker rooms with coin-operated lockers; and a family changing room.

www.pgparks.com/places/sportsfac/swim.html

301-853-9115

6122 Sargent Road, Chillum, MD
Capital Beltway (I-495) to Exit 28 south onto Rt. 650 (New Hampshire Avenue). Left on Rt. 193 (University Blvd). Proceed one mile and turn right onto Riggs Road. Turn left onto Sargent Road. The pool is on the right.

Prince George's County and Montgomery County residents: children, $4; adults, $5. Non-residents: children, $5; adults, $6.

Daily, noon–5; Fridays, noon–9:30.

South Germantown Recreational Park
Splash Playground and Miniature Golf

South Germantown Recreational Park's Central Park features two championship miniature golf courses, and a splash playground with a rain tree, a water tunnel, a tumbling buckets waterfall, a 36' water maze. Elsewhere in the park is an indoor pool (see Montgomery County Public Pools above). The two 18-hole putting courses provide real challenges with water features, sand traps, rough turf and natural obstacles that are part of the unique design. The miniature golf season may extend beyond October, weather permitting. Call for information.

www.mc-mncppc.org/parks/facilities/south_germantown

301-601-3580 (recording)**; 301-601-3581** (golf)**; 301-601-3582** (splash playground)

14501 Schaeffer Road, Boyds, MD
I-270 to exit 15B toward Germantown. Stay on MD Rt. 118 for 3 miles, passing Clopper Road (route 117). Turn right at Richter Farm Road, turn left at the traffic light at Schaeffer Road; follow signs.

Open end of May–early September; hours vary by season.

Splash Playground, $3.50; Miniature Golf, 18 holes, $5 per person. Discount books available.

Lockers, showers, dressing room, vending area.

Splash Down Water Park

Like a day at the beach without the drive, Splash Down Water Park offers 13 acres of fun with five unique water attraction areas, a shallow-entry beach area, water slides for all ages and thrill levels, water raindrops and bubblers, a 770 foot lazy river, special children's area and sand play area.

www.splashdownwaterpark.com

703-361-4451

7500 Ben Lomond Park Drive, Manassas, VA
I-66 west to Rt. 234; proceed on Rt. 234 south for one mile. Turn left on Sudley Manor Drive; after two miles, turn left into park.

Hours vary during season but are generally Sunday–Thursday, 11–7; Friday–Saturday, 11–8.

Over 48" tall, $13.50; under 48" tall, $10.50; ages 2 and under, free; $7 after 3 p.m. Group rates and season passes.

Athletic fields, playgrounds, tennis.

Water Mine Family Swimmin' Hole

This "old west" themed outdoor swimming facility offers more than an acre of water slides and interactive play features. While the main attractions are generally designed for elementary-aged children, there's something here for everyone. There are pint-sized slides and gentle bubblers for toddlers, and everyone can go with the flow in a tube on the lazy Rattlesnake River that circles the facility.

www.fairfaxcounty.gov/parks/watermine

703-471-5415

Lake Fairfax Park, 1400 Lake Fairfax Drive, Reston, VA
Capital Beltway Exit 47A (Leesburg Pike, Rt. 7) west for 6.5 miles. Turn left on Baron Cameron Avenue. (Rt. 606). Make your second left onto Lake Fairfax Drive. Follow until park entrance.

Daily, Memorial Day–Labor Day.

Anyone over 48", $13.50; under 48", $11; $8 after 5 p.m.; $7 chaperone fee.

9

INDOOR RECREATION

Maybe you've spent one too many days entertaining your children indoors. Fear not. Here are options to find fun indoors beyond even your heroic and extensive efforts. Check other chapters for details on indoor pools, skating, nature centers and museums.

BOWLING

Bowling is fun and inexpensive, and can be enjoyed by people of all ages. And unlike many other sports, bowling does not require extraordinary athletic ability.

Lightweight balls and gutter guards, which keep the ball out of the gutter, allow children as young as three to succeed at the game. Another option for young bowlers is duckpin bowling, using smaller balls and pins, offered at White Oak Duckpin Lanes in Silver Spring and AMF Bowling in College Park.

AMF Lanes

www.amf.com

301-948-1390

15720 Shady Grove Road, Gaithersburg, MD
I-270 north to Shady Grove Road/Redland Road exit. Veer right onto Redland Road; then turn left on Choke Cherry Road. Turn left onto Shady Grove Road. Bowling alley is next to Home Depot.

Monday, 10 a.m.–midnight; Tuesday–Thursday, 9 a.m.–midnight; Friday–Saturday, 9 a.m.–2 a.m.; Sunday, 9 a.m.–midnight.

$3.50 to $5 per person, per game. Shoe rental $4.68.

Also in Bowie, College Park (duckpin bowling), Glen Burnie, Hyattsville, Laurel, Temple Hills, Timonium and Waldorf, MD; Annandale, Alexandria, Centreville and Woodbridge, VA. Hours vary by location.

Bowl America

www.bowl-america.com

301-330-5200

1101 Clopper Road, Gaithersburg, MD
I-270 north, exit W. Diamond Avenue/Clopper Road (Rt. 117), and head west for 1.6 miles. Also in Glen Burnie, MD; Alexandria, Burke, Chantilly, Fairfax, Manassas, Sterling and Woodbridge, VA. Bowl America in Falls Church, VA is temporarily closed but plans to re-open.

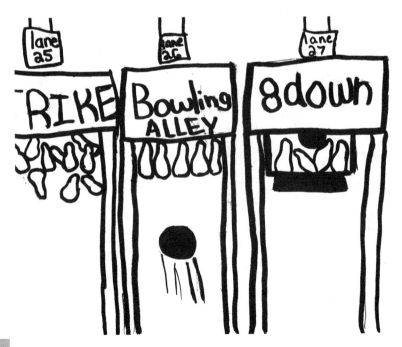

8:30 a.m.–1 a.m.

$2.49 to $5.25 per person, per game. Shoe rental, $3.40.

Also in Glen Burnie, MD; Alexandria, Burke, Chantilly, Fairfax, Manassas, Sterling and Woodbridge, VA. Bowl America in Falls Church, VA is temporarily closed but plans to re-open.

Strike Bethesda

www.bowlatstrike.com

301-652-0955

5353 Westbard Avenue, Bethesda, MD
Capital Beltway (I-495) to River Road/190 east toward Washington. Go 3.9 miles and turn right at Ridgefield Road, and immediately left at Westbard Avenue.

Monday 5 p.m.–2 a.m.; Tuesday–Thursday, 5 p.m.–midnight; Friday–Saturday, 11 a.m.–2 a.m.; Sunday, 11 a.m.–11:30 p.m. Must be 21 or older after 9 p.m.

$5.95 per game, weekdays. Other times, lanes, $25.95 to $34.95 per hour. Shoe rental, $5.

Take Note

When bowling, the floor approach—the place you release the ball—has dots to help you aim. Experiment to find the dot that marks your ideal spot to stand.

When you roll a ball with good results, pay attention to how you moved. Practice this again and again.

White Oak Duckpin Bowling Lanes

www.whiteoaklanes.com

301-593-3000

11207 New Hampshire Avenue, Silver Spring, MD
Capital Beltway (I-495), exit New Hampshire Avenue/650 north.

Monday–Thursday 9 a.m.–11 p.m.; Friday, 9 a.m.–midnight; Saturday, 9 a.m.–1 a.m.; Sunday, 10 a.m.–11 p.m.

$3.25 to $3.75 per person, per game. Shoe rental $3.25.

INDOOR PLAY

In addition to the sites mentioned here, check your local community center or municipal gym for open hours for children to run, play ball, tumble or otherwise burn up energy. Some shopping malls also have climbing and tumbling areas for young children.

 ### The Family Room

The Family Room is an indoor play area with a climbing structure, toys, art supplies and books for children, as well as books and magazines for adults. Also offering children's classes in music, foreign language and art.

www.thefamilyroomdc.com

202-640-1865

411 Eighth Street SE, 2nd floor, Washington DC
I-295 to Sixth Street SE exit toward Navy Yard. Turn left at Sixth Street SE, right at E Street SE and left at Eighth Street SE.

Metrorail Blue or Orange line (Eastern Market).

$10 per child per day; $5 per sibling. Memberships available.

Monday–Thursday, 9 a.m.–7 p.m.; Friday–Saturday, 9 a.m.–8 p.m.; Sunday, noon–6. Last entry one hour before closing.

 ### Funfit Family Fitness Center

A gym designed for both children and their parents, Funfit features kids' exercise bikes, hula-hoops, jump ropes, balls and other equipment for cardiovascular and strength exercise. Younger children can climb on soft wedges or jump in the moonbounce. Parents get a night out with a 'Just for Kids' party from 6:30 to 9:30 p.m. on the second Friday of every month.

www.funfitus.com

301-975-0099

17511 Redland Road, Gaithersburg, MD
I-270 north to Shady Grove Road/Redland Road exit. Stay in the right lane to exit onto Redland Road. Drive 3.7 miles. Look for the Redland Center on your right, before Muncaster Mill Road.

Open Gym: Wednesday and Friday, 1:30–8.

Children, 8 months and older, $6; siblings, $4; $12 maximum per family.

Hill's Gymnastics Training Center

Olympic winners including Dominique Dawes have trained at Hill's, which features an open gym in addition to classes.

www.hillsgymnastics.com

301-840-5900

7557 Lindbergh Drive, Gaithersburg, MD
From Rt. 355/Frederick Road, head east on Redland Road 2.6 miles. Left on Muncaster Mill Road for 1.3 miles to right at Woodfield Road/ Rt. 124; 0.4 miles to right on Lindbergh Drive.

Open gym Monday–Friday, 12:15–1:15; Sunday, 5:30–7.

Children, weekdays, $5; Sundays $10.

 ## JW Tumbles

A place where kids can run, jump, climb and tumble, JW Tumbles is an indoor gym that also offers classes and a Friday-night "Kids' Night Out" so parents get a night on their own.

www.jwtumbles.com

703-531-1470

2499 N. Harrison Street, #LL-12, Arlington, VA
George Washington Parkway, to Rt. 123 south toward McLean. Turn left on Kirby Road/Rt. 695, left onto ramp. Turn left onto Old Dominion Drive/Rt. 309. Turn right onto North George Mason Drive; Turn right onto Williamsburg Boulevard. Turn left onto North Harrison

Street. Also in Ashburn, VA. Plans to open in Rockville, MD and Alexandria, VA.

First child, $15; second child, $10. Discount for membership.

Open Gym, 4 months to 9 years, Wednesdays, 3:15–4:15; additional hours during the school year.

Little Sprouts Playtime Center

An indoor playground with Big Wheel tricycles, large balls, climbing and toys for children through age six. In addition to music, movement and cooking classes, Little Sprouts offers parents a night out on the first and third Friday of the month, as well as on Tuesday mornings.

www.littlesproutsplay.com

301-947-4356

12243 Darnestown Road, Gaithersburg, MD
At Quince Orchard and Darnestown Roads near Safeway.

Open play Tuesday, 11:30–5; Thursday, 11:30–6:30; Friday, 2:30–4:30.

Open play, $10/family.

Marvatots 'n' Teens

Do somersaults, bounce on the trampoline or try the bars at this gymnastic center. Also offering classes for toddlers to teenagers.

www.marvatotsnteens.com

301-468-9181

5636 Randolph Road, Rockville, MD
On Randolph Road, east of Rockville Pike/Rt. 355.

Open gyms Monday and Friday, 11 a.m.–noon.

$10 per session.

My Gym

Swings, slides, balls and climbing apparatus for babies six weeks to age 13. Also featuring classes in music, dance and gymnastics.

www.my-gym.com

301-983-5300

11325 Seven Locks Road, Potomac, MD
From I-270, exit Montrose Road/west. First left onto Seven Locks Road. My Gym is in Cabin John Mall at Seven Locks and Tuckerman Roads. Also in Bel Air, Columbia, Frederick, Gaithersburg and Timonium, MD; and Alexandria, Burke, Chantilly and Leesburg, VA.

Free Play Monday, 5:30–6:30; Wednesday and Friday, 2:15–3:15.

Children, $10.

Parent Resource Centers

The Parent Resource Centers provide a classroom-like setting for parents and children to play and learn together with the guidance of a parent educator. The centers have preschool toys, books, games and art activities; they also provide help with problem-solving for parents and a chance to share ideas and concerns.

www.hocmc.org/ParentCenters/ParentCenters.htm

301-279-8497

332 W. Edmonston Drive, Rm. D4, Rockville, MD
South on Rt. 355 from Rt. 28. Right on Wootton Parkway. Right on West Edmonston Drive. Go to first stop sign and turn left into parking lot. Also on Parkland Drive in Rockville and in Gaithersburg.

Tuesday–Friday, 10–2:30 during the school year. Open on a drop-in basis to families with infants, toddlers and preschoolers.

Families may register in person at any center. Annual fees based on income.

Appropriate for preschool children.

PlayWiseKids

PlayWiseKids is a hands-on activity center for children with exhibits that include a real fire truck and ambulance; a child-sized grocery store; a tap dance floor; a giant block room and an enormous indoor sand box. No reservations needed. One adult must accompany each group of up to five children.

www.playwisekids.com

410-772-1540

6570 Dobbin Road, Columbia, MD
Capital Beltway (I-495), exit Rt. 41 south/Rt. 175 west toward Columbia. Continue about two miles to left at Dobbin Road. Travel .7 miles and turn right into parking lot.

Monday–Friday, 9:30–5; Friday–Saturday, 9:30–7; Sunday 11:30–6.

Toddlers 12–23 months, $5.95; children ages 2–10, $8.95; adults, $3; babies free.

Café open during the school year on Saturdays, Sundays and school holidays.

INDOOR CLIMBING

Climbing the walls. If that sounds like your worst fear about long days inside with the kids, read on. At an indoor climbing gym, kids can scale the walls safely, get a great workout and have a blast.

Dick's Sporting Goods

Dick's offers one climbing wall within its retail store. A Dick's staffer serves as belayer while kids climb. A parent or guardian must be present during the climb.

www.dickssportinggoods.com

301-947-0200

Two Grand Corner Avenue, Washingtonian Center, Gaithersburg, MD
I-270 north to I-370 west, to the first exit. Turn left onto Rio Boulevard.
Follow the traffic circles; Dick's is the second circle, on the left. Also in
Fairfax, VA.

Tuesday–Friday, 5–9 p.m.; Saturday, noon–9 p.m.; Sunday, noon–5 p.m.

*$3 per child per climb, $5 per climb for adults. Prices include equipment.
Minimum height to climb: 4 feet.*

Earth Treks Climbing Center

Earth Treks Climbing Center is an indoor climbing gym
with 44-foot high walls and more than 15,000 square
feet of climbing surfaces. Extensive hours and programs
for beginning and experienced climbers. Climbers younger
than 14 must be accompanied by an adult unless otherwise noted.

www.earthtreksclimbing.com

240-283-9942

725 Rockville Pike, Rockville, MD
On Rockville Pike south of Rt. 28/Viers Mill Drive, in the back of the
Marlo Furniture building. From I-270, exit Falls Road toward Rockville
Town Center. Stay in the right lane, which becomes Maryland Avenue.
Turn right at Fleet Street. Earth Treks is one block down.

*Monday–Friday, noon–10.; weekends, 9–6; November–March, Satur-
days, 9–8.*

*$16/day; rental equipment, multi-day passes and annual memberships
available.*

*Metrorail: Red line (Rockville). Use overpass to cross Rockville Pike; walk
four blocks south. Also in Columbia and Timonium, MD.*

*Family Iintroduction to climbing: Adults learn basic safety skills, then
climb with their children ages 6–13. Call to register and for availability.
$30 per person, including equipment.*

*Open Climb: Up to three climbs for $15 per person, including harness fee;
$5 for each additional climb. Ages 5 and up. No reservations required.*

*Friday Nite Rox: Parents get a night on their own while kids 6 to 14 enjoy
supervised climbing activities, Fridays, 6:30–9, $25, including equipment.
Registration required.*

City of Rockville Indoor Climbing Gym

This indoor climbing gym has 20-foot-high walls and offers open climbing on Tuesday nights. It is also available for parties on weekend afternoons and evenings.

www.rockvillemd.gov/climbinggym

240-314-8643

603 Edmonston Drive, Rockville Civic Center Park, Rockville, MD
I-270 to West Montgomery Avenue/Rt. 28 east toward Rockville Town Center. Cross Rockville Pike/Rt. 355, turn left at the first light on 28 east. Go four blocks and turn right onto Baltimore Road. Go three blocks to Edmonston Drive and turn left into Civic Center Park. Pass the Rockville mansion on your right and continue downhill to parking lot on your left.

Open climbing, Tuesdays, 7–9 p.m. Adults who bring children for climbing must know how to belay. $10 per climber, equipment included. No credit cards.

The Rockville Climbing Gym also offers monthly evening classes for children and adults. Classes for a parent and child (age 7 to 12) cost $35 for Montgomery County residents. Classes for teens and adults are $20 for residents and $35 for nonresidents.

Recommended for ages 7 and older, accompanied by an experienced adult climber.

Take Note

Getting to the top of a climbing wall, said one seven-year-old, "feels awesome, especially when you look down at everyone watching you". His mother was convinced – and inspired. She's about to sign up for climbing lessons herself.

M Sportrock Climbing Center

Sportrock Climbing Center has 40-foot-high climbing walls and 12,000 square feet of climbing space. Extensive hours and programs for beginning and experienced climbers. Minors must be accompanied by an adult, except on Kids Nite.

www.sportrock.com

703-212-7625

5308 Eisenhower Avenue, Alexandria, VA
Capital Beltway (I-495), exit 173 toward Franconia. Turn left onto South Van Dorn Street/Rt. 613 north. Turn right onto Eisenhower Avenue. Also in Sterling, VA.

Monday–Friday, noon–11 p.m.; Weekends, 10–6; members only, 6–9 p.m.

Metrorail Blue line (Van Dorn). North 200 yards on Eisenhower Avenue.

Adults, $18/day; $14 for a member's guest, children, 12 or younger, $7. Rental equipment and memberships available.

Kids Nite: Parents get a break while kids 6 to 14 "get vertical." Friday, 6:30–8 p.m. $20, including equipment. Registration required.

Open Belay: Scale the walls for $5 per supervised climb, including equipment. Kids 6 and up, and adults. Weekends, noon–5. No reservation required.

Family Night: Parents and their children six or older can learn to climb for $20 per person, including equipment. First Friday of each month, 6:30 to 8 p.m. Registration required.

MAKE-YOUR-OWN ART STUDIOS

At most studios, you can walk in and start creating without an appointment, but call ahead to verify. The ceramic studios charge per piece of pottery you paint; some also charge a studio or supply fee.

All Fired Up

At All Fired Up, you can create a mosaic with colored tiles, returning 24 hours later to grout the tiles and take your creation home. (The store will grout for you for additional fee.)

www.allfiredupdc.com

301-654-3206

4923 Elm Street, Bethesda, MD
Capital Beltway (I-495) to Old Georgetown Road/Rt. 187 south. Drive 2.8 miles, to right on Woodmont Avenue. Go 0.2 miles to right on Elm Street. Also in northwest Washington, DC.

Metrorail Red line (Bethesda). Exit on Wisconsin Avenue and head three blocks south to right on Elm Street. Store is two blocks.

> **Take Note**
>
> At a pottery studio, your child can select and paint an unfinished ceramic piece—from fairies and frogs to picture frames and plates. The painted creations are glazed and fired later, so advise your child that you'll need to wait about a week for the finished product. Because these ceramic creations are popular gifts, it may take longer around holidays.

Monday–Wednesday, 11–7:30; Thursday–Friday, 11–9; Saturday, 10–9; Sunday, 11–6.

Pottery pieces range from $6 to $60 each. Mosaics are $25 to $55.

Amazing Art Studio

Amazing Art Studio also offers acrylic painting for plaster and some ceramic pieces, which you can take home immediately. Mosaic tiles are grouted 24 to 48 hours after creation, or you may bring home immediately and grout at home. Store will grout for additional fee.

www.amazingartstudio.com

301-762-5278

10066 Darnestown Road, Gaithersburg, MD
From I-270, exit Rt. 28 west toward Darnestown. Turn left onto Darnestown Road. Go 1.4 miles, crossing Great Seneca Highway. Turn left into shopping center.

Monday–Tuesday, 10–7; closed Wednesday except for school holidays; Thursday, noon–9 (adults only, 7–9); Friday, noon–9; Saturday, 10–7; Sunday, noon–6.

Ceramic pieces, $7.50 to $100; most $12 to $20. Mosaics, $15 and up; acrylic painting, $5 and up.

Clay Café Studio

In addition to pottery painting, Clay Café Studio offers fused glass.

www.claywire.com

703-534-7600

101 N. Maple Avenue, Falls Church, VA
Capital Beltway (I-495) to exit Rt. 7/Leesburg Pike east, which becomes West Broad Street in Falls Church. Turn left onto North Maple Avenue. Turn left into the first parking lot. Entrance is from the parking lot. Also in Chantilly, VA.

Monday–Thursday, 11–7; Friday–Saturday, 11–9; Sunday, noon–5.

Pottery, $3 to $50; most under $20; supplies, $6; Fused glass pieces, $10 to $60.

Color Me Mine

www.colormemine.com

301-565-5105

823 Ellsworth Drive, Silver Spring, MD
Capital Beltway (I-495), exit Colesville Road/29 south. Turn left onto Spring Street, then right onto Ellsworth Drive. Also in Gaithersburg and Waldorf, MD, and Fairfax, VA.

Metrorail Red line (Silver Spring). Head east on Colesville Road, cross Georgia Avenue. Walk one block to right on Fenton Street, two blocks to left on Ellsworth Drive.

Sunday–Monday, 11–7; Tuesday–Saturday, 11–9.

Studio fee: kids 12 and younger, $7; adults, $10. Pottery items, most less than $35; some as low as $4.

Kids 'N' Clay

In addition to ceramic pieces ready to paint, Kids 'N' Clay offers something rare among paint-your-own pottery studios: wet clay. Drop-ins are welcome in wet clay classes; call for availability.

www.kidsnclay.com

703-532-3738

6252 Old Dominion Drive, McLean, VA
Capital Beltway (I-495) , to I-66 east toward Washington. Merge onto 267 east, then merge onto Dolley Madison Boulevard/123 north toward McLean. Go 2.2 miles and turn right on Old Dominion Drive. Also in Stafford, VA.

Monday–Saturday, 10–5; Sunday, noon–4.

Studio fee: children, $7; adults, $9. Pottery is $4 to $44 per piece. Drop-in at wet clay class, $37.

The Mud Hut

www.mudhutstudios.com

301-260-8786

3231 Spartan Road, Olney, MD
From Georgia Avenue, travel 2.8 miles north of Rt. 28 to right on Spartan Road. Two blocks to store.

Monday–Thursday, 10–8; Friday, 10–9; Saturday, 10–6; Sunday, noon–5. Hours change during school year.

Ceramic pieces, $10–$65.

Paint Your Own Pottery

Select from a huge array of stencils, stamps and idea books, or create your own designs.

www.ciao-susanna.com

703-218-2881

10417 Main Street, Fairfax, VA
I-66 to Rt. 50 east, which becomes Main Street in Fairfax City. Store is on your right.

Monday, 10:30–5; Tuesday–Friday, 10:30–6; Saturday, 10–6; Sunday, noon–6. Reservations recommended Saturdays, Sundays and holidays.

Pottery, $7.50–$20. Studio fee, $7 per person, for two pieces of pottery, $4 for each additional piece.

Sunny Dyes

Tie-dye a hat, a pillowcase, a t-shirt or other clothes and bring your ultra-cool, dye-soaked creation home with you. You will need to wait 24 hours to wash your creation after the dye has set, but you don't need to return to the store, as you do with most make-your-own-pottery creations.

www.sunnydyes.com

301-881-2200

1701 Rockville Pike, Suite B9, Rockville, MD

Metrorail Red line (Twinbrook). Head west one block on Halpine and cross Rockville Pike to store, in back of building.

Drop in Tuesday–Thursday, 10:30–3; Friday, 3–5. Hours change during school year.

$5 for a hat to $16 for adult t-shirt or tank top. $10 charge to tie-dye your own item.

LASER TAG AND ARCADES

In laser tag, players don electronic vests and handsets and run through darkened or maze-like rooms, hoping to "tag" their opponents with laser beams while dodging attacks. Some would say it's a noisy and high-tech way to play guns; others find the experience exhilarating, with its special effects and team maneuvering.

 ### Dave and Buster's

Primarily an adult establishment, Dave and Buster's allows those under 21 when accompanied by a parent or guardian, one adult per up to three underage guests. This 60,000 square-foot high-tech video arcade also includes billiards and shuffleboard. The noise and lights can be intense for younger children.

www.daveandbusters.com

301-230-5151

11301 Rockville Pike, in White Flint Mall, Kensington, MD
I-270 south to Old Georgetown Road/187. Turn left from the exit ramp. Turn right on Tuckerman Lane, left on Rockville Pike/Rt. 355. White Flint Mall is on your right, at Edson Lane.

Sunday–Tuesday, 11:30 a.m.–midnight; Wednesday–Thursday, 11:30 a.m–1 a.m.; Friday and Saturday, 11:30 a.m.–2 a.m.

Fees per game played. After 10 p.m., Friday and Saturday, admission $5.

Metrorail Red line (White Flint).

ESPN Zone

This sports dining and entertainment complex has more than 100 interactive games and attractions in the sports arena. The Zone is also the place to catch a live broadcast on ESPN.

www.espnzone.com

202-783-3776

555 12th Street, NW, Washington, DC

Monday–Thursday, 11:30 a.m.–11 p.m.; Friday–Saturday, 11:30 a.m.– midnight. Last entry is one hour before closing time.

LaserNation/UltraZone

www.lasernation.net

703-578-6000

3447 Carlin Springs Road, Bailey's Crossroads, VA
Capital Beltway (I-495), exit onto Arlington Boulevard/50 east toward Arlington. Travel 4.3 miles, veer right on Leesburg Pike/7 east. Travel 2.4 miles to left onto Carlin Springs Road. Also in Sterling, VA.

Wednesday–Thursday, 4–10 p.m.; Friday, 4 p.m.–1 a.m.; Saturday, 10 a.m.–1 a.m. Longer hours in summer, school holidays.

$8.50 per game; $13 unlimited play Friday and Saturday after 8 p.m. $4 per game, 12 and younger Saturdays 10 a.m.–noon.

Laser Quest

www.laserquest.com

703-490-4180

14517 Potomac Mills Road, Woodbridge, VA
Capital Beltway (I-495) to I-95 south to Potomac Mills exit; turn right on Potomac Mills Road to Potomac Festival Mall.

Wednesday–Thursday, 6–9; Friday, 4–11; Saturday, 11–11; Sunday, noon–6. Longer hours in summer. Open Monday and Tuesday for private events.

$8; group rates available.

You may bring your own food; alcohol prohibited.

Shadowland

www.shadowlandadventures.com

301-330-5546

624 Quince Orchard Road, Gaithersburg, MD
From I-270, exit Clopper Road and turn right, one-half mile to left on Quince Orchard Road. Turn right shopping center. Also in Columbia, MD and Springfield and Chantilly, VA.

Monday, 11–6; Tuesday–Thursday, 11–10; Friday, 11 a.m.–midnight; Saturday, 10 a.m.–midnight; Sunday, 10–10. Private rentals Monday after 6 p.m.

$7.75 per 30-minute session; $14.75 for two sessions; $20.50 for three.

XP Laser Sport

www.xplasersport.com

301-953-2266

14705 A Baltimore Avenue, Laurel, MD
Capital Beltway (I-495), to I-95 north toward Baltimore. Exit Rt. 198 toward Laurel, pass six traffic lights and turn right onto Baltimore Avenue/Rt. 1 south. Go four traffic lights and turn left into the Red Sky Shopping Center.

Public play, Tuesday–Thursday, 3–9 p.m. and Friday, 3 p.m.–midnight. Saturday, noon–midnight; Sunday, 1 p.m.–8 p.m. Reservations required Friday through Sunday. Additional hours for reserved private rentals.

$15 per person for a 45-minute session/two 15-minute games or $24 per person for two 45-minute sessions/four 15-minute games.

Players must be at least 47" tall.

10

DAY TRIPS

The Washington, DC area is surrounded by fun and exciting places that make great day trips—natural wonders like the Chesapeake Bay and the Shenandoah and Allegheny mountains; significant sites from Civil War and Colonial history; fascinating cities and charming small towns.

With so many potential trips, we've stuck fairly close to home—within about two hours' drive. We've included a few of our favorites and provided references for you to search farther afield.

ANNAPOLIS

The waterfront area of Historic Annapolis is the center of activity in this charming city. Here you can enjoy Annapolis yachting facilities, water tours, restaurants, summer theater, specialty shops, galleries, Market House and strolling areas. Tour the harbor by boat. Day trips to other nearby locales operate from May to September. Schedules and fees are posted at the dock, or call Chesapeake Marine Tours, 410–268-7600 or 301-261-2719. The Annapolis Sailing School, 800-638-9192, offers weekday and weekend sailing lessons. For tours of Annapolis, call 410–267-7619; to receive a free children's kit, call 410–280-0445.

Take Note

Just along the City Dock, a sculptural tableau depicts Alex Haley reading to a group of children near the place where his ancestor, Kunta Kinte, arrived in Annapolis in 1767. The memorial incorporates the statues of Haley and Kunta Kinte, along with 10 markers dedicated to values such as diversity, family, love and forgiveness.

Special activities include Annapolis Arts Festival in June, Sailboat and Power Boat Shows in October, and the festive New Year's Eve celebration, First Night, with entertainment and fireworks.

Banneker-Douglass Museum

Named for scientist and inventor Benjamin Banneker and abolitionist Frederick Douglass, this museum is dedicated to preserving Maryland's African American history. Housed in the old Mount Moriah A.M.E Church, this museum includes art, photography, rare books and documents showing the role of African-Americans in Maryland history.

www.bdmuseum.com

410-216-6180

84 Franklin Street, Annapolis, MD
In the Annapolis historic district, off Church Circle. Capital Beltway (I-495) to Rt. 50 east to Annapolis. Exit Rowe Boulevard south; merge onto Rt. 70 east. Turn right on College Avenue/Rt. 450 west. Enter the next traffic circle and take second exit onto Franklin Street.

Parking available by shuttle from the Naval Academy Stadium parking lot and at commercial garages. Limited on-street parking.

Open Tuesday through Saturday, 10–4.

 ## Chesapeake Children's Museum

The Chesapeake Children's Museum offers a hands-on experience for children of all ages—but is especially appropriate for preschool and early elementary age children. The museum is all about discovery—of the peoples, technologies and ecology of the Chesapeake Bay.

Highlights include a "Bay Window" exhibit of live aquatic and land-dwelling animals; the seven-foot-tall human replica "Stuffee," which can be taken apart to see the internal organs; and a stage with dress-up costumes and audience seating for impromptu performances. An art and science workshop space is available for exploration by reservation. The museum includes an herb garden and the Harriet Tubman Walk—a simulated walk along the Underground Railroad.

www.theccm.org

410-990-1993

25 Silopanna Road, Annapolis, MD
Rt. 50 east to Exit 22, Aris T. Allen Boulevard Stay on Allen Boulevard—don't exit at Riva Road—as Allen becomes Forest Drive. Turn

left at the 4th traffic light, Hilltop Lane. Turn left at the first traffic light, Spa Road. Pass Gentry Court and Spindrift Way on your right, and turn right on Silopanna Road. Look for the CCM sign on your left at the stop sign. Plenty of parking in the lot.

Daily 10–4 except Wednesdays.

Age 1 or older, $3. Free for babies.

Wednesdays are reserved for groups of 10 or more; group reservations available other times.

Historic Annapolis Foundation
Welcome Center and Museum Store

Housed in the old Victualling Warehouse, this museum offers a diorama of Annapolis as the principal seaport of the Upper Chesapeake Bay 200 years ago.

www.annapolis.org

410-268-5576

77 Main Street, Annapolis, MD

Open Monday–Sunday, 10–5. Closed holidays.

Tour on foot with a colonial guide, in a horse-drawn carriage or on a trolley. You'll spend anywhere from $4 to $42 per person to learn about the architecture, African-American or colonial history—or even food history—of Annapolis. Or rent an audiotape for a self-guided walking tour for $10.

Maryland State House Visitor Center

The Maryland State House is the oldest state capitol in continuous legislative use and also the home of the flag that went to the moon in 1969, as well as a moon rock. Take a peek in the Old Senate Chamber to see a mannequin version of George Washington dressed in full uniform as he was on the day he resigned his commission as Commander-in Chief before the Continental Congress on December 23, 1783. The State House in Annapolis was the first peacetime Capitol, from November 1783 to August 1784. You can see the two rooms where the Maryland Legislature meets for 90 days every year (second Wednesday in January to April). Maryland school groups can arrange meetings with members of their county's senators or delegates during this time.

www.visitannapolis.org/index.asp?action=explore_house

410-974-3400

100 State Circle, Annapolis, MD
Capital Beltway (I-495) to Rt. 50 east and follow the signs to the State House.

Visitor Center is open daily.

State House open Monday–Friday, 8:30–5; Saturday and Sunday 10–4. Closed December 25. No tours on Thanksgiving and January 1.

Tours daily at 11 and 3. For large groups, special times may be arranged.

Wheelchair access from the back of the building.

Security: Photo ID required.

Best for children in grade 4 and up (and/or those who have studied the American Revolution).

Special activities include State House by Candlelight program the first weekend in December (Friday and Saturday evenings), featuring musical orchestras, bands and choral groups.

Quiet Waters Park

Scenically located on the South River and Harness Creek near Annapolis, Maryland, this 340-acre park offers natural beauty and a variety of recreational activities. The park has more than six miles of hiking/biking trails, six picnic pavilions available by reservation, open picnic areas (some with grills), scenic South River overlook, formal gardens, a large children's playground and a café. Visitors can rent bicycles, sailboats, pedal boats, rowboats, kayaks and canoes. Two art galleries are in the Visitor Center. Juried sculpture from across the country is displayed throughout the park.

www.friendsofquietwaterspark.homestead.com

410-222-1777

600 Quiet Waters Park Road, Annapolis, MD
Capital Beltway (I-495) to Rt. 50 east to Annapolis. Exit 22 (Aris T. Allen Blvd/Rt. 665) toward Riva Road. Stay on I-665 until it ends and merges with Forest Drive. Follow Forest Drive for two miles to right onto Hillsmere Drive. Park entrance is 100 yards on the right.

Daily 7–dusk except Tuesday. Outdoor ice rink open November–March. Boat rentals available spring–fall. Visitor Center open 9–4 weekdays and 11–4 weekends.

Cost is $5 per vehicle, handicapped plate $3 per vehicle; buses $30 each, school bus (school hours only Monday–Thursday) free with pavilion rental; walkers, runners, bikers, roller blades, free. Annual vehicle entry permits and senior citizen lifetime passes available. Free admittance to the art galleries in the Visitor Center.

Ramp access to the Visitor Center is at the main level in the rear.

Biking, boating, fishing, hiking, skating.

Special activities include Earth Day; Summer Concert Series in June–August; Arts Festival the second weekend in November.

U.S. Naval Academy

This is the part of Annapolis that many youngsters really want to see. Favorites are the Armel-Leftwich Visitor Center and the U.S. Naval Academy Museum, the crypt of John Paul Jones and the statue of Tecumseh. The Rogers Ship Model Collection contains 108 ship models dating from 1650–1850, and includes models of British Ships constructed by French prisoners of war during the Napoleonic conflict. At noon on some days, you may be lucky to see the midshipmen line up in front of Bancroft Hall and march with bugles and drums. Try *not* to visit during graduation (third week in May) because it is extremely crowded.

www.usna.edu

410-263-6933

Armel-Leftwich Visitor Center, 52 King George Street, Annapolis, MD

Grounds open daily, 9–5. Museum open Monday–Saturday, 9–5; Sunday, 11–5. Visitor Center open March–December, 9–5; January–February, 9–4; closed Thanksgiving, December 25 and January 1. Public walking tours available daily.

Museum, free. Tours, Adults, $8.50; age 62 and older, $7.50; students in grades 1–12, $6.50; preschoolers free.

Watermark Cruises

Take advantage of this wonderful way to see such sights as the U.S. Naval Academy, Historic Annapolis Harbor, the scenic Severn River, the Chesapeake Bay or even St. Michaels on the Eastern Shore of Maryland. Cruises depart from and return to the City Dock, located in the heart of historic downtown Annapolis. Cruises are available, from 40 minutes to 7.5 hours, on one of 11 vessels. Watermark also offers walking tours through historic Annapolis and the US Naval Academy. Pirate loving kids can join Captain Marcus Waters and become part of his pirate crew as they cruise the Chesapeake Bay and hear fictional tales of piracy from those dressed in 18th-century pirate garb. This interactive cruise is a swashbuckling adventure. Most vessels are equipped with beverage service. Harbor Queen also has a full concession stand onboard.

www.watermarkjourney.com

410-268-7600

Annapolis City Dock, Slip 20, Annapolis, MD
Capital Beltway (I-495) to Rt. 50 east toward Annapolis. Rowe Boulevard exit; follow signs to Annapolis. Stay on Rowe Boulevard to the end; turn right and enter traffic circle; exit onto Duke of Gloucester Street; proceed through one traffic light and turn left onto Green Street. Turn right on Dock Street; City Dock is at the end of the street.

Ticket prices vary depending on the cruise.

Wheelchair accessibility on the Harbor Queen.

A few events are perfect for children, such as the Pirate Pet Parade (typically held in May) where canines dressed as pirates parade around Annapolis City Dock.

William Paca House and Garden

This 37-room, five-part mansion was built by William Paca, a signer of the Declaration of Independence and three-term governor of Maryland. The two-acre terraced garden behind the house, hidden for many years, was uncovered through archaeological excavation in 1976. The garden includes roses, boxwoods, flowerbeds, hollies, a Chinese trellis bridge, domed summer house and fish-shaped pond. Children of all ages are welcome; tour guides are trained to tailor the tours when children are in the group.

www.hometownannapolis.com/tour_paca.html

800-603-4020, 410-267-7619

186 Prince George Street, Annapolis, MD

Daily, 10–5; Sunday, noon–5. Hours vary January–March.

Adults, $8; seniors, $7; children 6–18, $5.

Wheelchair access to garden. Strollers not permitted in the house.

Special events include children's colonial activities and garden event in the spring, Maryland Day (late March) and July 4 celebrations.

BALTIMORE

Baltimore has undergone an extensive makeover in the last two decades, transforming the historic tobacco and tin can warehouses into boutique hotels and thriving retail and restaurant complexes. This city on a harbor is a beautiful mix of historic architecture, unique neighborhoods and modern-day museums. The best part is that you can walk—or take a water-taxi—to many of the sites. You'll need several day trips to experience all that Baltimore offers. A weekend stay in one of the city's family-friendly harborside hotels will allow leisurely exploration.

Stop at the Baltimore Visitor Center, 401 Light Street, to find an array of information on the city's history, arts, neighborhoods, shopping and special events. You can purchase event and attraction tickets and make reservations for dining and lodging. The Visitor Center is open daily, 9–6. Call 877-BALTIMORE or visit www.baltimore.org.

To reach Baltimore, take the Capital Beltway (I-495) to I-95 or the Baltimore-Washington Parkway (Rt. 295) north. Follow signs to I-395/Downtown. On-street parking is limited; watch for commercial parking lots, some of which are beneath or adjacent to downtown hotels. Amtrak and MARC trains travel daily to Baltimore from Union Station in Washington, and from New Carrollton, MD.

American Visionary Art Museum

This national museum and education center features the extraordinary work of intuitive, self-taught artists, many of whom have no formal training or are experts in other fields, from farming to homemaking to medicine. Outside you'll find the 55-foot whirligig (created by 76-year-old Vollis Simpson) and the main building's eye-catching Community Mosaic Walls, created by Baltimore children. Inside is a gallery featuring the permanent collection, six second-floor galleries dedicated to an annual thematic mega-exhibition, and a smaller third-floor space featuring an exhibit that changes more frequently. The sculpture barn holds a collection of whimsical whirligigs along with one or two Artcars, lavishly decorated automobiles that are works of art in themselves.

www.avam.org

410-244-1900

800 Key Highway, Baltimore, MD
Capital Beltway (I-495) to I-95 north to Exit 55. Bear left at first light

onto Key Highway. Follow Key Highway two miles; museum is on the left at Covington Street. Metered on-street parking along Key Highway and on Covington Street.

Open Tuesday–Sunday, 10–6; closed December 25 and Thanksgiving.

Adults, $12; children, seniors, and students, $8; groups of ten or more, $7; children 6 and under, free.

Special activities include the annual Kinetic Sculpture race, featuring human-powered works of art (May); July 4 Pet Parade; Artcar parade during Baltimore's Artscape.

Babe Ruth Museum

Children who have read any of the Babe Ruth biographies will love visiting the house where baseball's great slugger and legendary sports celebrity was born. Here you'll find mementos and films from the life of George Herman "Babe" Ruth, like the jersey and glove worn by Babe during his 12 years at St. Mary's Industrial School for Boys (where he learned to play baseball), Babe's rookie baseball card, as well as a 1910s-era bat given to Babe Ruth by Shoeless Joe Jackson.

www.baberuthmuseum.com

410-727-1539

216 Emory Street, Baltimore, MD
Capital Beltway (I-495) to I-95 north to I-395; follow the signs for Martin Luther King, Jr. Blvd exit; turn right at second light on Pratt Street, then right on Emory. Or follow the painted baseballs on the street from the North Gate of Camden Yards to the museum, three blocks away.

Take Note

Baseball aficionados can enjoy artifacts from the 1932 World Series, in which the Babe "called his shot"—a towering home run. The exhibit includes a watch presented to him following the series, a souvenir mini-bat and a baseball autographed by the 1932 New York Yankees.

Daily, April–September, 10–6 (until 7:30 p.m. on Oriole home game days); October–March, 10–5, Tuesday–Sunday. Closed Thanksgiving, December 25 and January 1.

Adults, $6; senior citizens, $4; children 3–12, $3. Combination Birthplace and Sports Legends Museum at Camden Yards is $14 adults; seniors, $11; children 3–12, $9.

Limited parking in the museum lot on Pratt Street.

Limited wheelchair accessibility on the museum's first floor.

Baltimore and Ohio Railroad Museum

An affiliate of the Smithsonian, this 1884 roundhouse contains the world's most comprehensive collection of American railroading artifacts and locomotives, cabooses, freights and other cars dating to 1829. Children can climb through a caboose and the back of a mail car. The large model railroad station is always a hit.

www.borail.org

410-752-2490

901 West Pratt Street, Baltimore, MD
Capital Beltway (I-495) to I-95 north to I-395; exit at Martin Luther King, Jr. Boulevard; go three blocks to left turn on Lombard Street; turn left at first light on Poppleton; cross Pratt Street to museum entrance.

Take Note

The museum is spread across a 40-acre historic site so you'll need to do a bit of walking (or strolling) with little ones, or focus your visit on all that is in the roundhouse.

Monday–Friday, 10–4; Saturday, 10–5, Sunday 11–4. Closed major holidays.

Adults, $14; senior citizens (60+), $12; children 2–12, $8. Children under 2, free. Train rides are included in the price of admission, Tuesdays–Sundays, April–December.

Special activities: Annual KidsFest, festival of railroad and family fun in September. Holiday Festival of Trains beginning late November.

Baltimore Civil War Museum–President Street Station

The museum tells the stories of Baltimore's role in the Civil War, especially the Pratt Street Riot, which accounted for the first bloodshed of the war. The museum also explains the link between this railroad station and the Underground Railroad, as well as the story of the Philadelphia, Wilmington and Baltimore Railroads.

www.mdhs.org

410-385-5188

601 President Street, Baltimore, MD
At the end of I-83 north at Fleet and President streets, at the east end of the Inner Harbor.

Open Thursday–Monday, 10–5.

Adults, $4; seniors and students, $3; under 12 free.

Baltimore Maritime Museum

This is a great favorite for children. They always love the tours of these three vessels, even if they aren't old enough to truly understand the different naval technologies presented. The Taney I is the last surviving warship from the attack of Pearl Harbor, and the Torsk sank the last two Japanese combatant ships of WWII. Lightship Chesapeake, a floating lighthouse, marked entrance ways to harbors when other navigational devices were impractical. The seven-foot Knoll Lighthouse marked the mouth of the Patapsco River for 133 years before being moved to Pier 5 in Baltimore's Inner Harbor where it is home to the kid-friendly Mascots Exhibit, "Seagoing Dogs of the Coast Guard and Navy."

www.baltomaritimemuseum.org

410-396-3453

Piers 3 and 5, Pratt Street, Baltimore, MD
Capital Beltway (I-495) to I-95 north toward Baltimore to Exit 53, I-395 north/Downtown; stay left at the fork for downtown, then in the center lane, which becomes Howard Street. Stay straight, passing Oriole Park on your left. Turn right onto West Pratt Street and then continue on East Pratt Street to Piers 3 and 5.

Daily, 10–5, except winter, open only Friday–Sunday. Closed Thanksgiving, December 24 and 25.

Adults, $8; senior citizens, $6; children 6–14, $4; children 5 and under, free. Group rates available for ten or more.

Restaurants and food stalls at adjacent Harborplace.

Baltimore Museum of Art

This exceptional museum features the Cone Collection of early 20th-century art including several pieces from Matisse and Picasso. Be sure to pick up a special self-guided kit that encourages kids to dress up, sketch (and even sing) their way through the galleries. Learn to sketch, take a family art workshop or a special tour geared to families (at 2) during Family Fun Sundays.

www.artbma.org

443-573-1700

Art Museum Drive, Baltimore, MD
Capital Beltway (I-495) to I-95 north to I-395; follow the signs for
Martin Luther King, Jr. Boulevard exit; turn left on Howard Street;
continue north (past 29th Street); veer right at the fork on Art Museum Drive.

*Open Wednesday–Friday, 11–5; Saturday–Sunday, 11–6. Closed Thanks-
giving, December 25, January 1 and July 4th.*

*Gertrude's Restaurant serves regional cuisine. Reservations are strongly
recommended via separate reservationline: 410-889-3399.*

 ## Baltimore Museum of Industry

This hands-on museum, located in the heart of industrial south Baltimore (and housed in a harbor-side cannery), contains a print shop,
a machine shop, a garment loft and an assembly line where youngsters learn how parts become finished products. Before entering the
cannery exhibit, kids are given a name tag of a real Baltimore resident
from that time and assigned to one of the work stations labeling cans
or shucking oysters.

www.thebmi.org

410-727-4808

1415 Key Highway, Inner Harbor South, Baltimore, MD
Capital Beltway (I-495) to I-95 north to Key Highway/Fort McHenry
National Monument. Turn left at light; go under overpass; then left on
Key Highway. The museum is immediately on the right; look for the
big red crane.

*Open Tuesday–Saturday, 10–4. Closed Monday, Thanksgiving, Decem-
ber 24 and 25.*

*Adults, $10; senior citizens and students, $6. Group and family rates
available.*

Free parking available on site.

 ## Baltimore Public Works Museum

This hands-on museum should easily draw young children and
teens into understanding public works and how the water purifica-
tion process works thanks to a new exhibit. The museum is housed

in a 90-year-old red brick sewage pumping station completed in 1912. Children are introduced to the museum with a 15-minute kid-friendly video. If weather permits, the outdoor two-level exhibit, "streetscape," is definitely worth exploring. Here you'll find a fire hydrant, public telephone, parking meter, manhole, and alarm box—and a "peel back the pavement" look at the network of pipes and connections below. A stairway joins both levels for a closer look.

www.ci.baltimore.md.us/government/dpw/museum

410-396-5565

751 Eastern Avenue, Baltimore, MD
Capital Beltway (I-495) to I-95 north to the Inner Harbor exit; turn right on Pratt Street and right on President Street; follow President Street through the intersection with Eastern Avenue. The museum entrance is on Falls Way, facing the Inner Harbor. Museum is on the edge of Little Italy, and is a two-block walk from the National Aquarium over pedestrian bridges. Parking in nearby commercial lots at President and Fleet Streets.

Open Tuesday–Sunday, 10–4. Closed Good Friday, Thanksgiving, December 25, January 1, Martin Luther King's Birthday, and Baltimore City holidays.

General admission, $3; students, seniors and active military, $2.50; children under 6, free.

Group rate of $2 per person applies for ten or more.

Baltimore Streetcar Museum

This "rolling history" museum houses a collection of Baltimore streetcars, horse-drawn and electric, covering the 104-year history of this type of transportation in the city. Enjoy unlimited streetcar rides, tours, exhibits, and a video in addition to a collection of Baltimore streetcars from 1859-1944.

www.baltimorestreetcar.org

410-547-0264

1901 Falls Road, Baltimore, MD
Capital Beltway (I-495) to I-95 north to I-395; exit at Martin Luther King, Jr. Boulevard to left on Howard Street; turn right on North

Avenue; turn right on Maryland Avenue; turn right at Lafayette; turn right on Falls Road to museum.

Open June–October: Saturday and Sunday, noon–5; November–May: Sunday, noon–5.

Adults, $6; children, ages 4–11 and senior citizens, $3; children younger than 4, free. Maximum family admission: $24. Admission includes unlimited streetcar rides.

Wheelchair accessibility in the museum.

Special activities: Museum's birthday celebration the first Sunday in July, Antique Auto Meets twice a year and Tinsel Trolley in December.

Federal Hill Park

In the heart of downtown Baltimore and a short walk from the Maryland Science Center, the historical Federal Hill Park offers a beautiful country setting atop a hill, with a picnic area and playground—and excellent views of the Inner Harbor and Port of Baltimore.

www.FederalHillOnline.com

410-396-7946

800 Battery Avenue, Baltimore, MD
Capital Beltway (I-495) to I-95 north. Exit 53 to merge onto 395 north toward downtown. Martin Luther King Highway, veer right at Conway Street. Turn right at Light Street. Turn left at Key Highway. Turn right at Battery Avenue.

Open dawn–dusk.

Limited on-street parking.

Playgrounds.

Fire Museum

The museum contains more than 40 pieces of antique fire-fighting apparatus, dating from 1806–1957. See hand-pulled trucks that required 20+ men to pull them, horse-drawn steamers, hose wagons, and motorized vehicles from all over the country. Experience the thrill of sending an alarm over an antique fire alarm system. Preschoolers to early elementary aged children love visiting the Discovery Room to try on fire fighter boots and turnout gear, plus explore the exhibits on the Great Baltimore Fire, and uniforms and badges. Older children and adults can take audio tours of the Great Fire and the general museum collection.

www.firemuseummd.org

410-321-7500

1301 York Road, Lutherville, MD
Capital Beltway (I-495) to I-95 north toward Baltimore. Baltimore Beltway (I-695) west to York Road / Lutherville exit north (exit 26B). Go one block north, Museum is located behind the Heaver Plaza Office Building. Free on-site parking.

Open Saturdays, 10–4, May–December. Open Tuesday–Saturday, June, July and August. Closed federal holidays.

Adults, $8; firefighters and senior citizens 62+, $7; children ages 2–12, $4; under 2 free. Family membership is $45.

Food vendors outside during special events. Plenty of restaurant choices within a block of the museum.

Special activities include Movie Time, Wednesdays at 11:30; Craft Days, Thursdays at 10:30; Story Time on Fridays at 11:30, June–August. Also Great Baltimore Fire Tour of the Burnt District; Steam Day; Founders' Day; Antique Car Shows; Halloween Open House; Holiday Train Garden.

Flag House and Star-Spangled Banner Museum

This is the home of Mary Pickersgill, the woman who sewed the 30′ x 42′ flag that flew over Fort McHenry during the battle of Baltimore and inspired Francis Scott Key to write our National Anthem. The house is furnished with antiques of the Federal period. See the Great Flag Window which is the same size and design as the original Star-Spangled Banner flag at the adjacent Star-Spangled Banner Museum. The museum is best for children age 5 and older and includes a family activity room where children can try on clothing, play with puppets representing the characters from the Star-Spangled Banner story or make their own flag.

www.flaghouse.org

410-837-1793

844 East Pratt Street, Baltimore, MD
Capital Beltway (I-495) to I-95 north to I-395 to downtown Baltimore; follow signs for Inner Harbor to Pratt Street, go east on Pratt Street; to President Street (6 blocks from the Inner Harbor) and turn left; turn right from President Street behind the Reginald F. Lewis Museum of Maryland African American History and Culture onto Granby Street; where the street ends at Albemarle Street, turn right. Parking available on the street in front of the house on Albemarle Street. Ask for a parking permit to place on your windshield.

Open Tuesday–Saturday, 10–4. Closed Monday, Sunday, and major holidays.

Adults, $7; senior citizens, $6; children $5.

Many restaurants nearby in Little Italy and next door to the Reginald F. Lewis Museum of Maryland African American History and Culture.

The Star-Spangled Banner Museum and garden are wheelchair accessible. The Flag House is accessible on the first floor.

Fort McHenry National Monument and Historic Shrine

From a ship in Baltimore's outer harbor, Francis Scott Key saw the *Star-Spangled Banner* still flying from the ramparts of Fort McHenry after a 25-hour bombardment by the British in the War of 1812. There is a movie at the Visitor Center about the battle and the writing of the national anthem. Children are interested in the cannons and enjoy the soldiers in period uniforms on summer weekends.

www.nps.gov/fomc

410-962-4290

2400 East Fort Avenue, Baltimore, MD
Capital Beltway (I-495) to 95 north. Exit at Key Highway, the last exit before the Harbor Tunnel (you will see signs for Fort McHenry), and bear left. At third traffic light, make left on Lawrence Street; at first light, turn left on E. Fort Avenue and travel to the end of the street.

Daily, 8–4:45; summer hours (first weekend in June through Labor Day) 8 a.m–7:45. Closed Thanksgiving, December 25 and January 1.

Free admission to movie and grounds. Admission to historic area: adults age 16 and over, $7; children, free.

Audio tour is available in different languages.

Braille map is available on request.

Security: Museum staff may check bags.

Special activities include ranger-guided activities June–Labor Day, military demonstrations, drills, and special ceremonies presented by "soldiers" dressed in period uniforms, Saturday and Sunday afternoons, June through August. In the evening on Flag Day (June 14) and Defenders' Day (the second Saturday in September), see commemorative celebrations with band concerts and fireworks.

Harborplace and the Gallery

Harborplace and the Gallery are located in the heart of Baltimore's financial and business district, overlooking its Inner Harbor. Their three main buildings offer an exciting range of more than 200 shops, restaurants, stalls and harbor-side terraces, as well as easy access to several main attractions, such as the National Aquarium and the Maryland Science Center. Just outside (although not run by Harborplace), you can take a ride in paddleboats or travel on the Water Taxi or take a Duck Tour to sights on the Inner Harbor. The outdoor promenades are perfect for strolling, skipping, pushing a stroller or people-watching. In good weather, you may be lucky and run into street performers who will keep you and your children amused.

www.harborplace.com

410-332-4191

Inner Harbor at Pratt and Light Streets, Baltimore, MD
Just off of Interstates 95 and 83.

Stores open Monday–Saturday, 10–9; Sunday, 11–7. Restaurants close later. Light and Pratt Street Pavilions open until 10 p.m. Friday and Saturday.

Parking available in the Gallery Garage and numerous commercial lots.

Special activities include hundreds of free events annually with street performers, concerts, visiting ships, holiday fireworks and seasonal celebrations.

Ladew Topiary Gardens

Self-taught gardener Harvey Ladew created 15 garden "rooms" of topiary and flower gardens—each with its own theme—on his Maryland estate. The Garden Club of America called the Ladew Gardens "the most outstanding garden in America." A 1.5-mile nature walk leads through woods, fields and across a wetland board walk. Tours are self-guided, aided by a printed map and descriptions of each station.

A guided tour of Ladew Manor House offers an impressive collection of antique English furniture in this equestrian-inspired country house.

www.ladewgardens.com

410-557-9466

3535 Jarrettsville Pike, Monkton, MD
Capital Beltway (I-495) to I-95 north to Baltimore. Exit at I-695 west (the Baltimore Beltway) to I-83N via exit 24. Exit 20A Shawan Road East-toward Cockeysville. Right on Shawan Road to right on York Road (Rt. 45). Left onto Ashland Road (Rt. 145). Left onto Jarrettsville Pike (Rt. 146).

Open 10–4, Monday–Friday; Saturday and Sunday 10:30–5.

Adults, $13; seniors and students, $11; children, $5.

Special events include a summer concert series, story time for children age 2–4, an antique car show, Children's Day, and Christmas Open House.

The Gardens are partially accessible to wheelchairs, but Ladew can arrange a guided golf cart tour with five days advance notice.

Lexington Market

This world-famous market has been in operation since 1782 and is one of the oldest markets in the United States. Ralph Waldo Emerson referred to it as the "gastronomic capital of the universe." A recent renovation costing more than $2.6 million updated the market with new air conditioning, remodeled bathrooms, landscaping, new facades and awnings. More than 130 merchants sell food from all around the world, creating a bustling market with enticing sights, sounds, smells and tastes.

www.LexingtonMarket.com

410-685-6169

400 West Lexington Street, Baltimore, MD
Capital Beltway (I-495) to I-95 north to I-395 to Russell Street exit; continue on Paca Street five blocks north. You can enter the market from Paca or Lexington Streets. Additional small markets are sprinkled throughout downtown Baltimore. Parking adjacent to market.

Open Monday–Saturday, 8:30–6. Closed Sunday, Memorial Day, July 4, Labor Day, Thanksgiving, December 25 and January 1.

Special activities include free live music every Friday and Saturday (noon–2 p.m.) year round; Lunch with the Elephants in mid-March; a Preakness Crab Derby in mid-May; a Chocolate Festival in October; and a holiday concert series showcasing schools from around the state.

Maryland Historical Society

Pick up a "Passport to the Past" to explore the museum's permanent exhibitions. Highlights include a Hands-On-History Room with a rope bed, cast iron cook stove and butter churns. Young children love to play in "A Child's World," where they can try on period clothes as well as attempt some of the work a child in 1814 would have done. The original manuscript of the "Star-Spangled Banner" is housed here in an exhibit on the War of 1812.

www.mdhs.org

410-685-3750

201 West Monument Street, Baltimore, MD
Capital Beltway (I-495) to I-95 north to I-395; exit at Martin Luther King, Jr. Boulevard; right on Druid Hill Avenue; left on Howard Street; right on West Monument Street.

Open Wednesday–Sunday, and the first Thursday of every month until 8. Closed major holidays and Sundays, July–August.

Adults, $4; children under 12, free; senior citizens and students with I.D., $3. Family rate: $12 for two adults and children under 17.

Wheelchair access to all except Pratt House and the library. Strollers permitted, but it is preferred that they be left at the door.

 ### Maryland Science Center

You can easily spend a whole day in this excellent museum with its permanent exhibits on Earth Science, the Chesapeake Bay, Space, Dinosaurs and the Human Body. Little ones can play with giant microscopes, climb through undersea caves as well as have fun with water play and many other hands-on activities. Future paleontologists enjoy the Dinosaur Hall with its full-size dinosaur skeletons, field lab, and exhibits where visitors can excavate fossils. The center hosts temporary exhibits frequently.

www.mdsci.org

410-685-5225

601 Light Street, Baltimore, MD
Capital Beltway (I-495) to I-95 north toward Baltimore. Exit 53 onto I-395 north toward downtown/Martin Luther King Boulevard. Turn

right at Conway Street. Turn right at Sharp Street, left at Montgomery, left at Light Street.

Weekdays, 10–5; Saturday, 10–6; Sunday noon–5. Extended summer hours. Closed Thanksgiving and December 25.

Adults, $14.50; children 3–12, $10; and seniors 60+, $13.50. Special temporary exhibits and IMAX films additional.

Live demonstrations daily. Davis Planetarium and IMAX Theater presentations change several times throughout the year.

Memberships in the Maryland Science Center also provide access to more than 200 science centers and children's museums in North America.

Maryland Zoo in Baltimore (formerly the Baltimore Zoo)

The Maryland Zoo in Baltimore is home to more than 1,500 birds, mammals, amphibians and reptiles, representing nearly 200 species and divided into three main sections: Maryland Wilderness, the African Journey and Polar Bear Watch. The Children's Zoo (part of the Maryland Wilderness section and featuring animals native to Maryland) offers oodles of interactive exhibits. Here kids can burrow underground like woodchucks or hop on a lily pad like a frog. At the African Journey you'll find lions, cheetahs, African birds and penguins, chimpanzees, zebras, white rhinos, ostrich and leopards.

> **Take Note**
>
> See polar bears swim in their underwater viewing pool, Polar Bear Watch. This state-of-the-art exhibit teaches about life on the edge of the Arctic, and includes an authentic Tundra Buggy.

www.marylandzoo.org

410-366-LION

ZOO

Druid Hill Park, Baltimore, MD
Capital Beltway (I495) to I-95 north, then I-395 north (Exit 53). Continue onto Pratt Street, then turn left onto President Street. Continue straight on I-83 north to exit 7 west to Druid Park Lake Drive. Follow signs to the zoo. Parking is free.

Daily, March–December 10–4. Closed Thanksgiving, December 25 and on the second Friday in June.

Adults, $15; senior citizens 65+, $12, children 2–11, $10. Children under 2, free.

Tram runs from the main entrance to the central area of the zoo.

Strollers and wheelchairs available to rent.

Special activities include a Spring Event, Bunny BonanZOO; Halloween event, ZooBOO!; plus Keeper Chats and summer education camps. Camel rides in summer for an additional fee.

National Aquarium in Baltimore

The National Aquarium in Baltimore recently added a multimillion dollar immersion exhibit, "Animal Planet Australia: Wild Extremes." The exhibit depicts an Australian river gorge and contains the largest collection of Australian wildlife anywhere outside of Australia. Other popular exhibits include the high-energy dolphin show, where you'll see how dolphins, like humans, play to learn; and the Open Ocean exhibit, a four-floor viewing tank where you'll see nurse and sand tiger sharks, and which surrounds the ramp which you'll descend to exit. The Aquarium is one of Baltimore's most popular attractions; to avoid the heaviest crowds, visit before 11 a.m. or after 3 p.m.

www.aqua.org

410-576-3800, 410-576-3833, reservations

Pier 3, 501 East Pratt Street, Baltimore, MD
Capital Beltway (I-495) to I-95 north to I-395-downtown. Follow signs for Inner Harbor to Pratt and Gay Streets.

Take Note

If you've got preschoolers, head to Discovery Corner, a popular touch exhibit for little ones. Strollers are not permitted in the building, but the Aquarium will provide back-packs for babies and toddlers. Or visit the smaller National Aquarium in Washington, DC...and plan for a trip to Baltimore's aquarium in a few years.

Open November–February: Fridays, 10–8; all other days, 10–5; March–June, September–October: Fridays, 9–8; all other days, 9–5; July–August: Monday–Thursday, 9–6 and Friday–Sunday, 9–8. Note that the museum is the least crowded during January.

Adults, 12–59, $21.95; senior citizens, $20.95; children, 3–11, $12.95; children under 3, free. Advance timed tickets are available through the website, and it is possible to pick up advance tickets at the museum itself. You also can avoid the wait by buying a timed-entry ticket online for a $1.75 per ticket additional fee.

If you think your family will visit the Aquarium more than once a year, you'll save money by becoming a member; you'll also get discounts at the museum gift shops and, best of all, quicker entrance than general admission.

The Aquarium Café offers Maryland classics like crab cakes and Old Bay fries as well as other quick snacks.

The rain forest area is not accessible to wheelchairs.

National Museum of Dentistry

Discover the power of a healthy smile and the history of dentistry through hands-on exhibits. Visit George Washington's not-so-wooden teeth, sing along to vintage toothpaste commercials, and see how a visit to the dentist has changed for the better. Young kids can play in a child-size dental chair. Teenagers can explore genetics and scientific advances in dentistry. Learn to identify crime victims using dental clues, discover the wonders of saliva, and see how dentists may one day be able to grow new teeth.

Take Note

Don't miss the film shorts of Hollywood dentists featuring the Little Rascals, W.C. Fields and Charlie Chaplin.

www.dentalmuseum.org

410-706-0600

31 South Greene Street, Baltimore, MD
Capital Beltway (I-495) to I-95 to I-395 (downtown Baltimore) and exit onto Martin Luther King, Jr. Boulevard, staying in the right lane. At the fourth traffic light, turn right onto Baltimore Street. Turn right at the first traffic light onto Greene Street. Look for NMD banners on left.

Open Wednesday–Saturday, 10–4; Sunday, 1–4. Closed Monday, Tuesday, and major holidays.

Adults 19–59, $6; children 7–18, senior citizens, students with I.D., $3; children 6 and younger, free.

Light Rail (University Center stop located two blocks east of the museum).

Limited on-street metered parking, as well as a parking garage located on Paca Street and another north of Oriole Park at Camden Yards.

Special activities include a George Washington celebration in February and a Halloween event for children.

Port Discovery, the Children's Museum in Baltimore

Port Discovery offers educational and interactive exhibits, programs and events that are fun for the whole family. The museum comprises 80,000 square feet of interactive exhibits for children age 2–10.

Exhibits include Kidworks, the three-story elaborate climbing structure that forms the central core of the museum and the Adventure Expeditions exhibit, which lets you travel back to ancient Egypt. Future sleuths can solve a mystery in Miss Perceptions Mystery House, where they'll have to crawl through the sink to find clues on the other side. An exhibit called Five Friends from Japan allows children to "visit" Japan without using a passport. In Wonders of Water, another exhibit, children will be able to learn how important water is to the human body and global environment through play. And for children up to age 4, Sensation Station has mini-slides, a ball pit and toddler toys. Children can also build structures using giant Lincoln Logs.

Take Note

Stay close to younger children as they go through the tube mazes—or keep your eyes on them—because they come out at different levels.

www.portdiscovery.com

410-727-8120

35 Market Place, Baltimore, MD
Capital Beltway (I-495) to I-95 north to I-395-Baltimore (Inner Harbor) past Camden Yards to Pratt Street and turn right. Continue on Market Place and turn left. After crossing Lombard Street, Port Discovery is on the right.

Open Memorial Day–Labor Day: Monday–Saturday, 10–5; and Sunday, noon–5.

Open September: Friday, 9:30–4:30; Saturday, 10–5; and Sunday,
noon–5. Open October–May: Tuesday–Friday, 9:30–4:30;Saturday,
10–5; and Sunday noon–5.

Ages 2 and older, $10.75; younger than two, free.

Reginald F. Lewis Museum of Maryland African-American History and Culture

Opened to the public in 2005, this 82,000 square-foot
facility provides permanent and changing exhibits on
Maryland's rich African American history and culture,
along with an oral history studio and interactive learning
opportunities. The museum theater hosts dance and musical performances, film festivals and lectures.

www.africanamericanculture.org

443-263-1800

803 Pratt Street, Baltimore, MD
At President and Pratt Streets.

Open Tuesday–Saturday, 10–5; Sunday, 12–5.

General admission, $8; college students and seniors, $6; children 6 and
under, $6; members free.

For group tours, call at least three weeks in advance (443-263-1831).

Special activities include Martin Luther King and Black History Month
events in February; Freedom Week in July (includes reduced admission
and special events); Kwanzaa celebration.

Sports Legends at Camden Yards

Fans of all sports will find something to love in this interactive sports museum. Kids can sit on the bench in a
locker room and try on uniforms from the Frederick Keys,
Baltimore Ravens and other teams in the Locker Room–Kids'
Discovery Zone. See an array of products endorsed by the Babe from
a 1930s fountain pen, to the first Babe Ruth Home Run chocolate bar,
men's underwear and toys. Watch the moving video of Cal Ripken's
"2131" and see the banner that was unfurled that day when he broke
Lou Gehrig's record for the most consecutive games played.

www.sportslegendsatcamdenyards.com

410-727-1539

301 W. Camden Street, Baltimore MD
Capital Beltway (I-495) to I-95 north toward Baltimore. For public parking, exit 53 to I-395 north. Stay left at the split. Continue north on Howard Street to Pratt Street or Lombard Street for public parking garages. The museum is near the ticket windows for Camden Yards. For the stadium entrance and permit lots, use exit 52 (RussellStreet north) and turn right onto Lee Street for access to A, B/C, East or North permit lots.

> **Take Note**
>
> *Be sure to see the painting of Brooks Robinson titled "Gee Thanks, Brooks," one of Norman Rockwell's last full-size color paintings before his death. Try to find Rockwell's own caricature within it.*

Daily, April–September, 10–6 (until 7:30 p.m. on Oriole home game days); October–March: Tuesday–Sunday, 10–5. Closed Thanksgiving, December 25 and January 1.

Adults, $10; senior citizens, $8; children 3–12, $6.50. Combination Birthplace and Sports Legends Museum at Camden Yards is $14 adults, seniors $11, children 3–12, $9.

U.S.S. Constellation

This 1854 ship-of-war was the last sail ship built by the U.S. Navy and is the oldest Civil War era vessel still afloat. The U.S.S. Constellation offers hands-on activities and demonstrations for visitors as they explore life on board and see how thousands of sailors lived at sea.

www.constellation.org

410-539-1797

301 E. Pratt Street, Pier One, Baltimore, MD

> **Take Note**
>
> *The "Powder Monkey Tour" for kids runs Saturday and Sunday at 1 and 3 p.m. Kids can be members of the Constellation's crew and practice a gun drill, brace the yards and learn about life on board through presentations.*

Daily May 1–October 14, 10–6; October 15–April 30, 10–4. Closed Thanksgiving, December 25 and January 1.

Adults, $8.75; seniors, $7.50; youth 6–14, $4.75; children 5 and under are free. Group rates: adults, $7; senior citizens, $5; youth, $3. Last tickets for the day are sold 30 minutes before closing.

Special activities: The Second Saturday Series, Navigating Through History; Naval Tours and Living History Interpretations.

Walters Art Museum

The Walters recently celebrated the 100th anniversary of its original Palazzo Building with the reinstallation of more than 1,500 objects largely from the museum's Renaissance and Baroque collection—one of the largest troves of Italian paintings in North America. The Walters art gallery was modeled after Renaissance and Baroque palace designs. Paintings from the 14th through the 18th centuries are displayed with sculpture and decorative arts of the period. Children typically enjoy the collection of arms and armor, as well as the Egyptian mummy exhibit. The museum provides hands-on workshops, concerts, storytelling and docent-led tours for children.

www.thewalters.org

410-547-9000

600 North Charles Street, Baltimore, MD
Capital Beltway (I-495) to I-95 north to I-395 to Martin Luther King, Jr. Boulevard north; continue for one mile; turn right on Druid Hill Avenue (which becomes Center Street). Museum is on the left five blocks down at Center and Cathedral Streets.

Open Wednesday–Sunday, 11–5; Friday, 11–8. Closed January 1, July 4, Thanksgiving, and December 24 and 25.

Wheelchair access through entrance at corner of North Charles Street and West Mt. Vernon Place.

Special activities: Drop-in art activities Saturdays, 11–3.

World Trade Center "Top of the World"

Get an aerial overview of Baltimore from the 27th floor of the tallest pentagon-shaped building in the world. Here you'll find spectacular 360-degree panoramic views of Baltimore along with stationed binoculars and photo-map guides describing the local attractions, significant landmarks (like the Bromo Seltzer Tower, the world's largest four-dial gravity clock, and Baltimore's only Art Deco skyscraper) plus views of Camden Yards and a breathtaking view of the Inner Harbor.

www.viewbaltimore.org

410-837-8439

401 E. Pratt Street, Baltimore, MD
Capital Beltway (I-495) to I-95 north toward Baltimore. Continue
on I-395 north toward downtown Baltimore and the Inner Harbor.
Continue on South Howard Street, turn right onto West Pratt Street.
World Trade Center building is on the harbor side of the street near
the Inner Harbor shops and restaurants.

Wednesday–Sunday, 10–6. Last admission 30 minutes before closing.

*Adults, $5; seniors (60+), $4; military (with ID), $4; children 3–12, $3; free
under 3. Special rates apply during events.*

THE CHESAPEAKE BAY WESTERN SHORE

You don't need to cross the Bay Bridge to feel sand in your toes. You'll
find great beaches and attractions up and down the western side of
the Chesapeake Bay. They're far enough to make you feel you've got-
ten away from it all, and close enough for you to be home for dinner.

Breezy Point Beach

www.co.cal.md.us/residents/parks/getinvolved

410-535-0259

5230 Breezy Point Road, Chesapeake Beach, MD
Six miles south of Chesapeake Beach, MD. Capital
Beltway (I-495) to exit 11A, Rt. 4 south/east. Rt. 260 nine
miles to Chesapeake Beach. Turn right on MD 261, left on
Breezy Point Road to beach.

Daily, May 1–October 31.

*12 and over, $5; children 3–11 and
seniors, $3; 2 and under, free.*

*Camping, $25 per night for up to
four people.*

Bathhouses and playground.

Calvert Marine Museum

This museum offers a hands-on opportunity to learn about maritime history, paleontology and the unusual biology of the estuary (where salt and fresh water mix). Fifteen tanks display the amazing diversity of life in the Chesapeake Bay and Patuxent River (which meet where the museum stands). Boats, models, paintings and woodcarvings showcase the lives of water and cannery workers and shipbuilders. Outside, river otters frolic in the water next to a salt marsh that is home to crabs, herons and egrets. Take a walk to the Drum Point Lighthouse, behind the museum, which dates to 1883. Or experience the area by boarding an 1899 oyster boat.

www.calvertmarinemuseum.com

410-326-2042, 410-326-6691

14200 Solomons Island Road, Solomons, MD
I-95 to Rt. 4 south. Follow signs to Solomons Island.

Daily, 10–5.

Adults, $5; seniors, $4; children age 5–12, $2; children under 5, free.

Special activities include Winter Lights Festival in January; Meet the Lighthouse Keeper in April; Patuxent Family Discovery Day in May; Sharkfest in July; Cradle of Invasion (a WWII commemoration) in August; and Patuxent River Appreciation Day in October.

Chesapeake Beach and North Beach

These twin beaches hail from the days before World War II, when they were popular resort destinations. Small beaches and boardwalks make for a pleasant day to play in the sand or stroll past shops.

www.chesapeake-beach.md.us; www.nbeachmd.com

4155 Mears Avenue, Chesapeake Beach, MD
Capital Beltway (I-495) to exit 11, Rt. 4 south into Calvert County; at the cross-county line, left on Rt. 260. Proceed five miles to Chesapeake Beach. Turn right onto Rt. 261; left onto Mears Avenue.

North Beach admission: Calvert County residents, children 3–11, $3; ages 12 and older, $4. Nonresidents, children 3–11, $4; ages 12 and up, $5. All children younger than 3 are free, regardless of residence.

Chesapeake Beach admission free.

Chesapeake Beach Railway Museum

This museum is housed in a turn-of-the-century railroad station not much bigger than a railroad car. Although there are no full-size trains to see, children may enjoy the model trains, photos from the early railroad day and an old-fashioned toy locomotive.

www.chesapeake-beach.md.us

410-257-3892

4155 Mears Avenue, Chesapeake Beach, MD
Capital Beltway (I-495) to Rt. 4 south into Calvert County; at the cross-county line, left onto Rt. 260. Proceed five miles to Chesapeake Beach. Turn right onto Rt. 261; left onto Mears Avenue.

Open May 1–September 30, 1–4; in April and October, open weekends only, 1–4. By appointment in winter.

Chesapeake Beach Water Park

This water park is a great place to take a break from the heat and humidity of a Washington summer. This park offers eight water slides of varying thrill levels, including one that is wheelchair accessible. There is a separate pool for very little ones and a children's activity pool where kids can wrestle an alligator or swim with a giant serpent. Dreamland River, waterfalls and fountains add to the fun. Parents with older kids can pass the time swimming laps or playing water volleyball. Families can also watch the action while relaxing in the beach area.

www.chesapeake-beach.md.us

410-257-1404

4079 Gordon Stinnett Drive, Chesapeake Beach, MD
Capital Beltway (I-495) to exit 11, Rt. 4 south to Rt. 260. Turn right on Bay Side Road (Rt. 261) to Water Port.

Daily, 11–7 while Calvert County schools are not in session. Open weekends, Memorial Day weekend through the weekend after Labor Day, weather permitting.

Calvert County residents, $12, if 48 inches or taller; $10 if shorter than 48 inches and for seniors; nonresidents $18 for 48 inches or taller; $16 if shorter than 48 inches and for seniors. Ages 2 or younger free regardless of residence. Season passes available.

Flag Pond Nature Park

A mile of sandy beach and excellent shark's-tooth hunting await those willing to take the lovely but steep two-mile hike to the shore.

Hike, swim, fish, picnic and view wildlife at this 327-acre park and beach. Visit the nature center and talk to staff about the ponds, swamps, freshwater marshes and cliffs that support this ecosystem.

www.dnr.state.md.us/baylinks/14.html

410-535-5327

Capital Beltway (I-495) to the Rt. 50 exit to Upper Marlboro. From Upper Marlboro, follow Rt. 4 south for about 28 miles to the sign for Flag Ponds Nature Center.

Daily, Memorial Day to Labor Day, 9–6 p.m. In April–May and September–October, open 9–6 weekends only.

Calvert County residents, $4 per car; all others, $6 per car.

Sandy Point State Park

Swim, fish, hike, boat, bird-watch and picnic on this 786-acre park and beach at the foot of the eastern side of the Bay Bridge. Watch sailboats and freighters on the Bay. Playgrounds, marinas, cross-country skiing in winter.

www.dnr.state.md.us/publiclands/southern/sandypoint.html

410-974-2149

1100 East College Parkway, Annapolis, MD
Capital Beltway (I-495) to Rt. 50 east to Annapolis, to exit 29B for Cape St. Claire Road to East College Parkway; merge onto Rt. 179/St. Margarets Road. Turn right at College Parkway.

Open April 14–November 14, 6 a.m.–sunset; shorter hours other times. Boat launch and fishing is 24-hour access year-round.

Weekends and holidays, $5, Maryland residents, $6 non-residents; weekdays, $4 residents, $5 non-residents.

Concession stand.

OTHER MARYLAND SITES

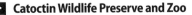

Catoctin Wildlife Preserve and Zoo

Catoctin Wildlife Preserve and Zoo is a shady 35 acres filled with natural wildlife and encounters with exotic animals. Exhibits include bears, boas, macaws, big cats and small mammals in an up-close manner—perfect for children. Shows called "Encounters" are scheduled seasonally and allow visitors to play with a baby animal, get the "bear facts" on grizzlies or explore the world of venomous snakes.

www.cwpzoo.com

301-271-3180

13019 Catoctin Furnace Road, Thurmont, MD
Capital Beltway (I-495) to I-270 north to Frederick, where I-270 becomes Rt. 15 north. Look for the brown Maryland State Attraction signs two miles south of Thurmont; the exit is almost exactly at mile marker 26.

Weekdays, 9–5 and weekends, 9–6, in summer; closed December–February; reduced hours other months. Visitors admitted up to one hour before closing.

Children ages 2–12, $8.95; 13–59, $13.95; seniors age 60 and older, $11.95; children under 2, free. Season passes and group rates available.

Paths are graveled.

Special activities include Catfish Derby, overnight camps for kids, Family Sleepover, Earth Weekend, and Boo-in-the-Zoo in October.

South Mountain Creamery

Feed calves, watch cows being milked or see the farm at this family-owned dairy and milk-processing plant. South Mountain Creamery boasts that it is Maryland's only on-the-farm processing plant, where they grow the crops, milk the cows, process the milk and deliver it.

www.southmountaincreamery.com

301-371-8565

8305 Bolivar Road, Middletown, MD
Capital Beltway (I-495) to I-270 to I-70 West to exit 49/Middletown/
Braddock Heights. Turn left onto Rt. 40A and continue about eight
miles. Turn left onto Bolivar Road and continue to the stop sign,
where you will turn left. Creamery is on your left.

*Free tours during farm hours. Farm and store open Monday–Saturday,
10–6; Sunday, noon–5. All operations except the milk plant are open to
the public. (Milk plant is open twice a year during festivals.)*

Cows are milked daily between 1:30 and 5. Calves are fed daily at 4.

*Special activities include the Cow Caper Festival, featuring hayrides, ice
cream– and butter-making demonstrations, and a petting zoo, held in
early May.*

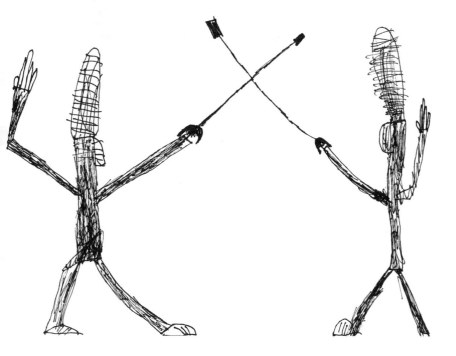

GETTYSBURG, PENNSYLVANIA

Eisenhower National Historic Site

This site adjacent to the Gettysburg Battlefield was the home and working farm of President Dwight D. Eisenhower before and after his presidency in the 1950s. It served as a weekend retreat, a refuge in times of illness and a relaxed setting to meet with world leaders like Premier Nikita Khruschev and President Charles de Gaulle.

In retirement, Eisenhower spent his time on the farm enjoying his hobbies and tending his show herd of black Angus cattle. The Eisenhower family deeded the farm to the National Park Service, which opened it to the public in 1980.

A visit to the farm includes a tour of the Eisenhower home, which retains all its original furnishings. Self-guided walks throughout the site's 690 acres allow for exploration of the skeet range, putting green, rose gardens, guest house and cattle, as well as barns still housing Eisenhower vehicles and farm equipment. In season, living history and park ranger programs are offered. A reception center features a video and exhibits on Eisenhower's life, including his military career. The bucolic setting includes streams, wetlands and endangered species.

www.nps.gov/eise

717-338-9114

97 Taneytown Road, Gettysburg, PA
Capital Beltway (I-495) to I-270 north to U.S. 15 north Business Rt. (Steinwehr Avenue Exit); follow for six miles to National Park Service Visitor Center on the right.

Daily, 9–4. Closed Thanksgiving, December 25 and January 1.

Adults, $6; children 13–16, $4.50; children 6–12, $3.50.

All visits are by shuttle bus from the Visitor Center. Wheelchair users may follow shuttle to the site. Strollers are carried on shuttle bus. The first floor of the Eisenhower home, the grounds, and the Reception Center are wheelchair accessible.

Special activities include the Junior Secret Service program for children 7–12, who earn a badge by performing activities from the Junior Secret Service Training Manual.

Explore & More

This hands-on children's museum and playhouse in a vintage 1860s house is designed for ages 3–8 and includes a Civil War playhouse with general store and battlefield encampment, a construction zone, giant bubbles and an art room.

www.exploreandmore.com

717-337-9151

70 East High Street, Gettysburg, PA
Capital Beltway (I-495) to I-270 north, which turns into Rt. 15 north to 30 east to Gettysburg Square. Head south onto Baltimore Street, left at second light at High Street. Museum on left.

Monday–Saturday, 10–5, April–September. Reduced hours off-season.

Ages 2–14, $6; ages 15 or older, $4.

Gettysburg National Military Park

This park is the site of a major battle of the American Civil War. The fighting July 2–3, 1863 is considered a turning point in the war and marked the second and final invasion of the North by Confederate forces. The Gettysburg National Cemetery adjoins the park and is where Abraham Lincoln delivered his famous Gettysburg Address.

The Visitor Center is south of the town of Gettysburg and is accessible from Routes 15 and 134. If you begin here, you will get tour information, see the Rosensteel Collection of Civil War artifacts, and see an electronic map of the battle. The first show starts at 8:15 and is held every 45 minutes until closing.

The Cyclorama Center, adjacent to the Visitor Center, contains the famous Cyclorama of "Pickett's Charge," painted by Paul Philippoteaux in 1884. The painting is displayed with a dramatic sound and light program. There are no advance reservations. Groups are admitted in order of arrival. This center also contains a number of free exhibits.

www.nps.gov/gett

717-334-1124

97 Taneytown Road, Gettysburg, PA
Capital Beltway (I-495) to I-270, which becomes Rt. 5 to Gettysburg.

Watch for signs to the National Park Service Visitor Center, at Taney-town Road/Rt. 134 and Steinwehr Avenue/Business Rt. 15.

Visitor center open daily 8–5 (to 6 p.m. in summer). Closed Thanksgiving, December 25 and January 1. The park is open daily, April 1–October 31, 6 a.m.–10 p.m.; and daily, November 1–March 31, 6 a.m.–7 p.m. The Cyclorama Center is open daily, 9–5, April–November.

Fees for the Electric Map and Cyclorama Program.

Licensed Battlefield Guides available for a personal two-hour guided tour in the visitor's vehicle.

Backpacks, daypacks, large handbags and large containers are prohibited in the Visitor and Cyclorama Centers.

Bicycling on paved park roads.

Camping, hiking.

Ghosts of Gettysburg Candlelight Walking Tours

These tours are popular evening destinations. They are based on the "Ghosts of Gettysburg" series by Mark Nesbitt which details the unexplained "sightings" of some of the soldiers who perished in the war. Trained guides in 19th-century garb take stories from Nesbitt's bestselling books and turn them into a fascinating 75-minute stroll through the darkened streets of Gettysburg. Each tour covers about a mile of leisurely walking and contains about ten different "haunted" sites.

www.ghostsofgettysburg.com

717-337-0445

271 Baltimore Street, Gettysburg, PA
Two blocks south of the circle in downtown Gettysburg on Business Rt. 15/Baltimore Street at Breckinridge Street.

Seven different tours, open daily, April–October; weekends March and November. Tours begin as early as 6:30 p.m. and as late as 9:45, varying by season and day of the week.

Land of Little Horses

Enjoy this delightful animal park featuring performances by Falabella miniature horses, which stand as small as 26″ high. The park also includes a petting farm, nature trails, rabbit races and goat milking, plus hay rides and pony rides.

www.landoflittlehorses.com

717-334-7259

125 Glenwood Drive, Gettysburg, PA
Capital Beltway (I-495) to I-270 north to Frederick to Rt. 15 toward Gettysburg. At the end York Street/Rt. 30 exit, turn left. Pass through the main circle of Gettysburg, continuing about three miles to left on Knoxlyn Road. Travel about two miles to right on Glennwood Drive. The farm is on your right.

Open in summer, Monday–Saturday, 10–5; Sunday, noon–5. Reduced hours April, May, September, October and early December.

Admission, $12; children under 2, free. Pony and hay rides $2 extra. Annual passes available.

Playgrounds.

Farther Afield

If you're willing to travel a bit more, head to Lancaster County, Pennsylvania to find charming small towns like Lititz; working farms and farm markets, some run by the Amish; elaborate corn mazes; and the Strasburg Railroad, a haven for train buffs and site of occasional visits from Thomas the Tank Engine and the inimitable Sir Topham Hatt. Helpful websites include www.padutchcountry.com; www.visitpa.com.

Or discover the beauty of western Maryland's mountains as you hike, swim or boat at state parks at Deep Creek Lake or Rocky Gap. You can take in the Alleghenys aboard the Western Maryland Scenic Railroad. Helpful websites include www.dnr.state.md.us/publiclands; www. wmsr.com; www.mdmountainside.com.

VIRGINIA

 Dinosaur Land

After a visit to Skyline Caverns, plan a quick stop at Dinosaur Land. Children will love to romp among the 36 life-size fiberglass dinosaurs, prehistoric mammals and fanciful creatures in a shaded outdoor setting. Take a self-guided tour of the dinosaurs; explanatory signs are beside each dinosaur. This is a great place for taking photos.

www.dinosaurland.com

540-969-2222

3848 Stonewall Jackson Highway, White Post, VA
Capital Beltway (I-495) to I-66 west toward Front Royal; exit 6, Rt. 522 north/340 north, and drive about seven miles. Dinosaur Land is at the intersection of Rt. s 227, 522, and 340.

Daily at 9:30, March–December. Closes at 6:30 in summer; 5:30 at other times.

Ages 11 and older, $5; ages 2–10, $4; children under 2, free.

 Flying Circus Air Show

The Flying Circus Air Show in Bealeton has more than 200 acres of Antique Airfields. From parachute jumpers to wing walkers, audiences are thrilled and amazed.

www.flyingcircusairshow.com

540-439-8661

Rt. 644 and Rt. 17, Bealeton, VA
Capital Beltway (I-495) to I-66 west toward Front Royal. Exit Highway 15 south to US-29/ 211. Turn left onto Meetze Road and right onto Rt. 28. In about a mile and a half turn right onto Germantown Road, which becomes Rt. 610/Midland Road.

Open every Sunday May–October; 11 a.m.–dusk. Gates and field open at 11 a.m. Air show begins at 2:30.

Adults, $10; children ages 3–12, $3; children under 3 are free; group rates available.

Bring sunglasses and binoculars for a better view.

If you are celebrating a special event, let one of the circus staff know and they will announce it during the show.

Special activities include an Annual Balloon Festival in August. Airplane rides are available before and after the Show. No reservation needed. Tickets sold at the gift shop, on a first-come, first-served basis.

Lake Anna State Park

Lake Anna offers fresh water for swimming, boating, fishing and water-skiing. The park features a sandy, life-guarded beach, wooded hiking trails, playground and concession stand, as well as camping and a stocked fishing pond for kids only. Nearby marinas rent boats and jet skis by the day or half day.

www.dcr.state.va.us/parks/lakeanna

540-854-5503

Spotsylvania, VA
Capital Beltway (I-495) to I-95 south. Two exits past Fredericksburg is the Lake Anna/Thornburg exit. Follow signs to the state park.

Fee for swimming: Memorial Day–Labor Day; ages 13 and older, $3 weekdays, $4 weekends; ages 3–12, $2 weekdays, $3 weekends; under 3 free.

Visitor Center open 11–5, Memorial Day–Labor Day.

Luray Caverns

Tour the largest and most popular cavern in eastern America. The profusion of formations and the variety of natural colors make this an underground wonderland. Hear the Great Stalacpipe Organ. See monumental columns, rooms with ceilings more than ten stories high, shimmering draperies, crystal clear pools, and glittering, glistening stone. Children will be amazed by the profusion of colorful formations. Admission includes tour of Luray Caverns and The Car and Carriage Caravan Museum. Tours last about 45 minutes.

www.luraycaverns.com

540-743-6551

Rt. 211 West, Luray, VA
I-66 west to Gainesville. Exit Rt. 29 south to Warrenton; then Rt. 211 west to Luray Caverns.

Open every day of the year. Tours daily, starting at 9 and departing approximately every 20 minutes. Time of last tour of the day changes throughout the year.

Ages 14 and older, $19; ages 6–13, $9; seniors, $16; children 5 and younger, free.

Bring a sweater; it is very cool inside.

Special features include the Garden Maze, a half-mile of twisting paths; and the Luray Singing Tower, which stands 117 feet high and includes 47 bells and features regular recitals. Additional fees for these attractions.

Monticello: The Home of Thomas Jefferson

Get an up close look at the house Thomas Jefferson built for himself and his family in the Piedmont region of Central Virginia. The guided house tour covers the rooms on Monticello's first floor and lasts about 30 minutes. Admission includes access to the grounds and two optional outdoor guided tours, in season: the Plantation Community and the Gardens and Grounds.

www.monticello.org

434-984-9822

931 Thomas Jefferson Parkway, Charlottesville, VA
Capital Beltway (I-495) to I-66 west to Rt. 29 south at Gainesville. Follow U.S. 29 south into Charlottesville and look for signs for the Rt. 250 west/29 south bypass. Follow bypass to I-64 east (direction Richmond), to exit 121A onto Rt. 20 south (direction Scottsville). At the second stoplight, turn left onto Rt. 53 East/Thomas Jefferson Parkway; drive 1.75 miles; immediately after passing under the stone-arch Saunders Bridge, exit right onto the roadway that leads over the bridge and to Monticello.

Daily, 8–5, March–October; and 9–4:30, November–February.

Adults, $15; children 6–11, $7; children younger than 6, free.

There are two ways to purchase tickets to Monticello: Same-day ticket available every day at the Monticello Ticket Office, and reserved tickets for specific times available online.

The Monticello Ticket Office is in the main visitor parking area. Tickets are sold to "walk up" visitors on a first-come, first-served basis. When you make a same-day purchase, you will be given a timed ticket for the next available house tour (conducted at 10-minute intervals throughout the day) or, if you prefer, a tour that starts later. As long as you arrive at Monticello before the gates close you are guaranteed a house tour.

Register at the Ticket Office for special tours for children and families, geared toward children 6–11. Tours include hands-on activities.

Leashed pets allowed on grounds.

Take Note

The tour guides are very child-friendly. Encourage children to ask questions of the tour guides. Have your children count the number of clocks or other gadgets in the house during the tour.

10+ National Museum of the Marine Corps

The National Museum of the Marine Corps features traveling exhibits on the history of WWII, the Korean War and the efforts to stop terrorism. An interactive boot camp experience might be cool for older kids, but photographs, movie footage and "fully immersive, interactive combat environments" are made to be realistic and will be too frightening for many younger or sensitive children.

www.usmcmuseum.org

877-653-1775

18900 Jefferson Davis Highway, Triangle, VA
I-95 to exit 150A to Rt. 1 (Jefferson Davis Highway); turn right (south) to Rt. 1; travel approximately 0.25 miles; museum entrance is on the right.

Daily, 9–5, except December 25. Free admission.

IMAX theatre.

New Market Battlefield State Historical Park and Hall of Valor Civil War Museum

Scavenger and matching games that guide children through the museum are available at the information desk, and younger visitors can dress up as a Union or Confederate soldier, or as a civilian of the era. Tour the historic farm on the grounds to learn how the Civil War affected a local farm family and explore 19th-century farming. Since the farmhouse served as a hospital during the Civil War, exhibits there also highlight Civil War medicine and medical procedures. Also enjoy scenic Shenandoah River overlooks, picnic spots and walking trails.

www.vmi.edu/newmarket

866-515-1864

9500 Collins Drive, New Market, VA
Capital Beltway (I-495) to I-66 west to I-81. Exit 264 onto Rt. 211 west, then immediate right onto Rt. 305/George Collins Parkway. Continue one mile to the circular Hall of Valor. A staff member will share park and ticketing information.

Civil War day camps for children ages 7–12 in July; space is limited and registration is required. Guided tours of the battlefield offered weekends 1 p.m. (battlefield) and 3 p.m. (farm complex) from June through October.

Daily, 9–5, closed Thanksgiving, December 24 and 25 and January 1.

Adults, $9; children 6–18, $5; seniors, $8; five or younger free.

Pink Box Visitor Center of Middleburg, VA

Middleburg is an historic, rural village in the heart of Virginia Hunt Country. Antique shops, specialty stores and great restaurants abound. Three top wineries and the Glenwood Park Race Course are located nearby.

www.cr.nps.gov/nr/travel/journey/mid.htm

540-687-8888, 540-687-5152

12 N. Madison Street, Middleburg, VA
Capital Beltway (I-495) to I-66 west toward Winchester to Rt. 50 west. Drive approximately 25 miles to Middleburg. Turn right at the only traffic light in town; the Pink Box will be on the left.

The Visitor Center, weekdays 11–3 and weekends 11–4, provides brochures and maps on what to do in Middleburg and Loudoun County.

Special activities include the Middleburg Garden Tour in the spring, the Hunt County Stable tour Memorial Day weekend, a Christmas parade the first Saturday in December, Christmas in Middleburg in December, and scores of special events at the Middleburg Community Center.

Shenandoah National Park

The Shenandoah National Park contains more than 196,000 acres and lies across the crest of the Blue Ridge Mountains in Virginia. Skyline Drive, a winding road that runs through the park, provides vistas of the spectacular landscape. This land was previously used by mountain farmers for grazing sheep and cattle, and farming and hunting.

The park was established in 1935 to bring the National Park experience to the millions of people living "within a day's drive," along the east coast. Trails totaling more than 500 miles provide short or long hiking adventures. Visitors can see plants and animals and experience the beauty and peace of this vast national park.

www.nps.gov/shen

540-999-3500

3655 U.S. Highway, 211 East, Luray, VA
Capital Beltway (I-495) to I-66 west to Front Royal, the north entrance of the park.

More than 500 miles of hiking trails, including 101 miles of the Appalachian National Scenic Trail.

Most facilities and one trail are wheelchair accessible. Waterfalls, camping, fishing, hiking.

Skyline Caverns

When visiting the Shenandoah National Park, don't miss the opportunity to visit the beautiful and unusual Skyline Caverns. These underground caves are filled with amazing geological formations that inspire the imagination while offering real life lessons about the physical history of the earth. The caverns—60 million years old—remained a secret until 1937.

Bring along a sweater; the temperature inside is 54 degrees all year round. The best way to see the caverns is on a guided walking tour conducted by a member of the knowledgeable staff. It lasts about 90 minutes. The spectacular lighting brings to life the aptly named wonders beneath the earth: the Capitol Dome, the Rainbow Trail, the Wishing Well, the Shrine, and Fairyland Lake, to name a few. There are also three underground streams, one of which forms a lovely 37-foot waterfall. Amid all this magic, the constant dripping of water throughout the caverns teaches children how the formations are made, and how long it takes nature to do the work. Anchorites, call "orchids of the mineral kingdom," grow an inch every seven thousand years.

After the tour, enjoy a half-mile ride on the Skyline Arrow, a miniature train.

---

www.skylinecaverns.com

540-635-4545

10344 Stonewall Jackson Street, Front Royal, VA
Capital Beltway (I-495) to I-66 west to Exit 13 toward Front Royal. Turn left on VA 79, then right on VA 55. Turn left on US Rt. 340. Caverns are about two miles.

Daily including holidays; hours vary by season.

Ages 14 and older, $16; children 7–13, $8. Train ride is $3 for everyone older than 3.

Stairs involved in tour.

HARPERS FERRY, WEST VIRGINIA

 Harpers Ferry National Historical Park

The story of Harpers Ferry is more than one event, one date or one individual. It involves many people and events that influenced the course of our nation's history. As you begin your tour of Harpers Ferry, look for the Information Center, where you will get an overview of the six main park themes: local industry, John Brown's raid, the Civil War, African-American history, transportation and environment. In addition to the museums listed below, there are hiking trails and fishing in the river nearby (licenses are required).

Black History Museum: This museum is devoted to the history of slaves and their struggle to gain freedom. It includes information before the Civil War and afterward.

Storer College Museum: Learn the history of the college that educated freedmen after the Civil War.

John Brown's Fort: This was the armory's fire-engine house, used by John Brown as a refuge during his 1859 raid.

John Brown Museum: On Shenandoah Street, look for this museum about the events of John Brown's raid. Video presentations describe events leading to the raid and its effect on the country.

Civil War Museum: On High Street, the museum depicts the way that the Civil War affected the town of Harpers Ferry. During the war, the town was occupied by either the Union or Confederate Armies.

Harper House: Built in 1782, this is the oldest surviving structure in the park. Climb the stone steps leading uphill from High Street to reach this historic site.

Dry Goods Store, Provost Marshall's Office, Blacksmith Shop: On Shenandoah Street, these sites give an appreciation of the social and economic history of the times. In summer, the office and shops are staffed with people in period clothing.

www.nps.gov/hafe/

304-535-6029

Shenandoah Street, Harpers Ferry, WV
Capital Beltway I-495 to I-270 North. Pass through Frederick to west on I-70. One mile to exit 52 (Charles Town and Leesburg) onto Rt. 340. Continue 22 miles southwest on 340 to Harpers Ferry. Cross the Potomac and Shenandoah Rivers; proceed to stoplight at top of hill; turn left into national park.

Visitors Center open daily, 8–5; Memorial Day–Labor Day, 8–6. Closed Thanksgiving, December 25 and January 1.

An entrance fee of $6 per vehicle secures a three-day pass to everything offered by the National Park Service. For those entering the park on foot, bicycle or tour bus, the entrance fee is $4 per person; children 17 and under, bus drivers and escorts are free. A variety of annual passes available at the Visitors Center.

Public walking tours are offered Memorial Day–Labor Day. The rest of the year, tours are by reservation only.

Some wheelchair access; wheelchairs are available for loan. Strollers are permitted, but the ride is bumpy.

Fishing, hiking.

AMUSEMENT PARKS

When it comes to amusement park rides, many families find they can get enough of a thrill at their local county or state fair. For a full course of rides, Six Flags America is right here in suburban Largo, MD. If you want to get yourself buckled into a ride right away, this is your best bet. Check out these parks:

Dutch Wonderland

Knights, dragons and princesses are the backdrop for Dutch Wonderland. Geared to children 12 and younger, Dutch Wonderland includes rides, water play and miniature golf.

www.dutchwonderland.com

866-386-2839

2249 Lincoln Highway East, Lancaster, PA

Hershey Park

HersheyPark is part of an entertainment complex based near the original Hershey chocolate factory. Roller coasters, water rides and kiddie rides are featured. You can get combination tickets for these and a visit to ZooAmerica, a zoo and wildlife park. Hershey's Chocolate World offers a dizzying (and delicious) display of chocolate for sale, a tour of a simulated chocolate factory and Hershey's product characters.

www.hersheypark.com

800-HERSHEY

100 Hersheypark Drive, Hershey, PA

Busch Gardens Williamsburg

Apollo's Chariot roller coaster and the Escape from Pompeii boat ride are among the attractions at Busch Gardens Williamsburg. Animal attractions at Busch Gardens include the Budweiser Clydesdales and an eagle habitat.

www.buschgardens.com/va

800-343-7946

1 Busch Gardens Boulevard, Williamsburg, VA

Knoebels Amusement Park and Resort

This no-admission, pay-per-ride amusement park (most rides are $1 or less) boasts excellent roller coasters, swimming, water slides and campgrounds—and a park well-suited to the youngest visitors. Knoebel's has a less commercial feel than other amusement parks; a family of four can buy $40 worth of tickets for the day.

www.knoebels.com

570-672-2572, 800-ITS-4FUN; 570-672-9555 (campground)

Rt. 487, Elysburg, PA (about three hours from Washington)

Paramount's Kings Dominion

Kings Dominion sports 12 roller coasters, including Ricochet, with a 50-foot drop, and the WaterWorks water park. For younger children, try Scooby-Doo's Ghoster Coaster or the SpongeBob SquarePants 3D movie.

www.kingsdominion.com

804-876-5000

Rt. 30 and 1-95, Doswell, VA

Six Flags America

Here families will find plenty of rides based on characters such as Bugs Bunny and Superman, as well as the Hurricane Harbor Water Park.

www.sixflags.com/america

301-249-1500

13710 Central Avenue, Largo, MD

RAILROADS

Strasburg Railroad (Lancaster County, Pennsylvania)

Explore the train engines and rail cars close up on America's oldest short-line railroad. Restored trains including a full-size, coal burning steam train—ride in coaches or in the open air for a 45-minute ride through the countryside. Stop for a picnic lunch on certain rides. Ride the miniature Cagney Steam Train. Operate a hand-powered Pump Car or watch little ones steer the pint-size Cranky Car. Tour the switch tower and freight equipment displays.

Arrive at least 45–60 minutes early, particularly on special event days. Weekends are crowded. Wear comfortable, closed-toes shoes for walking on rocks, gravel and sand. Beware of sitting close to the engine on the steam train with little ones in tow as ashes and soot can fall on passengers sitting close to the coal car.

www.strasburgrailroad.com

717-687-7522

Rt. 741 East, Strasburg, Lancaster County, PA
Capital Beltway (I-495) to I-95 north to I-695 (Baltimore Beltway) west to I-83 north toward York, PA. Exit at Rt. 30 east; turn left (South) onto Rt. 896 at Rockvale Square Factory Outlets. Turn left at the traffic light in the center of Strasburg, onto route 741 east. Follow Rt. 741 east to the Strasburg Rail Road. 1.5 miles east of the center square in historic Strasburg, Lancaster County, Pennsylvania).

Departures several times daily.

Tickets can be purchased online at the website for a $3 handling fee.

Day Out with Thomas the Train: Tickets for Day out with Thomas can be purchased online at www.ticketweb.com. Note that Day Out with Thomas can sell out.

Can accommodate special access needs; call in advance.

Walkersville Southern Railroad

The Walkersville Southern Railroad runs on the Frederick Branch of the old Pennsylvania Railroad. The turn-of-the-century railroad station, ticket office and freight house add to the feel of a trip back in time. Passengers ride a vintage 1920s car, a caboose or an open flat car into picturesque Maryland farm country at speeds limited to 10 mph.

www.wsrr.org

P.O. Box 651, Walkersville, MD 21793
I-270 North toward Frederick, MD. In Frederick I-270 becomes Rt. 15 North toward Gettysburg. Follow Rt. 15 North for 6 miles, then turn right onto Biggs Ford Road Travel 2.2 miles to the station and parking on the right.

Saturdays, May–October at 11, 1 and 3. Sundays in May, June, September and October at 11 and 1. Evenings and special events—contact WSRR for details.

Ticket office open 10:30–4 p.m. on excursion days.

Adults, $9; children, $5; seniors, $8; children under 3 free unless occupying a seat. Season pass for four, $85.

Seating on train rides is first-come, first-served. Excursions are held rain or shine.

Specialty theme train rides throughout the year: Teddy Bear Picnic; Fireworks; Fall Foliage; Costume Party; Santa Trains.

Museum includes model train displays.

Western Maryland Scenic Railroad

Mountain Thunder makes a 3.5-hour trip through the Allegheny Mountains from Cumberland. The 1916 Baldwin steam engine and the restored diesel engine climb 1,300 feet over 16 miles and chugs through a 900-foot tunnel and around horseshoe curves to Frostburg, where riders can stop for lunch and a visit to the Thrasher Carriage Museum.

www.wmsr.com

800-872-4650

13 Canal Street, Cumberland, MD
I-70 west to I-68 west at Hancock. Exit 43C, Cumberland; turn left at the bottom of the exit ramp into parking lot.

Adults, $25–48; children, $12–$31; seniors, $23–$46; children under 2 free if not occupying a seat. First-class tickets include lunch.

Trains operate May–December; standard excursions depart at 11:30 a.m.

Special excursions and rates for private celebrations, holidays and events. Annual Day Out with Thomas event.

Locomotive and caboose rides available.

11

FIELD TRIPS

Going Places with Children in Washington, DC originated half a century ago as a photocopied list of the many field trips students take as part of Green Acres School's hands-on, experiential curriculum. For this 50th anniversary edition, the editors asked current teachers about their favorite field trips—trips that families or groups could take both for education and for fun. This wide-ranging sample can serve as a jumping-off point for ideas for families and teachers looking for ways to bring to life topics their children are studying in school, from math to art to social studies.

American Visionary Art Museum

Inside the walls of this hip, unusual and very cool museum, wacky, eccentric and eclectic works of art beckon seductively from every angle—a perfect tonic for a potentially jaded group of middle school students. Even from the entrance, which is studded with whimsical treasures like broken china plates, cups and an assortment of broken colored glass bottles, students are catapulted out of the ordinary into the fantasy world of untrained artists on the fringes of society. Another building supports a fun house of mechanical figures in a hands-on, user-friendly sideshow alley, while the gift shop is bursting with the wackiest and most affordable Coney-Island souvenirs you could ever imagine.

www.avam.org/

410-244-1900

800 Key Highway, Baltimore, MD
Capital Beltway (I-495) to I-95 north toward Baltimore. Near Baltimore,

merge onto I-395 via exit 53 toward Martin Luther King Boulevard/ Downtown, to the Conway Street exit. Turn right onto Light Street/Rt. 2 south. Turn slight left onto Key Highway. Metered parking is available on Covington Street and Key Highway.

Tuesday–Sunday, 10–6. Closed Monday (except Martin Luther King, Jr. Day), Thanksgiving and December 25.

Admission: Adults $12; students and seniors $8; age 6 and under free.

Classroom in the Park

Each fall Gambrill State Park becomes the outdoor classroom that Green Acres middle school students visit to experience a school day in nature. For math, students jump between two lines, measuring the distance and calculating the average for each student and his or her group. A Spanish scavenger hunt combines Spanish and science. For art, students draw something in nature. Use your imagination, at this or any park, for a welcome break from the indoor classroom.

www.dnr.state.md.us/publiclands/western/gambrill.html

301-271-7574

Gambrill Park Road, Frederick, MD
I-270 north to Frederick, where it becomes U.S. Rt. 15. Continue to Rt. 40 west (West Patrick Street). Exit to the I-70 west/Rt. 40 split, bear right and continue on Rt. 40. Turn right on Gambrill Park Road and follow one mile to the Rock Run Area entrance on your left to reach the campground. Continue on Gambrill Park Road to reach the trail parking lot and to the top of the mountain to reach the scenic overlooks, pavilions and the Tea Room.

April–October, 8 a.m.–sunset; November–March, 10 a.m.–sunset.

Nature center, campsites and tea room.

Experimenting with International Cuisine

As part of a unit on Japan, first graders eat lunch at Hinode Japanese restaurant in Rockville. Prior to the visit, students practice eating rice with chopsticks in the classroom. They also learn how to write Japanese characters, read stories about Japan, make origami and dress up in kimonos and slippers. No matter what country or culture your children are study-ing, there's probably a restaurant in the Washington region where your children can literally get a "taste" of another culture.

---

www.hinode-restaurant.com/main.htm

301-816-2190

---

134 Congressional Lane, Rockville, MD

Fire Station Tours

You can't beat a trip to the fire station for the Pre-K crowd. At Rockville Volunteer Fire Department's Station 3—and most other fire stations in the region—firefighters will let children see fire trucks, engines, rescue squads and ambu-lances, and even sit in the driver's seat. They will often offer a tour of the facilities that includes the "watch room," kitchen, lounge, gym and sleeping quarters. Children can watch firefighters transform from their street clothes into their head-to-toe firefighting gear, touch the gear and learn all about the process of responding to emergency calls. If you're lucky enough to be there when a live call comes in, you can watch the firefighters and vehicles go into action.

---

www.rvfd.org/aboutrvfd/stations/station3/station3.htm

301-424-2311

---

380 Hungerford Drive, Rockville, MD
I-270 north to exit 5, MD 189, toward Falls Road north. Turn left onto Great Falls Road/MD 189, which becomes West Montgomery Avenue. Turn left onto North Van Buren Street, and right onto Beall Avenue. Fire station is where Beall Avenue ends.

Gettysburg Day Trip

Visit the Gettysburg Tour Center to see where Pickett's Charge took place, a site students proclaim "very cool." Students can re-enact some of the battles of the Civil War and can see for themselves where some of their forefathers (and foremothers) fought in this formative histori-cal period. History and the present collide as students strategize over geographic advantages and disadvantages of setting up an attack and begin to understand the psychological impact of war. For many, it is the first time students see that the Civil War was more than North fighting South; it was often friend fighting friend.

www.gettysburg.com

717-334-6020 or 800-447-8788

200 Steinwehr Ave., Gettysburg, PA
I-270 north toward Frederick, where it becomes US-40 west, and then US-15 north in Pennsylvania. Exit at Taneytown Road/PA-134, turning left onto Taneytown Road. Proceed about 3 miles; then turn sharp left onto Steinwehr Avenue.

Hands-on Optics

Try a visit to Hands-on Optics, a telescope store in Damascus owned and operated by Gary Hand, a Green Acres School alumnus. Gary can answer all your telescope needs and even schedules astronomy "events" for groups. Astronomy is not only for the few hobbyists who have the time and money to indulge an interest, but for anyone who would like to learn and observe the night sky. Stargazing nights led by volunteers at Green Acres have been very successful; parents, teachers and students point out constellations, track the motion of satellites, and look through a telescope at star clusters, galaxies and planets. Try creating a stargazing night of your own.

www.handsonoptics.com/index.html

301-482-0000

26437 Ridge Road (Rt. 27), Damascus, MD
I-270 north to exit 16A, Father Hurley Boulevard, toward Rt. 27 east. Father Hurley Boulevard becomes Ridge Road. After about 6 miles, turn right onto Main Street, then left onto Ridge Road.

Monday–Friday, 10–7; Saturday, 10–5

Hard Bargain Farm: Alice Ferguson Foundation

Picture yourself sitting on an idyllic hilltop looking over the Potomac River to Mt. Vernon. Wander along the wooden boardwalk, with the Potomac River on your right and the Chesapeake Bay watershed on your left. Grab your binoculars to track an eagle soaring through the sky. Catch a crayfish in the stream. Construct a watershed, complete with a "river," town and forest, and study the long-term effects of erosion. Milk a cow. Slop the pigs. Pet a newborn lamb. Help plan, prepare, serve and clean up your meals. Climb into your bunk after a long exciting day of adventures. This is what Green Acres fourth graders and thousands of other elementary and middle school students do every year at Hard Bargain Farm Environmental Center in Prince George's County, MD, where children learn about the environment and history of the area on an overnight trip that supports global awareness and community building.

www.hardbargainfarm.org

301-292-5665

2001 Bryan Point Road, Accokeek, VA
Capital Beltway (I-495) to exit 3A/Rt. 210 south, Indian Head Highway. Proceed about 10 miles to Accokeek and turn right on Livingston Road. Travel about 100 yards and turn right at Biddle Road. At the stop sign, go left on Bryan Point Road. Stay on Bryan Point Road for about 2.5 miles. Hard Bargain Farm is on the right.

 London Town

London Town, a scenic site on the South River near Annapolis, MD, offers middle schoolers the chance to experience 18th-century life and participate in an ongoing archaeological dig. Students sift through dirt from the site using real archaeological equipment such as tripod sifters. Anything found during this process is handed over to the docents to be recorded in London Town's historical documentation. Students also are taken into a 1700s style house to glimpse life for men and women in the 18th century and learn more about each gender's responsibilities. Students also have an up-close view of a cross section of earth that has been cut away by professional archaeologists, revealing the strata and the artifacts each layer contains. Students later tour the main building, an inn that George Washington used when traveling on business. The large building consists of model 18th-century dwellings, a lounge room, kitchen and additional rooms. As a last treat for the day, students try on period clothing for a glimpse of what it felt like to dress as a colonial American.

www.historiclondontown.com

410-222-1919

839 Londontown Road, Edgewater, MD
Capital Beltway (I-495) to US 50/MD 301 to Rt. 665 (Exit 22, Aris T. Allen Boulevard). Exit onto Rt. 2 south (Solomon's Island Road), go over South River Bridge. Continue about 0.6 miles (3 traffic lights); turn left at the third traffic light onto Mayo Road. Go about 0.8 miles; turn left at the second traffic light onto Londontown Road. Proceed about 1 mile to the end of the road, stay to the left and enter the site through the gates.

Tuesday–Saturday, 10–4; Sunday noon–4; closed Monday. Gardens open weather permitting. Tour hours: Tuesday–Saturday, 10–3; Sunday, noon–3. William Brown House closed January-March.

Guided house and self-guided garden tour $7; house tour $4; self-guided garden tour $4; children 7–12 $3; under 7 free. Field trip fees are $4 per student for half-day and $6 per student for full day.

Education programs are available at London Town on Tuesdays and Wednesdays from September through early November and from March through June. Contact the Education Department to arrange a field trip.

 ### National Gallery of Art: East Wing

Take a math trip to the East Wing of the National Gallery of Art. The building itself contains a plethora of two- and three-dimensional shapes, and the artwork adds to our study of geometry. How many geometric shapes can you find in the entranceway alone? Ride the elevator, and see if you can identify the 3-D shape in which you're traveling. From line segments to trapezoids, from rhombuses to pyramids, the East Wing is a geometric treasure. (See National Gallery of Art, p. 22.)

www.nga.gov

202-737-4215

4th and Constitution Avenue, Washington, DC

Metrorail Red line (Gallery Place).

Walking Tour of Alexandria, Virginia

What better way is there to learn about history than to take on the role of someone who lived at that time and imagine what life was like for that person? As part of a study of colonial Alexandria, students take a walking tour of Alexandria led by docents from the Lyceum. Through role-playing during the tour, they learn how the townspeople lived and worked two hundred years ago. Children take great delight in pretending to be the doctor, ship builder or dress maker in Old Town. They come to realize the interdependence of the people living in the town: the doctor may tend sick sailors from the ships or his wife might need a new dress. Children also enjoy walking on a cobblestone street while looking for boot scrapers, gossip mirrors and historical artifacts.

oha.alexandriava.gov/lyceum/

703-838-4994

The Lyceum: Alexandria's History Museum, 201 S. Washington Street, Alexandria, VA
Capital Beltway (I-495) to US Rt. 1 north exit (first exit on the Virginia side of the Woodrow Wilson Bridge). Follow Rt. 1 (Patrick Street) about one mile. Turn right on Prince Street; turn right on South Washington Street. The Lyceum is on the right.

Monday–Saturday, 10–5; Sunday, 1–5. Closed January 1, Thanksgiving, December 24–25.

Metrorail Yellow or Blue line (King Street).

12

QUICK GUIDE

Editors' Choices

The Air and Space Museum and Steven F. Udvar-Hazy Center

American Visionary Art Museum

Clark Griffith/ Cal Ripken Sr. League Baseball

Bureau of Engraving and Printing, U.S. Treasury

Calvert Cliffs State Park

Glen Echo Park

Great Falls National Park

Kennedy Center's Millennium Stage and National Symphony Petting Zoo

Land of Little Horses

The Lincoln and Jefferson Memorials at night

Maryland Science Center

Mount Vernon

National Building Museum Family Programs

National Gallery of Art Sculpture Garden

Old Rag in Shenandoah National Park

Oxon Hill Farm Park

Port Discovery

Smithsonian American Art Museum and National Portrait Gallery

Smithsonian Carousel

Sports Legends at Camden Yards

Storytimes at libraries, bookstores and museums

Sugarloaf Mountain

U.S. Botanic Garden

Textile Museum

Vietnam Veterans Memorial

The Washington Monument (especially the top)

New for the 17th Edition

Amazing Art Studio

AMF Lanes

Arlington Cinema 'n' Drafthouse

The Banneker Douglass Museum

Belle Haven Marina

Bowl America

City of Rockville Indoor Climbing

Classika Theater

Claude Moore Recreation Center

Clemyjontri Park

Color Me Mine

DC United Soccer

Earth Treks Climbing

The Family Room

Flag Pond Nature Park

Funfit Family Fitness Center

Herbert W. Wells Ice Rink

Hill's Gymnastics

JW Tumbles
Kids 'N' Clay
Koshland Science Museum
LaserNation/Ultra Zone
Lincoln Cottage
Little Sprouts Playtime Center
Madame Tussauds Washington, DC
MarVaTots 'n' Teens
Mid Atlantic Golf Center
Monticello: Home of Thomas Jefferson
Mount Vernon Ice Arena
The Mud Hut
My Gym
National Gallery of Art Children's Film
    Program
National Museum of the Marine Corps
Norwood Local Park
Nottoway Park
Old Rag Mountain, Shenandoah
    National Park
Olney Manor Skate Park
Paint Your Own Pottery
PlaywiseKids
Potomac Nationals Baseball

Robert E. Parilla Performing Art Center
Rollingcrest-Chillum Splash Pool
Sandy Point State Park
Sculpture Garden Ice Rink
South Mountain Creamery
Sports Legends at Camden Yards
Steven F. Udar-Hazy Center
Strike Bethesda
Sunny Dyes
TopGolf
Tucker Road Ice Rink
Turtle Park
Walkersville Southern Railroad
Washington Ballet
Washington Capitals Hockey
Washington Freedom
Washington Nationals
Washington Wizards
Water Mine Family Swimming Hole
Wheaton/Glenmont Outdoor Pool
Wheaton Ice Rink
White Oak Duckpin Bowling Lanes
World Trade Center "Top of the World"
XP Laser Sport

Birthdays and Other Celebrations

This book is meant for anyone in the region—tourists, residents, families hosting out-of-town guests, and people looking to spark ideas for birthday parties or other celebrations. Many, many of the places listed in this book offer party packages; you can be as adventurous or low-key in your celebrations as you are when you go places with children on a normal day. Call or check websites for more information—and have a wonderful time "going places."

ACTIVITY GUIDE

Appropriate for Preschoolers

Adventure Theater
Arlington Cinema 'n' Drafthouse
Books and Toys—Chapter 7
Bowling—Chapter 8
Bull Run Regional Park
Burke Lake Park
Cabin John Regional Park
Classika Theater
Claude Moore Recreation Center
DC United Soccer
ExploraWorld
The Family Room
Funfit Family Fitness Center
Glen Echo Park and Carousel
Hadley's Park
Hidden Oaks Nature Center
Hill's Gymnastics
Ice Skating—Chapter 8
Imagination Stage
JW Tumbles
Little Sprout Playtime Center
Lake Accotink Park
Lake Fairfax Park

Locust Grove Nature Center
Make-Your-Own Art—Chapter 9
MarVaTots 'n Teens
Minor League Baseball—Chapter 8
My Gym
National Aquarium, Washington
National Gallery of Art – Children's
    Film Program
Noyes Library for Young Children
Oxon Hill Farm
Parenting Resource Centers
PlaywiseKids
Public Swimming Pools—Chapter 7
Puppet Company Playhouse
Robert E. Parilla Performing Art Center
Smithsonian Discovery Theater
South Mountain Creamery
Sports Legends at Camden Yards
Steven F. Udvar-Hazy Center
Watkins Regional Park
Wheaton Regional Park
World Trade Center "Top of the World"

Of Special Interest to Teenagers

African Art Museum of Maryland
Alexandria Archaeology Museum
Arlington Cinema 'n' Drafthouse
Arlington House, the Robert E. Lee
    Memorial
Arthur M. Sackler Gallery
Baltimore Orioles
Beall-Dawson House and Stonestreet
    Museum of 19th Century Medicine
Belle Haven Marina
Bowling—Chapter 8
Brookside Gardens
Carlyle House Historic Park
City of Rockville Indoor Climbing
Classika Theater

Claude Moore Recreation Center
Corcoran Gallery of Art
Dave and Buster's
DC United
Drug Enforcement Administration
    Museum and Visitors Center
Earth Treks Climbing
Fairland Batting Cages
Folger Shakespeare Library
Fort Washington Park
Frederick Douglass Home (Cedar Hill)
Gadsby's Tavern Museum
Golf—Chapter 8
Hirshhorn Museum and Sculpture
    Garden

Airplanes/Space

Aquariums

Arboretums/Gardens

Batting Cages

Cameron Run Regional Park and Great
    Waves Water Park
Fairland Batting Cages

Occoquan Regional Park
Upton Hill Regional Park
Rocky Gorge

Battlefields/Forts

Antietam National Battlefield
Ball's Bluff Regional Park
Bedford Park and Museum
Federal Hill Park
Fort McHenry National Monument
    and Historic Shrine
Fort Ward Museum and Historic Site
Fort Washington Park

Fredericksburg and Spotsylvania
    National Military Park
Gettysburg National Military Park
Manassas National Battlefield Park
New Market Battlefield Military
    Museum
Patapsco Valley State Park

Biking

Allen Pond Park
Black Hill Regional Park
Bluemont Park
Capital Crescent Trail
Cedarville State Forest
Chesapeake and Ohio (C&O) Canal
    Historical Park Great Falls, MD
East Potomac Park
Fletcher's Boathouse
Fountainhead Regional Park
Gettysburg National Military Park
Lake Accotink Park
Lake Artemesia Park
Mount Vernon Trail
Occoquan Regional Park

Patapsco Valley State Park
Prince William Forest Park
Quiet Waters Park
Rock Creek Park
Rocky Gap State Park
Seneca Creek State Park
Sligo Creek Park
Thompson's Boat Center
Washington and Old Dominion
    (W&OD) Railroad Regional Park
Watkins Regional Park
Wheaton Regional Park
White's Ferry
Whitetail Resort

Boating

Algonkian Regional Park
Allen Pond Park
Anacostia Park
Belle Haven Marina
Black Hill Regional Park
Bull Run Marina
Burke Lake Park

Calvert Marine Museum
Chesapeake and Ohio (C&O) Canal at
    Great Falls, MD
Cosca Regional Park
Cunningham Falls State Park
Fletcher's Boathouse
Fountainhead Regional Park

Harborplace and The Gallery
Jack's Boats
Lake Accotink Park
Lake Fairfax Park
Lake Needwood Park
Mount Vernon Trail
Occoquan Regional Park
Patapsco Valley State Park
Patuxent River State Park, Jug Bay
　　Natural Area
Piscataway National Park

Pohick Bay Regional Park and Golf
　　Course
Quiet Waters Park
Riverbend Park
Rock Creek Park
Seneca Creek State Park
Spirit Cruises
Theodore Roosevelt Island
Thompson's Boat Center
Watermark Cruises
White's Ferry

Canoe and Kayak Rentals

Belle Haven Marina
Bull Run Marina
Fletcher's Boathouse

Pohick Bay Regional Park and Golf
　　Course
Quiet Waters Park

Carousels

Burke Lake Park
Glen Echo Park and Carousel
Lake Accotink Park
Lake Fairfax Park
Lee District Park and Robert E. Lee
　　Recreation Center

Smithsonian Information Center ("The
　　Castle")
Watkins Regional Park
Wheaton Regional Park

Children's Museums

The Children's Museum of Rose Hill
　　Manor Park
Discovery Creek Children's Museum
　　of Washington

Explore and More
Port Discovery Children's Museum

Disk Golf

Bull Run Regional Park
Pohick Bay Regional Park and Golf
　　Course

Seneca Creek State Park

Equestrian

Bluemont Park

Bull Run Marina

Bull Run Regional Park

Meadowbrook Stables

Patapsco Valley State Park

Potomac Horse Center

Riverbend Park

Rock Creek Park Horse Center

Shenandoah National Park

Wheaton Regional Park

Fishing

Algonkian Regional Park

Allen Pond Park

Anacostia Park

Ball's Bluff Regional Park

Black Hill Regional Park

Bluemont Park

Bull Run Marina

Burke Lake Park

Calvert Cliffs State Park

Cameron Run Regional Park and Great
    Waves Water Park

Catoctin Mountain Park

Cedarville State Forest

Chesapeake and Ohio (C&O) Canal
    Historical Park Great Falls, MD

Cosca Regional Park

Cunningham Falls State Park

Dickerson Conservation Area

Fort Washington Park

Fountainhead Regional Park

Great Falls Park

Harpers Ferry National Historical Park

Lake Accotink Park

Lake Anna State Park

Lake Artemesia Park

Lake Fairfax Park

Lake Frank

Lake Needwood Park

Mount Vernon Trail

National Wildlife Visitor Ctr., Patuxent
    Research Refuge

Occoquan Regional Park

Oxon Hill Farm

Patapsco Valley State Park

Patuxent River State Park, Jug Bay
    Natural Area

Pohick Bay Regional Park and Golf
    Course

Quiet Waters Park

Riverbend Park

Seneca Creek State Park

Shenandoah National Park

Theodore Roosevelt Island

Wheaton Regional Park

White's Ferry

Whitetail Resort

Golf Courses

Algonkian Regional Park

Anacostia Park

Brambleton Regional Park

East Potomac Park

Jefferson District Park

Lake Needwood Park

Pohick Bay Regional Park

Rock Creek Park

Sligo Creek Park

Wisp

Miniature Golf

Algonkian Regional Park
Bohrer Park at Summit Hall Farm
Bull Run Regional Park
Cameron Run Regional ParkandGreat
    Waves Water Park
East Potomac Park
Fountainhead Regional Park
Jefferson District Park and Golf Course
Lake Accotink Park

Mid Atlantic Golf Center
Pohick Bay Regional Park and Golf
    Course
Rocky Gorge
South Germantown Recreational Park
TopGolf
Upton Hill Regional Park
Watkins Regional Park

Nature Centers

Brookside Nature Center
Clearwater Nature Center
Cosca Regional Park
Croydon Creek Nature Center
Gulf Branch Nature Center
Hidden Oaks Nature Center
Hidden Pond Nature Center
Little Bennett Regional Park
Locust Grove Nature Center
Long Branch Nature Center

Meadowside Nature Center
Potomac Overlook Regional Park
Riverbend Park
Rock Creek Nature Center and
    Planetarium
Rust Sanctuary (Audubon Naturalist
    Society)
Watkins Regional Park
Woodend Nature Sanctuary (Audubon
    Naturalist Society)

Observatories/Planetariums

Arlington Public Schools Planetarium
Howard B. Owens Science Center and
    Planetarium
Maryland Science Center
Einstein Planetarium at National Air
    and Space Museum

Rock Creek Nature Center and
    Planetarium
Steven F. Udvar-Hazy Center
U.S. Naval Observatory
University of Maryland Observatory

Railroads/Miniature Trains

Baltimore and Ohio Railroad Museum
The Baltimore Civil War Museum
Baltimore Streetcar Museum
Burke Lake Park
Cabin John Regional Park
Chesapeake Beach Railway Museum
Day Trips and Train Rides—Chapter 10

Lake Fairfax Park
National Capital Trolley Museum
Skyline Caverns
W&OD Railroad Regional Park
Watkins Regional Park
Wheaton Regional Park

Ships

Baltimore Maritime Museum
Calvert Marine Museum
Maryland Tours

The Navy Museum
U.S. Naval Academy Museum
U.S.S. Constellation

Swimming

Algonkian Regional Park
Anacostia Park
Audrey Moore RECenter
Bohrer Park at Summit Hall Farm
Bull Run Regional Park
Calvert Cliffs State Park
Cameron Run Regional Park and Great
    Waves Water Park
Chesapeake Beach Water Park
Chinquapin Center and Park
Claude Moore Recreation Center
Cunningham Falls State Park
Downpour at Algonkian Regional Park
East Potomac Park
Fairland Regional Park
Greenbrier State Park

Lake Fairfax Park
Lee District Park and Robert E. Lee
    Recreation Center
Paramount's Kings Dominion
Pohick Bay Regional Park and Golf
    Course
Prince William Forest Park
Public Swimming Pools—Chapter 8
Rollingcrest-Chillum Splash Pool
Six Flags America and Paradise Island
    Water Park
South Germantown Recreational Park
Splash Down Water Park
Upton Hill Regional Park
Water Mine Family Swimmin' Hole

Tennis

Audrey Moore RECenter
Bluemont Park
Cabin John Regional Park
Candy Cane City
Chinquapin Center and Park
Cosca Regional Park
East Potomac Park
Fort Ward Park
Hidden Pond Nature Center
Jefferson District Park and Golf Course
Lee District Park and Robert E. Lee
    Recreation Center

Martin Luther King, Jr. Swim Center
Mason District Park
Montrose Park
Rock Creek Park
Rockville Municipal Swim Center
Sligo Creek Park
Splash Down Water Park
Tuckahoe Park and Playfield
Watkins Regional Park
Wheaton Regional Park

Zoos

Catoctin Wildlife Preserve and Zoo
The Maryland Zoo in Baltimore
National Museum of Natural History

National Zoo
ZooAmerica, North American Wildlife
    Park

INDEX

D

H

I

J